The Starmer Symptom

'A vital kickback against national decline, ranging over the aimless, joyless landscape of Britain under Grey Labour. Mark Perryman has persuaded some of the fiercest, most eloquent polemicists in the land to examine, expose and ultimately eviscerate one of the lamest leaders in Labour history.'

—Alex Niven, Editor, *Tribune*

'Packed with insightful commentary focusing on Labour lacking a two-way dialogue between members and leadership which is driving many of the party's activists away. Via a critique of Labour's resistance to coalition-building, so vital under our undemocratic voting system, *The Starmer Symptom* pinpoints the reasons why Labour is failing to reverse the rise of the Far Right agenda.'

—Cat Arnold, member, Labour Party National Executive Committee

'The core of the argument is that Labour needs to break out of Labourism and remake itself as part of a broader pluralist bloc. Labour absolutely should be like this, here is a book that brilliantly explains why it has never been.'

—Alan Finlayson, Chair of the Editorial Board,
Renewal: A Journal of Social Democracy

'Had me cheering on the writers and their arguments as they interrogated the symptoms of a Labour Party that has undermined its own potential for change. Left me asking, what is this bloody huge parliamentary majority for?!'

—Laura Parker, Private Secretary to Jeremy Corbyn, Leader of
the Opposition 2016–17 before prominently endorsing
Keir Starmer in the 2020 Labour leadership election

'Keir Starmer decries the existence of Starmerism. Yet his actions as prime minister tell a different story – he has a discernible political project. Mark Perryman and the authors tease out the underlying shape of what this "Starmerism" is and could still be. An invaluable contribution to thinking about Labour politics today.'
—John McTernan, Tony Blair's Director of Political Operations 2005–2007 and Special Adviser to two Cabinet Ministers in Gordon Brown's government 2007–2010

'A conceptually strong and timely contribution to understanding Keir Starmer's Labour Party. Essential and thought-provoking reading for anyone interested in understanding how Labour ended up where it is now and looking for where it might go next.'
—Sasha Das Gupta, co-chair of Momentum

'A very stimulating, accessible and engaging read. By drawing on a wide range of theoretical and historical sources, Mark Perryman advances our understanding of Starmer's project, its prospects, and its implications.'
—Colm Murphy author of *Futures of Socialism: 'Modernisation', the Labour Party, and the British Left, 1973–1997*

'A book that provides a theoretical critique of Starmerism which is both extremely accessible and entirely non-intimidating; no mean feat when drawing on thinkers such as Gramsci and Stuart Hall.'
—Pat Stack, 'Stack on the Back' column, *Socialist Review 1987–2004*

The Starmer Symptom

Edited by
Mark Perryman

Foreword by Clive Lewis MP

First published 2025 by Pluto Press
New Wing, Somerset House, Strand, London WC2R 1LA
and Pluto Press, Inc.
1930 Village Center Circle, 3-834, Las Vegas, NV 89134

www.plutobooks.com

British Library Cataloguing in Publication Data
A catalogue record for this book is available from the British Library

ISBN 978 0 7453 5109 4   Paperback
ISBN 978 0 7453 5111 7   PDF
ISBN 978 0 7453 5110 0   EPUB

This book is printed on paper suitable for recycling and made from
fully managed and sustained forest sources. Logging, pulping and
manufacturing processes are expected to conform to the environmental
standards of the country of origin.

Typeset by Stanford DTP Services, Northampton, England

Simultaneously printed in the United Kingdom and United States of
America

EU GPSR Authorised Representative
LOGOS EUROPE, 9 rue Nicolas Poussin, 17000, LA ROCHELLE, France
Email: Contact@logoseurope.eu

For the Lewes Labour events and Keir Hardie Café crews keeping the morbid symptoms at bay via an organic intellectual culture and the conviviality of home baked cake.

Contents

CONTENTS

Change, Stability, Contradictions

The Outcomes

Understanding Keir Starmer's Labour Party

Afterwords

Foreword
Clive Lewis MP

So choppy are the waters of the perma-crisis, and so flat-bottomed the life raft known as Starmerism, decisions once thought impossible at the outset of Starmer's initial soft-left, 'Corbyn-in-a-suit' journey have become the defining realities of Labour's present course. The Starmer Symptom? Don't say you haven't been suitably warned.

The Jeremy Corbyn wave that swept Labour in 2015 was more than just a political surge – it was a redefinition of the possible, a moment when grassroots activism, radical ideas and the audacity of political hope took centre stage. It represented a demand for genuine democracy, pluralism and transformative change, articulated most powerfully by a generation alienated by the empty managerialism and technocratic minimalism that had dominated politics for decades. For many, it was the first time in living memory that Labour had felt like a movement rather than a machine. Yet even amidst the promise, a clear tension existed between traditional Labourist centralism and a more expansive, pluralistic politics. Today, Keir Starmer's absolute determination to distance Labour from that era speaks volumes – not only of strategic pragmatism, but of a deeper ideological retreat, symptomatic of Labour's internal contradictions and unresolved anxieties.

Starmer's relentless drive to move on from the Corbyn era reflects Labour's enduring aversion to genuine pluralism. At its heart lies an instinctive recoil from the messiness and unpredictability of democratic participation, preferring instead the perceived security and tidiness of centralised control. The party leadership views unity not as something cultivated through respectful dialogue and representation of diverse perspectives, but something enforced through control. This aversion is not merely tactical – it's existential. The Corbyn moment threatened Labour precisely because it signalled a party potentially ungovernable by conventional managerial methods.

Starmerism, therefore, is less an ideological renewal than a reassertion of centralised managerialism, because this is a party unsure how to reconcile democratic participation with electoral success.

Parliamentary candidate selections have been increasingly centralised, grassroots members marginalised and left-wing voices within the party targeted. What this amounts to is the pathologising of dissent while conformity is rewarded. Those who once championed community wealth-building, a Green New Deal and public ownership have been either disciplined into silence or ejected altogether. These processes amount to a hollowing out of Labour – not just of ideas, but of a political culture. A party once brimming with energy, ideas and volunteers has become, under Starmer, a professionalised bureaucracy aimed at maintaining power rather than transforming society.

Labour's aversion to pluralism manifests itself most vividly in its reluctance toward coalition politics. Labourism is framed by the idea that true strength comes from an absolutist monopoly – an electoral juggernaut capable of winning alone or not at all. Yet contemporary crises – climate breakdown, authoritarian populism, stark economic inequality – demand co-operation beyond narrow party lines. Coalition-building is not simply electoral pragmatism; it's an acknowledgment of complex, interdependent realities. No one party alone can solve the polycrisis we face. Collaboration between Labour, the Greens, the Liberal Democrats and other progressive forces is not a sign of weakness, but maturity.

The rigid refusal to engage in electoral pacts or meaningful dialogue with potential allies is telling. Starmerism's allergy to coalition-building isn't new. The Labourist tradition with few, dissenting, exceptions has always been fixated on the myth of majoritarianism, and seemingly indifferent to the necessity of broad-based alliances in a fractured political landscape. The stakes now, however, are as high as the very future of our democracy, our planet. Such a refusal to share power becomes not just strategically foolish, but morally questionable.

Nowhere is Labour's aversion to transformative politics clearer than in its avoidance of public ownership. Consider water, the most fundamental human necessity and a natural monopoly uniquely suited to democratic management. Public opinion consistently favours reversing privatisation – not as nostalgia, but as a pragmatic response to corporate failures, ecological crises and profound erosion of trust in privatised utilities. From the droughts in the south-east to sewage dumped into rivers and seas, privatised water is a textbook case of extractive capitalism failing the public.

And yet Labour's reluctance to commit to public ownership reveals more than mere caution. It is symptomatic of a deeper ideological capitulation to market logic and implicit endorsement of the corporate status quo. Refusing public ownership as a serious policy option signals abandonment of democratic control over our collective future, showing Labour's alignment not with popular sentiment or ecological necessity, but with neoliberal orthodoxy that has repeatedly failed. Instead of empowering people to take back control of essential services, Labour is all too ready simply to tinker at the edges while leaving in place the corporate structures that produced this crisis.

This alignment finds its starkest symbol in the party's increasing proximity to corporations like BlackRock. Labour's embrace of corporate influence and management-by-consultancy is more than simply the tactical pragmatism of parliamentary politics. Rather, it is the basis of an ideological drift toward technocratic neoliberalism. This is governance defined by financial markets and consultancy reports rather than communities, workers or public deliberation. This undermines democracy itself by nourishing popular cynicism. When voters see politicians cosying up to the same firms that caused the 2008 crash, or profited during the Covid pandemic, the social contract frays further. Democratic parties surrendering policymaking to investment firms relinquish political imagination, ceding ground to an economic orthodoxy incapable of confronting the profound crises of our age – whether ecological collapse, rampant inequality or erosion of democratic legitimacy.

Labour's timidity on the climate emergency underscores this problem further. The climate emergency, the defining crisis of our times, demands bold, courageous and imaginative responses. Yet Labour's approach has been notably cautious and incrementally timid, perpetually afraid of alienating swing voters or corporate backers. Starmer's climate strategy increasingly resembles an exercise in political triangulation rather than a plan of ecological salvation.

Net zero is framed only in terms of competitiveness, not adaption and survival. Green investment is promised, but always secondary to fiscal rules set by an economic consensus long past its sell-by date. Treating climate change as peripheral rather than fundamental further signals Labour's inability to imagine politics beyond short-term economic calculations and electoral cycles. While floods devastate communities, food prices rise due to crop failures and corporate price-gouging; while air quality worsens in cities, Labour dithers.

This cautiousness is not prudent. It is political timidity produced by a party paralysed by institutional pressures and geopolitical alignments rather than guided by moral clarity or ecological urgency. Of course, finding a balance between these, often opposing, forces is what makes for great governments and leaders. But Starmer has shown no such inclination. As prime minister, he faces substantial institutional and diplomatic constraints, particularly regarding established alliances such as those with the United States, whose stance on Israel and Gaza amounts to an unwavering alignment with Israel's most hardline factions. Starmer's careful neutrality over the humanitarian crisis in Gaza, continued arms sales and quiet acquiescence to harsh immigration policies reflect an institutional inclination toward diplomatic continuity and strategic pragmatism rather than ethical clarity. Such institutional caution severely limits the space available for moral leadership, even as the moral and humanitarian imperatives remain clear and urgent.

In this vacuum, the populist right seizes ground, offering nativist, nationalist solutions to problems that demand internationalist, ecological and equitable solidarity.

And yet – despite these profound concerns, hope persists. Not because the current Labour leadership inspires it, but in spite of it. A hope that arises from deeper commitments to democratic renewal, community empowerment and transformative politics. A hope underscored by the belief that the 2015 moment was not a fleeting aberration, but a vital reminder of what is possible when people rediscover political agency. Hope, here, is not naive optimism, but political necessity – a grounded resilience against managerial centralism, corporate capture and ecological inertia.

Hope survives in the growing networks of community organisers, co-operative movements, union branches, citizen assemblies and environmental campaigns. It flourishes in places ignored by Westminster – municipal projects reclaiming public land, local councils experimenting with participatory budgeting, workers organising in Amazon warehouses and Uber ranks. These spaces show that politics is not the property of party elites, but of people acting in concert to change their lives.

Ultimately, Starmerism reveals profound symptoms: ideological ambiguity, technocratic managerialism, corporate influence, aversion to pluralism, and political timidity in facing existential threats. These are not temporary conditions, but structural ailments that risk rendering Labour unfit for the purpose it was created for: to give political voice to working people and deliver collective solutions to collective problems.

Openly addressing the Starmer Symptom is essential for Labour – and British politics broadly – to recover clarity, purpose and genuine democratic legitimacy. The crisis is real, yet so too is potential renewal. But that renewal cannot come from above. It must come from below – from a revitalised political culture that sees people not as voters to be harvested, but as citizens to be empowered. Recognising what this symptom represents is the first critical step toward a politics daring enough to imagine and urgently act upon the challenges we collectively face. And if this moment is indeed one of endings, then let it also be a moment of beginnings – a time to organise, to imagine and to build anew.

Introduction

The Starmer Symptom is an attempt to understand Keir Starmer, his Labour Party and his government. Its starting point is a quote from Gramsci: 'The crisis consists precisely in the fact that the old is dying and the new cannot be born; in this interregnum a great variety of morbid symptoms appear.'

This is neither a Keir Starmer biography nor a potted history of his career. It is not a 2024 general election campaign diary either, nor a survey of how and why the country voted – or didn't vote – in 2024. Instead this collection presents a plurality of views on the 'symptom' that is a Keir Starmer government. Our contributors' brief was simple: to make readers think.

Mark Perryman opens *The Starmer Symptom* with a keynote essay applying the ideas and theories of Gramsci and Stuart Hall to a Labourism framed by 1945's 'Now Win the Peace' general election victory, via waves of modernisation under Neil Kinnock and Tony Blair, to Keir Starmer. How do Gramscian concepts of hegemony, passive revolution, war of position and the party as organic intellectual help us to understand Labourism today?

The book is divided into four thematic parts, each consisting of four essays. The format allows readers to follow the plurality of views in any order and direction they choose, to dip in and out whilst they think through how our writers' ideas and experiences interact with their own, or not. It includes suggestions for further reading, and other resources listings, together with a guide to Labour's 2029 battleground defences against Tory, Reform, SNP, Green and Independent gains.

'Mapping the Hope' assesses the causes of Labour's 2024 landslide. Or, as Paula Surridge asks in her essay, did Labour win or the Tories lose? Jeremy Gilbert offers a critique of Starmerism as a kind of non-politics. Gargi Bhattacharya argues that the boredom this generates serves to produce something far more dangerous than simply apathy. To conclude, Joe Kennedy applies his theory of 'authentocracy' to Keir Starmer's much-trumpeted backstory as the son of a toolmaker, leaving readers to question whether anything is 'authentic' in politics.

'The Fallout' provides a critical account of how, since the general election, party politics is being reconfigured. To open, Neal Lawson critiques Starmer Labour's lack of pluralism; as an alternative, Neal explores what a 21st-century Labour left might look like. Phil Burton-Cartledge follows with an update of his theorisation of the Tories' long-term failure to renew both party and electoral support and analyses how the Tories might yet recover. Or might they fall victim to the resistible rise of Nigel Farage and Reform UK? This is the subject of Joe Mulhall's essay, which details Reform's emergence as part of a European and trans-Atlantic far right with a mass electoral base. In contrast, Hilary Wainwright offers a more hopeful alternative via an analysis of the options facing Jeremy Corbyn, the independent left and the Green Party as they seek to mount parliamentary and extra-parliamentary challenges.

'Change, Stability, Contradictions' begins with Danny Dorling detailing the scale of inequality that the British variant of neoliberalism has enabled and describes the kind of programme of 'change' Labour needs if Keir Starmer is going to get anywhere close to reversing it. James Meadway combines a critique of Starmer and Reeves' economic strategy with his case for an alternative. Jess Garland argues that any programme of economic change has to have a foundational commitment to democratic reform. Andrew Simms catalogues the evidence of what is happening now to our climate and the deadly consequences of insufficiently radical action being taken by Labour to reverse it.

The 2029 general election already looms large in Labour thinking. To conclude, 'The Outcomes' anticipates the socio-political destination to which Keir Starmer will take his Labour party and government. Emma Burnell unpicks a Labour Party according to the rule of Morgan McSweeney – good, bad, or more complicated than that? Gregor Gall assesses the likelihood of a revival of a trade union militancy as a focus of resistance to this Labour government. Yasmin Alibhai-Brown contextualises how Gaza has become an issue that defines Labour's collapsing support from communities which for too long it took for granted.

The book argues that, if he is not to disappoint, Keir Starmer has to find the ways and means to combine the pragmatic, the social democratic and the radical. Eunice Goes concludes the collection by arguing that such a combination is not impossible. More than anything else, it is the success or failure of this combination that will define the Starmer government's journey.

The Starmer Symptom offers readers a way to understand the processes along the way.

Testing the Limits of Labourism

Mark Perryman

The crisis consists precisely in the fact that the old is dying and the new cannot be born; in this interregnum a great variety of morbid symptoms appear.

Antonio Gramsci[1]

To start a book on Keir Starmer's Labour Party and government with a 100-year-old quote from an imprisoned Italian communist is surely bordering on the intellectually perverse. Gramsci's ideas had a certain currency amongst a section of the British left intelligentsia through the 1970s and 1980s, but even that was 50-odd years ago.[2]

So a word of explanation and caution. There is an unhealthy habit among those who frame their politics in the words of centuries-old sages, Marx and Lenin in particular, to treat these founding texts as a kind of catechism masquerading as revolutionary politics. That is not what is being suggested here.

Rather, Gramsci's idea of 'symptom' acts as a tool to help us develop and deepen our own understanding of this Keir Starmer 'moment'. Gramsci was writing in 1930, at which time he was a prisoner of one of the most morbid 'symptoms' of the entire 20th century: fascism, in this case the Mussolini version. The argument of this book is that between the old and the new there appear a variety of 'symptoms', some negative but some positive. Symptom not in the sense of a disease, but in the sense of an indicator of what comes next. And for those who suggest this is a revisionism too far, the committed Marxist and academic Gilbert Achcar points out[3] that in his original text, Gramsci used the word *fenomeni*. 'Phenomenon' is clearly a neutral term. 'Symptom' is used in the same way. The purpose of this collection is not to offer a lexicon of self-fulfilling prophecies, but to explore politics as the art of the possible.

In the post-2024 general election issue of the journal *Soundings*, John Clarke echoed this approach by pointing out how multifaceted these 'symptoms' are. As a result, any outcomes are likely to be the same:

> As a starting point, Gramsci's observations generate a set of difficult questions about the shifting alignments of consent and force; about who the 'great masses' are (and who they think they are); about the spatial and temporal conditions of the 'interregnum' (and how to address its 'morbid symptoms'); and about how the instabilities of the interregnum might be resolved.[4]

Clarke brilliantly sums up our lived experience of these symptoms: 'from the shit in our rivers and seas through to the collapse of collective infrastructures, including welfare and care'.[5]

HEGEMONY AND COUNTER-HEGEMONY

Concerning that 'shit', nothing illustrates the obverse of the morbid in these symptoms as the sight of the lead singer from 1970s Northern Irish punk band The Undertones emerging as the effective leader of the movement against inland and coastal waters pollution. Who would have thought when Feargal Sharkey was belting out 'Get teenage kicks right through the night, all right' he'd end up being the eloquent spokesperson for the unanswerable case to renationalise the water boards.

Poster boy of the counter-hegemony? Sharkey fits the bill perfectly. Because what Sharkey does is place the inconvenience of swimming, paddleboarding, surfing our way through shit, never mind washing ourselves in or drinking the horrible stuff, in the context of a decades-long neoliberal hegemony.

Thatcherism was the post-1979 'common sense' that replaced citizens with customers and turned the foundations of the nation into a business. The ideas behind Thatcherism went first transatlantic, via Reagonomics, and then, after the 1989 fall of the Berlin Wall and the widely trumpeted 'end of history', rebranded as neoliberalism to become both global and hegemonic. By the turn of the century, the political choice seemed to have narrowed down to between progressive neoliberalism and hyper-reactionary neoliberalism. It was – and is – no choice at all.[6]

Hegemonies don't last for ever. What was once the 'new' becomes the 'old', or to use appropriate market vocabulary, 'past its sell-by date'. Nancy Fraser identifies this particular interregnum/interval and the symptoms/signs that accompany it:

> Neither variant of neoliberalism can successfully resolve the objective system blockages that underlie our hegemonic crisis. Since both are in bed with global finance, neither can challenge financialization, deindustrialization, or corporate globalization. Neither can redress declining living standards, ballooning debt, care deficits or intolerable stresses on community life.[7]

Fraser's variants are the unashamed neoliberalism of the right and the accommodation of neoliberalism by postmodern social democracy. Their mutual failure to resolve a hegemonic crisis is how she describes our current interregnum. Is this therefore one of those 'there is no alternative' moments? She argues not, suggesting instead that populism, in one of two very different and competing versions, is the most likely candidate to forge a 'counterhegemonic bloc'. The first form, 'Reactionary Populism', is familiar: we see it in Trump and Farage, in Germany's AfD, Viktor Orbán in Hungary, and in the so-called post-fascists, Giorgia Meloni in Italy and Marine Le Pen in France.

However, rather too optimistically it turned out, Fraser, writing in 2019, suggested that the more likely candidate for the 'new' being born would be the second version, what she called 'Progressive Populism':

> Only by joining a robustly egalitarian politics of distribution to a substantially inclusive, class-sensitive politics of recognition can we build a counterhegemonic bloc capable of leading us beyond the current crisis to a better world.[8]

In other words, Jeremy Corbyn, Bernie Sanders, Jean-Luc Mélenchon – that triumvirate of ageing super-socialists – who, alongside younger variants in Syriza, Podemos, Die Linke and others, had some success in pursuing the kind of politics Fraser promotes.[9]

Of course, there is nothing necessarily wrong with the reassuring certainties Fraser offers for her version of the counter-hegemonic bloc. The trouble is, they sound so familiar because they are irretrievably associated with decades' worth of marginalisation and defeat.

BEYOND THE COMFORT OF CERTAINTIES

John Clarke's response to the 2024 Labour landslide was more nuanced. He describes the immediate aftermath, the 'political-cultural moment' as:

> characterised by widespread disaffection, dissent and a deeply felt desire for change. The crumbling of the dominant bloc and its political representation in Johnson's Conservatism testify to this depth and diversity of disaffection. Hardly a fraction of society exists that does not hope for something different, even as those somethings may differ widely. It is this multiplicity of desires for change that is encompassed in the Starmerite slogan: *Change*. Meanwhile, its relative emptiness serves as a warning about the risks of Labourist containment.[10]

Clarke's cataloguing of this 'multiplicity of desires' illustrates precisely the ways in which symptoms can be both negative (morbid) and positive (joyful). He picks out three in particular:

1. 'Global and international dynamics that the UK inhabits are more turbulent and pressing – from the climate catastrophe to wars and their shifting alliances.'
2. 'Domestic fractures are more complex than in the early 2000s, particularly around forms of 'nativist' populism, and grating realignments of class, race and gender.'
3. 'The forms in which dissent is lived have multiplied – from new sites and practices of activism to a deepening pool of what might best be described as passive dissent, one of whose significant forms is the proliferation of political scepticism and cynicism.'[11]

CATALOGUING THE SYMPTOMS

Whatever the differences, it was surely significant that Starmer and Reeves echoed Corbyn and McDonnell in the centrality they set out to give a green economics of sufficient magnitude to reverse the climate emergency. The Corbynite 'Green New Deal' was replaced by 'Great British Energy'. But at each stage of implementation they beat a retreat to the soundtrack of their mantra of 'growth'.

Gaza marked another very obvious dividing line. 'Israel has a right to defend itself,' Starmer said on 7 October – a right he hasn't once, before or after the Hamas atrocity, extended to Palestine, Lebanon or Iran. In doing so, Starmer has cut himself off from a constituency that stretches considerably wider than what remains of the Corbynite left. Because this is a 'moment', like Guernica, Vietnam, Soweto and Iraq. It is defining a political generation stretching way beyond any preconceived definition of the 'left'. Starmer has ended up positioning himself and Labour in opposition to those defined in this way by Gaza.

A third symptom of what is to come is the well-publicised strategy of recapturing Labour voters who deserted Labour in 2019.[12] Immigration and asylum were identified as the key issues. Fine, but heaven forbid this might mean making the argument that immigration is a foundational principle for Britain to have a functional economy and the social infrastructure we all depend upon. Or that asylum is a fundamental, human right, or at least it should be. And when Jewish refugees who sought it in the 1930s escaping from Nazi Germany were refused entry because of a demonisation eerily similar to today, it didn't end happily, rather it ended in the gas chambers Starmer very publicly visited ahead of the 2025 anniversary of the liberation of Auschwitz. Labour seeks to trump the Tories' 'Stop the Boats' with 'Smash the Criminal Gangs'. What kind of argument is Labour making when it cannot bring itself to explain why people seek asylum and the consequences for them when it is denied?

The Starmer 'moment' is, inevitably, visible in the so-called 'culture wars', most obviously around transgender issues – a subject seemingly almost everyone actively involved in politics, and beyond too, has a position on, usually entrenched and bitterly opposed to those who hold a different point of view, who are labelled as either transphobic or misogynist. I say 'almost everyone'. Prominent exceptions include Keir Starmer and the Labour Party, who have been at pains not to have a position.

And, as a final symptom of 'multiplication of forms of dissent', a revived Scottish National Party and Plaid Cymru cannot be ruled out. Meanwhile, there is Sinn Fein's increasing dominance of Northern Irish politics. It is and seems likely to remain difficult for a Unionist Labour Party, despite the landslide, to prevent the break-up of Britain.[13] And in England, despite Starmer's prominent appearances in an England shirt, Reform UK have successfully positioned themselves as the party of English nationalism.

Add this list to John Clarke's, and together these are symptoms that spell: F-R-A-C-T-U-R-E.[14]

CLAUSE ONE SOCIALISM

Keir Starmer and his allies have a disregard for those who don't fit his particular definition of what constitutes 'doing politics'.

During his first leader's speech as prime minister at Labour Conference, Starmer was interrupted by a heckler because of Gaza. His response? – 'While he's been protesting, we've been changing the party. That's why we've got a Labour government,' adding by way of carefully scripted witticism, 'This guy's obviously got a pass from the 2019 conference. We've changed the party.'[15] Starmer couldn't have been more wrong. It was later revealed that the heckler, 18-year-old Daniel Riley, had joined the party in 2022 *because* of the hope he believed Keir offered his generation.

The day before, Rachel Reeves had also been heckled during her first set piece speech as chancellor. Her retort was short, if not sweet. She declared that Labour had become 'a party that represents working people not a party of protest'.

The 'not a party of protest' put-down was entirely ignorant. Labour's history of protest stretches a lot further back than Jeremy Corbyn's brief tenure as leader.

Reeves has been an outspoken campaigner to honour the legacy of the Suffragettes, perhaps the country's most famous protestors.

Above her desk at Number Eleven, Reeves has a portrait of Ellen Wilkinson, the Labour MP and leader of the Jarrow March in 1936.

The British Battalion of the International Brigades fought Franco's fascists in the Spanish Civil War. When they returned in 1938, Labour leader Clement Attlee and frontbencher Stafford Cripps joined Communist Party MP Willie Gallagher and Communist Party leader Harry Pollitt to welcome them home. Those who'd taken up arms in defence of Spain's republican government were embraced by the then Labour leader.

And then there's equal pay for women. How was that secured? By an alliance between Labour's Barbara Castle and the first all-women strike, in 1968 at Ford, where women workers refused to accept unequal pay.

Labour is a party that from its very beginning has consisted of both individual members and affiliated trade unions. How do the latter defend and improve wages and working conditions? By industrial action, including strikes and pickets.

But the put-down is typical of the Starmer moment. It is rooted in what Starmer and his backers call 'Clause I Socialism'. It can be found on page one of the party rulebook:

CLAUSE ONE
NAME AND OBJECTS

1. This organisation shall be known as 'The Labour Party' (hereinafter referred to as 'the Party').
2. Its purpose is to organise and maintain in Parliament and in the country a political Labour Party.
3. The Party shall bring together members and supporters who share its values to develop policies, make communities stronger through collective action and support, and promote the election of Labour Party representatives at all levels of the democratic process.
4. The Party shall give effect, as far as may be practicable, to the principles from time to time approved by Party conference.

This, naturally, is open to a variety of interpretations. The self-identified 'Clause One Socialists' choose the simplest version: get Labour elected. Nothing else matters, certainly not why, nor what for.

In an article for *Labour List*, Morgan Jones described the process by which these 'Clause One Socialists' have, under Starmer, become Labour's 'organising class'. She identified a number of key signifiers:

> The rise of Ridley [Hollie Ridley, Labour Party General Secretary] and McSweeney [Morgan McSweeney, Downing Street Chief of Staff] ... reflects the coming to power of the organiser class. ...
>
> ... Labour Together has displaced traditional intellectual hubs like the Fabians or the IPPR ....
>
> ... the persistent assertions one encounters the party intends to govern in campaign mode (something that will no doubt be aided by organisers flooding into parliament as aides to new MPs). ...
>
> Labour ran an incredible field campaign in 2024, and there seems little reason to doubt that that level of rigour will continue. ...
>
> But at a certain level, you need to govern in governing mode; I remember discussion amongst organisers under Corbyn of how a good ground game was 'necessary but not sufficient' to win elections. The question arising is: is it enough to be organised?[16]

STARMER'S PASSIVE REVOLUTION

The 2024 landslide is what Gramsci called a 'passive revolution'. Deborah Lynn Steinberg and Richard Johnson define a 'passive revolution' as:

> The demobilisation or disorganisation of forms of popular agency and therefore of the possibility of organic change. ...
>
> It seeks to contain and control popular forces from outside. ...
>
> This may involve making real concessions, but always within the limits of existing social arrangements. ...
>
> ... an attempt to solve structural, problems within the terms of existing structures.[17]

Is this all bad? Not necessarily. It's been a long while, centuries long, since the last time a movement threatened the revolutionary overthrow of the English establishment, monarchy and the rest: The Levellers.[18] Despite the worst efforts of Saturday morning *Socialist Worker* sellers, nobody would seriously suggest that we're on the verge of another such moment. So it isn't entirely unreasonable to argue that if the best we can manage is a passive revolution, it's surely better than nothing.

However, when we connect Steinberg and Johnson's definition to how John Clarke uses the concept to describe the Starmer 2024 landslide, we begin to see how things might only get bitter:

> A revolution of declining expectations about the difference that politics might make – an intensification of very long-standing sentiments driven by fourteen years of Conservative incompetence, lies and corruption. Together these elements shape a strangely flat popular reaction to the promise of Starmer's Labour – not just a response to an uninspiring leader, but a sense of sceptical distance from the political process itself.[19]

FOR FOLK'S SAKE

Nick Srnicek and Alex Williams, in their 2016 book *Inventing the Future: Postcapitalism and a World Without Work*,[20] offered an intellectual underpinning for an outlier version of the Corbynite left. It was an outlier that to the end was bedevilled by a duality; the conservatism of the traditional Labour hard left and the romanticism of a new-generation left they rather wonderfully called 'folk politics':

> At its heart folk politics is the guiding intuition that immediacy is always better and often more authentic, with the corollary being a deep suspicion of abstraction and mediation.
>
> ... Typically [it] remains reactive (responding to actions initiated by corporations and governments, rather than initiating actions); ignores long-term strategic goals in favour of tactics (mobilising around single issue-politics or emphasising process); prefers practices that are often inherently fleeting (such as occupations

and temporary autonomous zones); chooses the familiarities of the past over the unknowns of the future (for instance, the repeated dreams of a return to 'good' Keynesian capitalism); and expresses itself as a predilection for the voluntarist and spontaneous over the institutional (as in the romanticisation of rioting and insurrection.[21]

And the consequence? '[It] often rejects the project of hegemony, valuing withdrawal or exit rather than building a broad counter-hegemony.'[22]

For Srnicek and Williams, a hegemonic project means: 'Changing the conditions which determine the trajectory of societies, by transforming the means by which subjectivities and desires are articulated and formed'.[23]

And they add: 'This is politics, pure and simple.'

That there is a singular lack of a Labour politics resembling such a hegemonic politics more than anything points toward the morbidity element in the Starmer symptom. Starmer's core message of 'change' has the potential breadth of appeal any hegemonic politics depends upon. That's the hope. But a party that actively disavows, polices even, a plural, coalition-building politics fundamentally undermines any such potential and leaves any prospect for real 'change' remote indeed. And that's being generous.

WHOSE HEGEMONY? NOT OURS

In 1979, that most fateful of years for the British variant of social democracy, a.k.a. the post-war settlement, Stuart Hall wrote an essay for *Marxism Today*. It was this essay, 'The Great Moving Right Show',[24] that sparked a wide-ranging debate for a left recovering from the 1979 general election defeat. This was not only a debate about Thatcherism, but also a deep structural and ideological crisis of the left that had been prefaced, also in *Marxism Today*, by Eric Hobsbawm as 'The Forward March of Labour Halted?'[25]

As Hall developed his description of the Thatcherite project, it became more and more terrifying, but inspiring too. Terrifying in what Thatcher was able to achieve, inflicting defeat after defeat on her opponents, most spectacularly in the miners' strike of 1984–85.

Inspiring in what Labour, and the wider left, could achieve with a hegemonic project on the scale of Thatcherism.

Hall listed those elements required for a hegemonic project to succeed:

> The attempt to put together a new 'historical bloc'; new political configurations and 'philosophies': a profound restructuring of the state and the ideological discourses which construct the crisis and represent it as it is 'lived' as a practical reality; new programmes and policies, pointing to a new result, a new sort of 'settlement'.[26]

The question is, why was Thatcher's victory a 'revolution', but the equally impressive landslide victories of Blair and Starmer not? Hall's argument was that Thatcherism's triumph was its destruction of the post-war consensus that had lasted since 1945. In contrast, there is the failure of Blair and Starmer to replace the fundamentals of Thatcherism, or what it evolved into globally, neoliberalism. Hall detailed the process that would be required for such a break: 'These do not "emerge": they have to be constructed. Political and ideological work is required to disarticulate old formations, and to rework their elements into new configurations.'[27]

Blair's legacy, and Starmer's prospects, should be judged precisely in how far they fulfil this task. For all the good, and there was a lot, that Blair did, and all the good that Starmer will do, which I entirely expect there will be, this surely is the least we can expect of Labour governments. But, to use a favourite word in Labour's current lexicon, if there is 'change' without that construction, disarticulation and reworking, no new consensus will be established.

1945: LABOUR'S HEGEMONIC MOMENT

In the nostalgia industry for the Churchillian and all things World War Two, one date is missing: 5 July 1945. The war in Europe was barely over, the war in the Pacific and South-East Asia was still raging. And the wartime leader Winston Churchill, feted ever since, led the Tories to a landslide defeat by Labour.

Owen Hatherley is a critic of a politics rooted in 'The Ministry of Nostalgia' and all things '45:

1945 remains the English left's eternal benchmark, the moment when war led to its greatest parliamentary triumph. That this combination is utterly unrepeatable is seldom considered. But in theory the left is impelled to a more inclusive, more humane version of 'socialism and the English genius' to use Orwell's phrase.[28]

Hatherley will not concede ground to those who might suggest this is sufficient, that Labour's renewal could be founded on that faraway moment when it won the peace. He describes any such tendency as the 'social democracy of fear' and it produces a Labour politics: 'which tries to annex ground from the right without partaking in any of the sad passions that actually makes much of the right's politics so powerful – resentment, hatred, bitterness'.[29]

I would argue that it is no kind of fudge to combine Hatherley's critical thinking with a deep-seated appreciation of the monumental changes Attlee's Labour governments achieved in 1945–51. The latter is a recognition of the wider social forces and cultural shifts this government came to represent – forces and shifts first formed in the Popular Front of the 1930s.

In his essay 'Days of Hope: The Meaning of 1945',[30] Jim Fyrth describes British society in the 1930s as one in which 'a conservative moral and cultural dominance was all pervading',[31] and what happened next: 'Then, during the war, the tide turned and by 1945, threatened to overwhelm this conservative hegemony with a flood of progressive and radical ideas, and giving these ideas popular power, an emotional desire for a new and better Britain,'[32] fusing a movement politics with electoral purpose, and in the process building a hegemonic bloc.

This, both the possibility and the fact, arose out of the very particular conditions of the triumphant rise of fascism. In Spain this took the dramatic shape of a civil war: the Spanish army led by the fascist General Franco, armed and supported by Mussolini and Hitler, going to war against the Republican government. The Republican side was supported by the International Brigades from across the world. The British Battalion's Number One Company was named 'The Major Attlee Company'. Attlee took the huge political, not to mention physical, risk of visiting them on the front line in 1937.

In early 1939, both Attlee's future chancellor, Stafford Cripps, and his future minister of health who more than anybody was responsible for founding the NHS, Nye Bevan, were expelled from the Labour Party for publicly advocating Labour joining an anti-fascist popular front stretching from the Communist Party and Independent Labour Party to the Liberal Party and anti-appeasement Tories.

In 1942 came the Beveridge Report, the foundational document of Attlee's welfare state. Beveridge was a social reformer influenced by the Fabian thinkers Sidney and Beatrice Webb. But he identified with the Liberal Party: for a time he was a Liberal MP, and later led the Liberal Party in the House of Lords.

Fyrth describes what this combination amounted to:

A mixture of Socialist, Labour, Keynesian, Fabian/Liberal and anti-Fascist ideas that was strongly anti-establishment and anti-capitalist, and was hostile to those who were held responsible for poverty and unemployment and for appeasement of the Fascist dictators.[33]

This was the basis of Labour's 1945 strength, what Fyrth admiringly dubs a 'popular front of the mind'.[34] It had a plurality of influences and ideas, and a breadth of support. And it is this which produced an historically unique moment: 'It looked as though Conservative supremacy in society might be quite overthrown and a new hegemony of the Left be established.'[35]

But despite the populist idealism of Bevan, who in 1945 declared, 'We have been the dreamers, we have been the sufferers, and now we are the builders,'[36] any hegemony was replaced by 'a consensus between right-wing Labour and progressive conservatism'.[37] Popularly known as 'Butskellism', fusing the names of Hugh Gaitskell (Labour leader 1955–63) and Rab Butler (Tory Cabinet minister 1951–64), it was better than what followed, when another '-ism', Thatcherism, dismantled the consensus, but it was by no means as good as it might have been.

1979: THATCHERISM AND THE CRISIS OF THE LEFT

In his post-1979 general election *Marxism Today* essay 'Thatcherism: The Impasse Broken?',[38] the magazine's editor Martin Jacques mapped out why the Thatcherite hegemony was as much a product of a crisis of what this Labour vision had turned into as a victory of the right.

Jacques described this shift as being from a project of transformation to an ever-increasing emphasis on modernisation. The newly elected Labour leader, Harold Wilson, had prefaced this change in his speech to the 1963 Labour Conference:

> In all our plans for the future, we are re-defining and we are re-stating our socialism in terms of the scientific revolution. But that revolution cannot become a reality unless we are prepared to make far-reaching changes in economic and social attitudes which permeate our whole system of society.
>
> The Britain that is going to be forged in the white heat of this revolution will be no place for restrictive practices or for outdated methods on either side of industry.[39]

Jacques set out what this produced in turn:

> The strategy of modernisation it sought to carry through – aimed at a major transformation of the economy and society – proved not only completely inadequate relative to the nature and scope of the problem but, crucially, it also involved a new kind of attack on the position of the unions and, more widely, the working class, that is on its own social base.[40]

The effect wasn't immediate. Labour's 1945 election-winning vote share of 47.8% was still as high as 47.9% when Harold Wilson won in 1966, an impressive holding of the electoral ground. But after that, the decline was non-stop, reaching as low as 36.9% in 1979, and even lower in 1983. Labour membership reached a post-war high of 908,000 in 1950, but after 1964 fell every year to reach 676,000 in 1978.

At the same time, Jacques argued: 'Labour has become identified with the increasing use of the state in an administrative, impersonal, bureaucratic and even authoritarian manner.'

He described the implications as 'profound':

The Labour Party for many people, *especially* young people, is no longer seen as an effective oppositional, anti-establishment force; on the contrary, for many it has become an establishment party, partially incorporated into the state structures. ...

Inevitably, this has undermined the position of the Labour Party as a *party*, rooted in society, enjoying a popular activist base, and committed to reforming society.[41]

The post-war consensus, which Labour had founded in 1945, followed by Labour's 1960s flirtation with a technocratic modernism, ignominiously ended in the 1978–79 Winter of Discontent. There was a surge in angry strike action as layer after layer of low-paid workers resisted the poverty imposed on them by Labour's state-sanctioned programme of wage restraint. It was a crisis of Labour's making. Statism, which was once the glorious shock of the 1945 new, was replaced by an alien, bureaucratic, inefficient state that was no match for a new set of Tory promises: the right to buy your own home, the opportunity to become a shareholder in an unfettered public utility, the chance to bring bright, shiny, new management practices to a failing NHS. This was modernisation, and then some. Labour had no effective answer because it had helped create the need for such drastic, if disastrous, action in the first place.

CHANGE BUT NO CHANGE

When Tony Blair gave his speech to the 2005 Labour Conference following his historic third successive Labour general election victory, he set out precisely why his time in office would never break with the core belief of what Thatcher, more than anyone, had instilled as the neoliberal consensus: 'I hear people say we have to stop and debate globalisation. You might as well debate whether autumn should follow summer.'[42]

Keir Starmer hasn't wasted any time in setting out the basis of his version of continuity-neoliberalism. This being the modern age, he did this via a tweet:

I'm determined to deliver growth, create wealth and put more money in people's pockets. This can only be achieved by working in

partnership with leading businesses like @BlackRock, to capitalise on the UK's position as a world leading hub for investment.[43]

That word 'only' is doing a lot of work here to identify precisely
where the Starmer 'symptom' lies between the old and the new that
cannot be born, yet.

Before the general election, the academic Daniela Gabor had
warned where Labour's widely trumpeted plan[44] for BlackRock and
companies like it would end up:

> Starmer's vision for government-by-BlackRock reduces the
> question of state capacity to 'how do I get BlackRock to invest in
> infrastructure assets?' This model involves the state in effect sub-
> sidising the privatisation of everyday life. This doesn't only make
> it harder to bring public goods back into public ownership; it also
> allows big finance to tighten the grip on the social contract with
> citizens, and to become the ultimate arbiter of climate, energy
> and welfare politics, which will have profound distributional,
> structural and political consequences.[45]

Of course, no such critique appeared in Labour's manifesto, *Change*.
Which is precisely why, despite the title, it won't.

AGAINST MISERABILISM

> There is a real danger of getting too depressed about the apparent
> triumph of a particularly tawdry and irresponsible sort of finance
> capitalism and the state of the labour movement and the cow-
> ardice and lack of vision of its leadership. But I'm very against
> miserabilism.
>
> David Widgery[46]

The Thatcherite hegemony was reinforced by the flag-waving
aftermath to the 1982 Falklands War. Labour was drifting under
the leadership of Kinnock, who, having once led CND marches,
promptly dropped any commitment to nuclear disarmament. From
the White House Ronald Reagan was implementing 'Reagonomics'
an early version of neoliberalism. The list of possible reasons to be

miserable was very long. David Widgery was 'against miserabilism' because what precisely did being miserable achieve?

And Widgery had form on the subject. He was the architect of the greatest fusion of a popular agitational politics with a popular joyful music, Rock Against Racism. And he had no time for those on 'our side' who couldn't grasp the significance: 'Marxists who turn socialism into something as obscure as particle mechanics'.[47]

Ouch! And then ouch again. I didn't then, and don't now, share David Widgery's Trotskyist politics, but a foundational ideal of mine is a belief that, if a left politics is to be effective, it not only has to be rooted in mass movements, but those movements have to be fun and interesting to be part of. Widgery's 'against miserabilism' brilliantly summed this up with wit, humour and political bite. What was there for an unashamed revisionist turncoat like me not to like? Nothing remotely at all.

LIFTING THE GLOOM

Widgery wrote his case against miserabilism in 1984. That Christmas, like many, I would stand outside supermarkets collecting food for striking miners. Forty years later, I was outside a Lewes supermarket once more collecting food, but this time for those in my community who without the food we'd collected for our town's three food banks would go hungry.

There's a new version of what Widgery diagnosed as miserabilism, generated by a moralistic left around food banks. 'The point is to change the government, change the system. With food banks, all we are doing is replacing politics with charity. We're giving a legitimacy to a system that produces poverty.' So the argument goes.

No tin of beans will ever rid us of food poverty, but I've never met a single person on our Lewes Food Bank collections who collects or donates who thinks it will. And again, neither will miserabilism.

Those who, like me, occasionally need their spirits lifting need look no further than the surrounds of a football stadium on a matchday. At grounds up and down the country, there are food bank collections organised by fans.[48] These fans' food bank collections are huge. This brilliant initiative was founded by usually deadly rivals, Liverpool and Everton fans, with the superb message, 'Hunger doesn't wear colours'. One of the founders of Fans Supporting Food-banks, Ian Byrne, went on to be elected a Labour MP. Instead of Labour calling Ian in to find out how his experience could help ignite a wave of food poverty activism across local parties, a tawdry attempt was made to deselect him. And when that failed, he was suspended as an MP for (checks notes) opposing the two-child benefit cap. Which says it all, and it's not good.

To ground a brighter politics amidst the greyness that threatens to overwhelm us means understanding the ways and means by which this can take shape outside of what we'd conventionally think of as the 'political'. Aditya Chakrabortty is the *Guardian*'s senior economics commentator and a weekly columnist. In 2018, Chakrabortty joined a Saturday morning park run and wrote about it. Much as I enjoy his columns, it is in this piece that for me Chakrabortty best describes the kind of intellectual and practical resources a counter-hegemony requires, not that many involved in park runs would describe them as such:

> What they share is an ethos. Parkruns are free to all, and all are treated equally. No hierarchy intrudes between the hares and the tortoises, the old-timers and the debs ... devoid of government nagging or corporate profiteering, but reliant instead on mutual aid and human kindness.[49]

No, it doesn't sound like most familiar versions of 'doing politics'. But Chakrabortty identified the park run as something more: a hugely successful version of what has been termed 'people's innovation':

> Driven by users rather than producers, by volunteers rather than professionals; they're horizontal rather than hierarchical, and they're not primarily about making money. What drives these citizen innovators isn't pay, but purpose; to have fun, gain work experience or just help others. This is an inversion of how we have come to think of work – it is more the gentle anarchism that you see in your local park every Saturday.[50]

Football fans supporting foodbanks, park runs as motors of change does sound a tad like what Srnicek and Williams deride as 'folk politics'. And if that's all we have left to cling on to, they'd be right. But they are resources of hope, pointers towards what's possible, and a way to lift spirits and expand horizons.

That said, the underlying critique of 'folk politics' is correct. If we fetishise the small as beautiful because the intimacy of what we experience as being part of it matters more than anything, we'd lose sight of the scale of change required. For how to link the two, look no further than Preston.

Preston is today the source of a political project that links the local to the national: community wealth-building.

Matthew Brown, Labour leader of Preston City Council, with co-author Rhian E. Jones, set out the case in their book *Paint Your Town Red*:

> Community wealth-building is not merely about tinkering at the edges of existing systems but forms part of an overarching social, political and economic strategy to address the most urgent and equally overarching threats and challenges of the day.[51]

The basis for such claims? The 'Preston Model', rather than being founded on the spurious idea that change can *only* be achieved in partnership with the likes of BlackRock, is entirely unafraid of the idea that it is the state, in their case the local state, that is best placed to create such change.

From dustbin collections to street cleaning, parking wardens to park-keeping, leisure centres to our children's school meals, and most disastrously of all, council housing, virtually every aspect of the local state has been 'out-sourced' to faceless and faraway multinational corporations. Preston's answer was very simple: reverse all of this with 'in-sourcing', to the benefit of both local people and the local economy.

Joe Guinan and Martin O'Neill, in their book *The Case for Community Wealth Building*, explain how such apparently small changes can spark the kind of break with neoliberalism Blair and Brown failed to make, and that Starmer and Reeves refuse to consider:

> With the increasingly evident exhaustion of the neoliberal model, the search is on for the next political-economic paradigm capable

of replacing it. Community Wealth Building is a way to start at the local level and begin systemic economic change that can, in the end, bring about a fundamental shift in the balance of power and wealth in favour of ordinary people.[52]

MY FRONT IS POPULAR

In December 2023, Labour made public its full list of 'non-battleground seats'[53] for a 2024 general election. Not only did these include those seats with huge and unbeatable Tory majorities, but all of those where the Liberal Democrats were best placed to win, including my own, Lewes. The Lib Dems did something similar, putting next to no effort and resources into Tory seats they couldn't win, but Labour could.

For Labour, was this the party signalling its support for 'tactical voting'? It obviously was. But, as always, Labour couldn't bring itself to admit this.

It was a tactic, not a strategy, with no attempt to have a discussion with local parties affected, brutally enforced where required.[54] And it was a product of Labourism's – left or right varieties – outright aversion to embracing actually existing pluralism.

Or, as Neal Lawson once put it, 'monopoly socialism'.[55]

Lawson coined the phrase at the time of peak Corbynism, following all the optimism generated by the 2017 general election. It was, and remains, a sobering analysis now Starmerism is in the ascendant.

Labour, despite all manner of modernisations, retains its own identity. Those who join are mostly of a social democratic bent. And despite changes in the relationship, no other parliamentary party comes close to Labour insofar as it retains a rootedness in the trade unions. And if we don't want a Tory (or please to goodness no, Reform UK) government, the only alternative is a Labour majority.

But does any of this mean Labour is substantially more progressive and matters so much more than the Liberal Democrats, Green Party, Scottish National Party or Plaid Cymru, to the extent that Labour need not co-operate with them? Although each has different antecedents to Labour, all surely have their place in any sort of progressive bloc.

Neal argues that this requires a fundamental shift away from monopoly socialism's political practice:

> Labour must move from the politics of the Big Tent, with everyone under its suffocating roof, to the politics of the campsite, where progressive parties, movements and organisations keep their identity but share and help others whenever and wherever progressive politics can be advanced.[56]

Which means Labour ceding its historic role as a party of government? He argues, no:

> If Labour were to let go in this way, the party could be the biggest tent in a new ecosystem, and gain the power to transform our country. It would be the end of all or nothing politics for Labour – especially when the 'all' bit turns out to be an infrequent and often hollow promise.[57]

While leadership is important in instituting such a transformation, what is key is cultural shift. Bryn Griffiths reported for the *Labour Hub* website on one of the events organised by Lewes Labour Party as a practical example of what this might look like:[58]

> The only requirement for attendance at a Lewes Labour Party festival of ideas event is that you come with an open mind. The result of this unusual approach to Labour politics is that you find yourself in a room full of left-wing socialists, Labour centrists, Labour loyalists, Green Party members, single issue campaigners, community activists, people of no party at all and even the odd radical liberal. Open, robust and serious political discussion at a Labour Party-hosted event might sound unusual but believe me it really works![59]

And he described the cause of all this: 'the principle of radical pluralism seems to be part of their political DNA'.[60] I'm not entirely sure whether Bryn meant this as a compliment or as a critique, but I fully endorse his description.

Radical and plural, my Front is Popular.

WHAT WOULD GRAMSCI SAY?

In April 1987 Stuart Hall gave a talk at 'Gramsci '87' a *Marxism Today* event to mark the 50 years since Gramsci's death. He argued: 'I do believe we must "think" our problems in a Gramscian way.'[61]

Then he warned: 'We mustn't *use* Gramsci (as we have for so long abused Marx) like an Old Testament prophet who, at the correct moment, will offer us the consoling and appropriate quotation.'[62]

When using Hall's work to think through our problems with the current *interregnum*, I am conscious of his warning. A lot has changed since 1987, but some hasn't.

Hall described the post-war consensus:

I'm perfectly well aware that socialism was not inaugurated in 1945. I'm talking about the taken-for granted popular base of welfare social democracy, which formed the real, concrete ground on which any socialism worth the name has to be built.[63]

He was depressingly accurate in his assessment of Thatcherism. It destroyed the post-war consensus, but it: 'entered the political field in a historic contest, not just for power, but for popular authority, for *hegemony*'.[64]

And Thatcherism in the form of neoliberalism has been *hegemonic* ever since.

How? Hall described the process as follows:

In modern societies, *hegemony* must be constructed, contested and won, on many different sites, as the modern state and society complexify and the points of social antagonism proliferate.[65]

Stuart Hall's final essay was published in the summer 2011 edition of the journal *Soundings*, which he co-founded. Writing in the wake of the end of the Tony Blair and Gordon Brown version of the interregnum and the start of 14 years of Tory government, he reminded those of us of a certain political age what Thatcherism was, and for a 21st-century Generation Left what it had become: a 'neoliberal revolution':

According to the neoliberal narrative, the welfare state (propelled by working-class reaction to the Depression of the 1930s and the popular mobilisation of World War Two) *mistakenly* saw its task as intervening in the economy, redistributing wealth, universalising life chances, attacking unemployment, protecting the socially vulnerable, ameliorating the condition of oppressed or marginalised groups and addressing social justice.[66]

Did Blair and Brown – do Starmer and Reeves – subscribe to such a view? No, of course not.

But then Hall added the core economic philosophy that underpins it:

State intervention must never compromise the right of private capital to 'grow the business', improve share value, pay dividends and reward its agents with enormous salaries, benefits and bonuses.[67]

Did Blair and Brown – will Starmer and Reeves – govern in opposition to any of this? It is hardly asking a lot – but, hmmm.

Stuart Hall didn't live to see Ed Miliband's defeat in 2015, the rise of Corbynism, and Starmer's landslide victory in 2024. His closing remarks in that 2011 final article, however, proved prescient:

Hegemony is a tricky concept and provokes muddled thinking. No project achieves 'hegemony' as a completed project. It is a process, not a state of being. No victories are permanent or final. Hegemony has constantly to be 'worked on', maintained, renewed, revised. Excluded social forces, whose consent has not been won, whose interests have not been taken into account, form the basis of counter-movements, resistance, alternative strategies and visions ... and the struggle over a hegemonic system starts anew.[68]

NOSTALGIA ISN'T DEAD

Provided Starmer doesn't decide to go early, or is somehow forced to, the next general election will be in July 2029. Give or take a month, it will be 50 years on from Thatcher's 1979 victory and all that has meant for the ensuing half-century.

For those who, like me, were first-time voters in 1979, we're now of pensionable vintage. In 1978, I was doing my A-levels, my Surrey school a comprehensive – such schools were known back then as 'state schools', not a whiff of a private corporation running an ever-expanding chain of such schools rebranded as 'academies' for profit.

The school was in the middle of a sizeable council estate. Council houses, owned by the council. The weasel-worded phrases 'social housing' and 'affordable housing' didn't exist back then, the houses defined instead by who owned them – the local state – rented out and maintained for local people.

Once I'd passed my A-Levels, it was off up north to Hull University, the train to get there and the buses to get around the city publicly owned. The student house I lived in for my first year was owned and managed by the university for the good of their undergraduates and duty of care, not sold off to some private outfit for a quick buck by an entirely monetised higher education system. At Christmas I worked as a seasonal postman for the Royal Mail, wholly publicly owned, and in the summer, for a local hospital as a cleaner, the cleaning carried out by NHS employees, not some outsourced outfit.

Back home, the water out of our taps, the gas and electricity that kept us warm, the telephone line that kept us in touch with relatives and friends – all publicly owned. The district nurses who visited each day to care for my disabled mum were provided by the NHS, not a business making a profit out of the plight of those who couldn't care for themselves.

These memories today read like a fairy story. Until 1979, they were what we all expected as the very least our society should look like.

In 1979, the year of Thatcher's election, *In and Against the State*[69] was published. The authors were unafraid to hold back their criticism of the state provision that I now remember so fondly:

We seem to need things from the state, such as child care, houses, medical treatment. But what we are given is often shoddy or penny-pinching, and besides it comes to us in a way that seems to limit our freedom, reduce the control we have over our lives.[70]

Highly critical of traditional Labour politics and existing versions of trade union campaigning, the authors were equally unimpressed by the Leninist revolutionary left. Instead, they advocated a politics built out of the lived experience of the state. This would, they argued, produce an entirely different set of relations: 'It is about infusing all aspects of everyday life, from work and health to child care and personal relationships with oppositional practice.'[71]

The language and ambition are both very much the product of a particular late 1970s moment, perhaps best summarised by the one-sentence philosophy of another hugely influential book from this era, *Beyond the Fragments*:[72] 'The personal is political.'

In and Against the State was republished in 2021, with an afterword by John McDonnell[73] in which he regretted that Corbynism failed to establish something similar to an 'in and against' tendency. His reasoning? 'A lot of our attention, unfortunately, was just on survival. And what happens when you're fighting for survival is the danger that you bureaucratise.'[74]

McDonnell described the consequences of this struggle to survive as a defensiveness, a closed circle of only the most loyal and trusted, a shutting down of potential alliances. And, most disastrously, a failure to recognise what had powered Corbynism in the first place: 'Our strength was not a ring of steel around us; our strength was to go further outwards and build the social movement anyway.'[75]

In and against Labourism – round one to Labourism.

LABOURISM'S PERMA-CRISIS

Stuart Hall addressed the causes of Labour's 1983 defeat in the context of 'the crisis of Labourism'.[76]

First:

Labour understands perfectly well, but is incapable of organising, a popular political and ideological struggle .... It can mobilise the vote, provided it remains habitually solid. But it shows less and less capacity to connect with popular feelings and sentiments, let alone transform them or articulate them to the left.[77]

This was true then, and all the empirical evidence[78] from the 2024 'loveless landslide' suggests that nothing much has changed for the better.

Second:

Extra-parliamentary activity – politics and campaigning in any political space other than that directed to the House of Commons or within the confines of the formal electoral system – produces in its leadership the deepest traumas and the most sycophantic poems of praise for parliamentarism. Yet it is precisely the confinement within the parliamentary mould and Labour's formal definition of the 'political' which has been its undoing.[79]

Or, as Labour MP and Chief Secretary to the Treasury Darren Jones helpfully put it:

Many Jeremy Corbyn supporters preferred a party of protest as opposed to a party who have had to make difficult decisions around the trade-offs in its preparation for government in the hope that we get to run this country.[80]

Jones, like his boss, Rachel Reeves, betrays a wilful ignorance of Labour, history and protest.

He also seems to have a less than cursory knowledge of how he came to be elected an MP. In 2015, he'd stood for the first time in Bristol North West, and came a distant second. In 2017, he stood again, and won with a +16.4% swing. He held the seat in 2019, with his majority reduced by just 70 votes and a swing against him of just -1.4%. In the 2024 general election, after four years' worth of Starmer changing Labour from a party of protest to a party of government and a landslide, Jones' majority was down by 3,272 votes, the 'landslide' swing just +0.7, and the Green Party was up from fourth to second place. Darren – who was Labour leader in 2017? And wasn't it testament to the coupling of protest and parliamentary politics that in 2017 you signed a path-breaking local agreement with the

Green candidate to campaign in parliament on a shared agenda against Brexit, for PR, and on environmental issues. And as a result, the Green Party ceased campaigning in Bristol North West for that election.[81] As a participant in overcoming this binary opposition, party of government versus party of protest, Jones was well placed to point out how unhelpful it is. The fact he didn't? Welcome to cynicism.

Hall's final point on Labourism was:

Apart from the handful of experts who advise its committees on policy matters – it has not organised a core of 'organic intellectuals'. Labour, then looks like a party which has never heard of the strategy of a 'war of position' – that is, struggling for leadership and mastery over a whole number of different fronts in the course of making itself the focal point of popular aspirations, the leading popular political force.[82]

Hall's conclusion was damning. A party with no organic intellectual culture while lacking a 'war of position' strategy would fail: 'Labour does not believe such a struggle to be necessary because it does not take mass political-ideological struggle seriously.'[83]

A bit harsh? Inappropriate even? Hall refutes any such suggestion:

Labourism is profoundly 'economistic' in outlook and ideology. It really does suppose that economic facts transmit themselves directly into working-class heads, without passing through the real world. Working-class consciousness is as automatic as self-programming underground trains: once Labour, always Labour. And yet the clear signs are that political automatism is certainly at an end – if ever it existed.[84]

JOLTS TO THE SYSTEM

Stuart Hall's exploration and critique of Labourism didn't appear in *Marxism Today*, but in *New Socialist*, which, ironically, was a magazine published by the Labour Party. It was a jolt to the very systemic 'Labourism' Hall was criticising. The aims of the magazine, described by the founding editor James Curran, were 'partly to develop analysis and debate about the principles of democratic socialism but also to tap into the new movements of the post-1968 left and promising veins of popular culture'.[85] The range of authors was decisively pluralist: Hall, alongside well-established Labour intellectuals including Anna Coote, Bernard Crick and Ben Pimlott, and dissident feminists such as Doreen Massey, Lynne Segal and Hilary Wainwright.

The May 1987 'How to Nobble Thatcher' issue of the magazine which preceded the general election carried a cautious endorsement by Stuart Weir, Curran's successor as editor, of tactical voting. Weir was realistic about what the Labour Party could and should do. Calling on members and supporters to vote for another party, for example, was a non-starter. But that didn't mean the party should condemn this embryonic movement of voters whose sole objective was to get Labour into government. Weir proposed:

The Labour Party cannot endorse TV 87 [the organised tactical voting campaign] or disavow any of its candidates. But it can adopt a strategy which is more likely to encourage the tactical voting by potential Alliance voters that could put the party in power in the next parliament. This means, inescapably, declaring now for electoral reform. The media will give tactical voting a big push in the next election. Labour could give it a radical edge and cure the 'asymmetric effect' by committing itself to electoral reform.[86]

Weir was forced to resign, replaced by the editor of the extraordinarily dull party newspaper *Labour Weekly*. Within three years, *New Socialist* was closed down. Nothing has come close to replacing this popular, occasionally irreverent, intellectual Labour venture since. Jolt ended.

The Kinnock model of modernisation saw a second venture, one framed by a politics we could both dance and laugh along to: Red Wedge.[87] The key architects were Annajoy David, previously the driving force behind the youth wing of CND, and Phill Jupitus, mainstay of the 'alternative cabaret' circuit latterly best known as a team captain on the TV show *Never Mind the Buzzcocks*. Driving the Red Wedge van as they toured round the country was none other than Geoff Mulgan, later to become Tony Blair's director of policy. Mixing pop, politics and comedy is no mean feat, but with the help of Ben Elton, Billy Bragg, Mark Steel, Tracey Thorn's' Everything but the Girl, Robbie Coltrane and more, the Labour Party became the hottest ticket in town.

Stuart Cosgrove, music writer mainstay at what, in the mid-1980s, remained the weekly must-read for all that was hip, happening and political, the *New Musical Express*, had a neat line on the scale of Red Wedge's popular-cultural ambition:

> So what happens when the Red Wedge circus moves on? What does it leave behind, some satisfied souls and a few hangovers? Red Wedge has to become the animator not the afterthought, it has to *generate* events and not simply provide them.[88]

Adding as an afterthought his own version of such an animation, Cosgrove concluded: 'Red Wedge has to chase the improbable and fast. It has to unite the night away. Labour: it ain't nothing but a *parrrty*.'[89]

No, despite Red Wedge's best efforts, it doesn't sound like any Labour Party I've ever known. Once Labour lost the 1987 general election, Red Wedge was wound up, job not done.

Tony Manwaring was head of the Labour Party general secretary's office during 1983–93 and was involved in Red Wedge from the beginning. His reflections on what might have been describe precisely why this jolt petered out:

> It was brilliant and beautiful to see and Red Wedge was reconfiguring the DNA. But I don't think the Labour Party had the reflective capability to draw and learn and honour what was being done ... the answer isn't what Red Wedge brought to the Labour Party, it's what kind of politics we could have created together.[90]

All Labour was left with from this precious 'moment' was a grinning Tony Blair rubbing shoulders with Noel Gallagher at Number Ten[91] and thinking this was the dawning of the age of 'Cool Britannia'. It wasn't. Jeremy Corbyn made the same error, mistaking his adoring reception at Glastonbury for a social movement. It wasn't.[92]

Jolts to the system come from all of Labour's different political directions, because in so many ways the system serves and protects the interests of Labour's left, right and soft in-between once any of them are in control. The biggest single jolt came in 2014 from the centre and right of the party, bitterly opposed by the left and only grudgingly accepted, 'this far and no further', by most of the affiliated trade unions.

The 2014 Collins Review is an obscure document.[93] David Kogan analysed the changes it ushered in: 'the unexpected consequences were a mass movement, and the return and election of the left after so many years in the wilderness'.[94]

Neither was what Labour's right had in mind!

They thought that reducing the threshold of MPs' nominations would ensure a veneer of pluralism while producing humiliation of any candidate from the hard left.

By largely replacing the affiliated trade unions' block vote with ballots of individual members paying into their unions' political funds, they confidently expected the ordinary members to be to the right of their general secretaries. Hence the left's opposition to the change.

But the most significant change was to open any future leadership and deputy leadership elections to 'Labour supporters' as well as Labour members. Confident this would swamp a declining Labour left activist base with 'ordinary' voters who'd always plump for a centre-right candidate, the Labour right couldn't have been happier and more in favour. The Labour left was opposed. The changes went through.

The result? The 2015 leadership election and the 2016 re-election were both won decisively by Jeremy Corbyn in what were effectively open primaries. Labour's doors were wide open.

But almost as soon as this change was introduced, the process was in retreat.

First, the fee for becoming a registered supporter was increased. Then an ever-longer cut-off point to register as a supporter was introduced, thus preventing new supporters from voting in leadership elections despite the fact, or because, this was the reason why most would register! And finally, the number of MPs' nominations needed to get on the ballot paper was increased, thus narrowing the range of candidates likely to win, and given the low number of Labour left MPs, designed to exclude any of them from being a candidate.

Jess Garland described the experiment as 'changing what it means to support a party and embracing the needs of twenty-first century partisans'.[95] But the experiment was ended by the combined forces of a left that never really grasped how an 'open party' might function and a right that did, so they promptly ensured that the 'open' party would remain closed as long as they were in charge. The jolt that shook labourism up for a while, fixed.

Labour's long years out of office, 1979–97, focused members' minds. The Tories governed with a vote share that never topped 43.9%, while Labour and the Liberal Democrats (and briefly, the Social Democratic Party) remained in opposition with a combined vote share that never fell below 50.7%. Labour support for proportional representation grew, but remained a minority-activist pursuit.

The second long spell out of office, 2010–24, focused minds a lot more. The result was a hugely successful 'Labour for a New Democracy' campaign.[96] At the 2022 Labour Conference, constituency party delegates and affiliated unions overwhelmingly passed a motion rejecting an electoral system that the motion identified as having 'catastrophically failed to represent people's wishes, needs and votes'. The resolution insisted that 'Labour must make a commitment to introduce proportional representation for general elections in the next manifesto.'[97] Starmer's position on its inclusion? 'No, it's not a priority for me.'[98]

The vote wasn't simply historic because of the party's change of position on PR, but because of how it was delivered – support that was non-factional. Spokespersons for PR ranged from John McDonnell of the hard left, Andy Burnham from the centre left to the Labour right's key organiser, Luke Akehurst. It was Labour combining the plural and the radical.

Unsurprisingly, the 2024 landslide has meant the issue has receded,[99] but it is clear that, with Labour enjoying a huge majority despite winning only 33.7% of the popular vote, the iniquities of first past the post will come back to haunt it. Jolt unfinished.

Meanwhile Starmer, the advocate of ill-defined 'change', reigns supreme. His party's conference is reduced to a rapturous rally with no significant influence on Labour's direction and policy.

The morning after the 2024 general election, one more jolt came to an end, but this time it was of its own choosing. The World Transformed (TWT) project announced that its annual festival of ideas on the fringe of Labour conference was no more.[100] The festival had been a huge presence on the party's conference fringe since 2016. *Guardian* columnist John Harris went to the first TWT and liked what he saw:

> These were not the hardliners and ideological desperadoes that some people might imagine: their politics felt open, self-critical and realistic about the huge tasks it faces. They may not yet have a clear idea of how a new left politics might decisively cohere – but no one (not even gobby newspaper columnists) does, as yet. The point is to at least begin with a sense of how it might start to mesh, and the breadth of people who will have to be involved.[101]

But despite all that, TWT, with an entire world to transform, absented itself from a sustained effort at transforming the world on its political doorstep, the Labour Party, and as a result, largely failed[102] to generate any sort of culture that would produce within Labour what Gramsci called a culture of 'organic intellectuals':

> The mode of being of the new intellectual can no longer consist in eloquence, which is an exterior and momentary mover of feelings and passions, but in active participation in practical life, as constructor, 'permanent persuader' and not just a simple orator.[103]

Jolt abandoned.

TESTING THE LIMITS OF LABOURISM

Gramsci's most famous maxim is 'Pessimism of the intellect, optimism of the will'.[104]

John Clarke has a neat line on what to expect from Keir Starmer for adherents of the 'pessimism of the intellect' position: 'a thin, but profoundly pacifying and restorationist, version of social democracy, seeking to reassure us that all will be well'.[105]

The obverse, however, 'optimism of the will', can be just as disheartening – supercharging all efforts towards Starmer defying his critics' pessimism, only to come down with a crushing intellectual bump so severe any will is extinguished.

To date, Starmer has been a disappointment, including to many of those who supported him, voted for his Labour Party and revelled in Labour's general election victory.

His unwillingness ever since to be radical manifests as a number of symptoms, symptoms in the sense of being signs of what is to come, even worse.

Signs can be warnings – but they also offer the prospect that the 'new' can yet be born.[106]

A Labour Party that fosters a culture that is organically intellectual.

Labour building pluralism into every way it works, internally and externally.

A convivial party in which taking part is as much about pleasure and fun as duty and formality.

A Labour party that is unafraid to act, to campaign and to govern as the leading party of a much broader progressive bloc.

Testing the limits of Labourism. To destruction.

ENDNOTES

1.   Antonio Gramsci 'Wave of Materialism and Crisis of Authority' in Quintin Hoare and Geoffrey Nowell Smith (eds) *Antonio Gramsci: Selections from Prison Notebooks* Lawrence and Wishart, London 1971 p. 276.
2.   See David Forgacs 'Gramsci and Marxism in Britain' *New Left Review* 1/176 (July/August 1989) pp. 70–88.
3.   Gilbert Achcar 'Morbid Symptoms: What Did Gramsci Really Mean?' *Notebooks: The Journal for Studies on Power* 1 (2021) p. 379.
4.   John Clarke 'Change! (in Moderation): Labourism, Starmer and the Conjuncture' *Soundings: A Journal of Politics and Culture* 87 (Summer–Autumn 2024) p. 147.
5.   Ibid. p. 148.
6.   See Nancy Fraser *The Old Is Dying and the New Cannot Be Born* Verso, London 2019.
7.   Ibid. p. 29.
8.   Ibid. pp. 39–40.

9. For a description of this missed opportunity moment, see James Doran 'Liquidating Labour' Novara Media 15 September 2013 www.novara-media.com and James Doran 'An Antidote to Pasokification' in Mark Perryman (ed.) *The Corbyn Effect* Lawrence and Wishart, London 2017. For a pan-European survey of the mid-2010s populist left at its peak, see Catarina Principe and Bhaskar Sunkara (eds) *Europe in Revolt* Haymarket Books, Chicago 2016.

10. Clarke, 'Change! (in Moderation)' p. 157.

11. Ibid. p. 18.

12. For various theories that lie behind this, see: Claire Ainsley *The New Working Class: How To Win Hearts, Minds and Votes* Policy Press, Bristol 2018; 'Labour Together General Election Review 2019' 18 June 2020 www.labourtogether.uk; Deborah Mattinson *Beyond the Red Wall: Why Labour Lost, How the Conservatives Won and What Will Happen Next?* Biteback, London 2020.

13. See Mark Perryman (ed.) *Breaking Up Britain: Four Nations after a Union* Lawrence and Wishart, London 2009.

14. See Satnam Virdee and Brendan McGeever *Britain in Fragments: Why Things Are Falling Apart* Manchester University Press, Manchester 2023.

15. Keir Starmer's retort to a heckler during the leader's speech at Labour Party Conference on 24 September 2024.

16. Morgan Jones 'Ridley, McSweeney, McDonagh and the Rise of the Organiser Class' Labour List 10 October 2024 www.labourlist.org.

17. Richard Johnson and Deborah Lynn Steinberg 'Distinctiveness and Difference within New Labour' in Richard Johnson and Deborah Lynn Steinberg (eds) *Blairism and the War of Persuasion* Lawrence and Wishart, London 2004, pp. 12–13.

18. See John Rees *The Leveller Revolution: Radical Political Organisation in England, 1640–1650* Verso, London 2017.

19. Clarke 'Change! (in Moderation)' p. 158.

20. Nick Srnicek and Alex Williams *Postcapitalism and the World Without Work* Verso, London 2016.

21. Ibid. pp. 10–11.

22. Ibid. p. 11.

23. Ibid. p. 198.

24. Stuart Hall 'The Great Moving Right Show' *Marxism Today* (January 1979) www.banmarchive.org.uk.

25. Eric Hobsbawm 'The Forward March of Labour Halted?' *Marxism Today* (September 1978) www.banmarchive.org.uk.

26. Hall 'The Great Moving Right Show' p. 15.

27. Ibid.

28. Owen Hatherley *The Ministry of Nostalgia* Verso, London 2016 pp. 47–48.

29. Ibid. p. 48.

30. Jim Fyrth 'Days of Hope: The Meaning of 1945' in Jim Fryth (ed.) *Labour's Promised Land? Culture and Society in Labour Britain 1945–51* Lawrence and Wishart, London 1995 p. 4.
31. Ibid.
32. Ibid.
33. Ibid.
34. A term recycled in the 1980s by the long-forgotten UK magazine *Samizdat* to describe its advocacy of a broad coalition against Thatcherism.
35. Fyrth 'Days of Hope' p. 5.
36. Quoted in Michel Sheen 'Full Text of Michael Sheen's speech' *The Guardian* 2 March 2015 www.theguardian.com.
37. Fyrth 'Days of Hope' p. 5.
38. Martin Jacques 'Thatcherism: The Impasse Broken?' *Marxism Today* (October 1979) pp. 6–15 www.banmarchive.org.uk.
39. Harold Wilson' Labour and the Scientific Revolution' speech to Labour Party Annual Conference 1963.
40. Jacques 'Thatcherism' p. 11.
41. Ibid. pp. 11–12.
42. Tony Blair, Labour Conference speech, 27 September 2005.
43. @Keir_Starmer on X 21 November 2024.
44. Alex Wickham, Alibhe Rea and Joe Mayes 'Labour Banks on Billions of Private Investment Post-Election' Bloomberg 27 June 2024 www.bloomberg.com.
45. Daniela Gabor 'Labour Is Putting Its Plans for Britain in the Hands of Private Finance. It Could End Badly' *The Guardian* 2 July 2024 www.theguardian.com.
46. David Widgery, unpublished biographical piece written in 1984 quoted in David Widgery *Against Miserabilism: Writings 1968–1992* Vagabond Voices, Glasgow 2017 p. 3.
47. David Widgery *Beating Time: Riot 'n' Race 'n' Rock 'n Roll* Chatto & Windus, London 1986 p. 122.
48. See www.fanssupportingfoodbanks.co.uk.
49. Aditya Chakrabortty 'Forget Profit. It's Love and Fun That Drive Innovations Like Parkrun' *The Guardian* 20 August 2018 www.theguardian.com.
50. Ibid.
51. Matthew Brown and Rhian E. Jones *Painting Your Town Red: How Preston Took Back Control and Your Town Can Too* Repeater Books, London 2021 p. 21.
52. Joe Guinan and Martin O'Neill *The Case for Community Wealth Building* Polity Press, Cambridge 2020 pp. 34–35.
53. See 'Non Battleground Seats 2024' The Labour Party www.labour.org.uk.
54. See James Moules, Tom Belger and Daniel Green 'May Elections: Party Warned GE Handling of "Non-Battlegrounds" Could Cost Votes' Labour List www.labourlist.org 14 November 2024.

55. Neal Lawson *Beyond Monopoly Socialism: Why Labour Needs to Learn to Live with Complexity and Seek Power with Others, Not over Them* Compass Think Piece #94 March 2018 www.compassonline.org.uk.
56. Ibid. p. 13.
57. Ibid.
58. To declare an interest, I am the organiser of Lewes Labour events.
59. Bryn Griffiths 'How to Transform Unequal Britain' 25 November 2024 www.labourhub.org.uk.
60. Ibid.
61. Stuart Hall's talk was republished as 'Gramsci and Us' *Marxism Today* (June 1987) p. 16 www.banmarchive.org.uk.
62. Ibid. p. 16.
63. Ibid. p.17.
64. Ibid.
65. Ibid. p. 20.
66. Stuart Hall 'The Neoliberal Revolution' *Soundings* 48 (2011), p. 11.
67. Ibid.
68. Ibid. p. 26.
69. Originally self-published in 1979 as a pamphlet, then in a revised and expanded book version, London Edinburgh Weekend Return Group *In and Against the State: Discussion Notes for Socialists* Pluto Press, London 1980. All references from Seth Wheeler (ed.) London Edinburgh Weekend Return Group *In and Against the State: Discussion Notes for Socialists* (2nd edn) Pluto Press, London 2021.
70. Ibid. p. 8.
71. Ibid. p. 121.
72. Sheila Rowbotham, Lynne Segal and Hilary Wainwright *Beyond the Fragments: Feminism and he Making of Socialism* Merlin Press, London 1979.
73. 'Interview with John McDonnell' in Wheeler (ed.) *In and Against the State* pp. 135–150.
74. Ibid. p. 144.
75. Ibid.
76. Stuart Hall 'Whistling in the Void' *New Socialist* (May/June 1983), published as a revised and updated version as 'The Crisis of Labourism' in James Curran (ed.) *The Future of the Left* New Socialist and Polity Press, Cambridge 1984. All references from latter version.
77. Ibid. p. 32.
78. See Paula Surridge in this collection and John Curtice 'After the 2024 Election: Parliamentary Strength, Electoral Weakness' in Gerry Hassan and Simon Barrow (eds) *Britain Needs Change: The Politics of Hope and Labour's Challenge* Biteback, London 2024.
79. Hall 'The Crisis of Labourism' p. 33.
80. Peter Walker 'Labour No Longer a "Party of Protest" Says Shadow Minister after Drop in Numbers' *The Guardian* 3 April 2024 www.theguardian.com.

81. See 'Green and Labour Candidates Agree to Work Together in Bristol North West' Bristol Green Party 30 May 2017 www.bristolgreenparty.org.uk.

82. Hall 'The Crisis of Labourism' p. 33.

83. Ibid.

84. Ibid. pp. 33–34.

85. Cited in Colm Murphy 'The Forgotten Rival of *Marxism Today*: The British Labour Party's *New Socialist* and the business of Political Culture in the Late Twentieth Century' *English Historical Review* 138/593 (August 2023) p. 883 www.academic.oup.com.

86. Stuart Weir 'How to Nobble Thatcher' *New Socialist* (May 1987) p. 19.

87. See 'Book Three: Red Wedge' in Daniel Rachel *Walls Come Tumbling Down: The Music and Politics of Rock against Racism, 2 Tone and Red Wedge* Picador, London 2016 pp. 337–534.

88. Stuart Cosgrove 'Bands on the Wagon' *New Socialist* (March 1986) p. 10.

89. Ibid.

90. Interview in Rachel *Walls Come Tumbling Down* p. 513.

91. For a comprehensive account of this episode, see John Harris *The Last Party: Britpop, Blair and the Demise of English Rock* Fourth Estate, London 2003.

92. The potential of #Grime4Corbyn is described by Monique Charles in 'Generation Grime' in Perryman (ed.) *The Corbyn Effect* pp. 138–149.

93. For a very good account, see David Kogan *Protest and Power: The Battle for the Labour Party* Bloomsbury, London 2019 pp. 184–200.

94. Ibid. p. 184.

95. Jess Garland 'Labour's New Model Party' in Perryman (ed.) *The Corbyn Effect* p. 79.

96. See www.labourforanewdemocracy.org.uk.

97. See Peter Walker and Aubrey Allegretti 'Labour Delegates Back Motion Calling on Party to Back PR' 26 September 2022 *The Guardian* www.theguardian.com.

98. Michael Savage and Toby Helm 'Keir Starmer Defies Calls for Changes to First Past the Post System' *The Guardian* 24 September 2022 www.theguardian.com.

99. See Peter Walker 'Labour Divided over Calls to Scrap First Past the Post after Landslide Win' *The Guardian* 17 July 2024 www.theguardian.com.

100. See 'What's Next for TWT?' The World Transformed 20 August 2024 www.theworldtransformed.org.

101. John Harris 'A Labour Party of the Future Is Beginning to Emerge' *The Guardian* 29 September 2016 www.theguardian.com.

102. For a critique, see Isaac Kneebone-Hopkins 'After the Party Was Over: Looking Back at the World Transformed' *Morning Star* 17 July 2024 www.morningstaronline.co.uk.

103. Antonio Gramsci 'The Formation of the Intellectuals' in Quintin Hoare and Geoffrey Nowell Smith (eds) *Selections from the Prison Notebooks of Antonio Gramsci* Lawrence and Wishart, London 1971 p. 10.

104. Antonio Gramsci 'Address to the Anarchists' *l'Ordine Nuovo* (3–10 April 1920) in Quintin Hoare (ed.) *Antonio Gramsci: Political Writings 1910–1920*, Lawrence and Wishart, London 1977 p. 188. In the text, Gramsci attributes what was to become his most famous maxim to the original source, the French dramatist and novelist Romain Rolland.

105. Clarke 'Change! (in Moderation)' p. 159.

106. For an excellent, and complementary, distillation of these 'signs', see Kirsten Forkert and Sally Davison 'Moving Right: The Circus Continues' *Soundings* 88 (Winter/Spring 2024–25) pp. 4–14.

MAPPING THE HOPE

Did Labour Win or the Tories Lose?

Paula Surridge

The outcome of the 2024 election could not be clearer. Voters returned a government with a three-figure majority, giving Keir Starmer's administration the kind of parliamentary power many had thought a thing of the past. After a series of elections which resulted in hung parliaments or small and difficult to manage majorities, Boris Johnson's 80-seat majority in 2019 had seemed an outlier, but in 2024 Labour doubled it. It was delivered on the lowest winning vote share on record. Of those who turned out to vote, just over one in three voted Labour. Given the second lowest turnout on record, across the entire electorate it was closer to one in five.

Labour undoubtedly won the election, but the extent to which this was because of how voters viewed it rather than how they viewed the Conservative government is a key question. It is important not only for understanding the 2024 results, but also for assessing how easy, or difficult, Labour will find it in government.

VALENCE AND THE CONSERVATIVE DECLINE

This election delivered a clear verdict on the performance of the Conservative government. Valence issues are those on which there is broad agreement about what the outcomes should be (for example, most people would prefer inflation to be lower), so focus turns to who is best placed to deliver those outcomes. Competence, leadership and delivery are the key elements of valence politics.[1] The Conservatives were failing on all of them.

As the public went to the polls, Rishi Sunak's government was seen by more than two-thirds of voters as incompetent. More than four-fifths of the public were dissatisfied with it, and two-thirds said it did not deserve to be re-elected.[2]

45

It is no surprise that the Conservatives lost almost 20 percentage points from their 2019 vote share. What is more difficult to explain in terms of valence politics alone is where those votes went. They went in all directions.[3] Critical for the Labour majority was the traditional 'swing' vote between the two major parties. But there were other swings which contributed to Labour's success. Conservative voters in seats in the south of England went to the Liberal Democrats. A larger but less electorally successful group went to Reform UK, and a much smaller but nonetheless important group voted for the Green Party.

In a year that proved difficult for incumbent parties across the world,[4] the SNP also struggled in Scotland, losing 15 percentage points from its vote share and 40 seats (36 to Labour).

Perhaps more surprising is that, in an election the voters saw primarily in terms of 'change', the winning party also lost votes. Fragmentation occurred across the electorate and across the country. While the vote share of incumbent parties of government (the Conservatives, the SNP, and to a lesser extent the Labour Party in Wales) collapsed, it was not always a simple story of the main opposition party gaining. The result is a new sort of political battleground that will shape the nature of party competition and their interactions with the electorate across the parliament, as how voters chose to vote varied depending on the type of party competition in their constituency.[5]

NEGATIVE PARTISANSHIP AND TACTICAL VOTING

The last two years of the previous parliament had made it clear that voters at local elections and by-elections were willing to vote for whichever party they thought was best placed to remove an incumbent Conservative.

The British Election Study internet panel (BESIP)[6] asked voters to say how much they liked all parties on a zero to ten scale. When asked to rate the Conservative Party, the average was just 3.0, compared with 4.3 in 2019. More than one in three of the electorate gave it a score of zero out of ten.

Figure 1[7] shows how these ratings changed across the parliament for different groups of voters. As we would expect, those who voted

Conservative in both elections rated the party highly throughout, although even this group saw a drop from an average of almost eight to an average of seven.

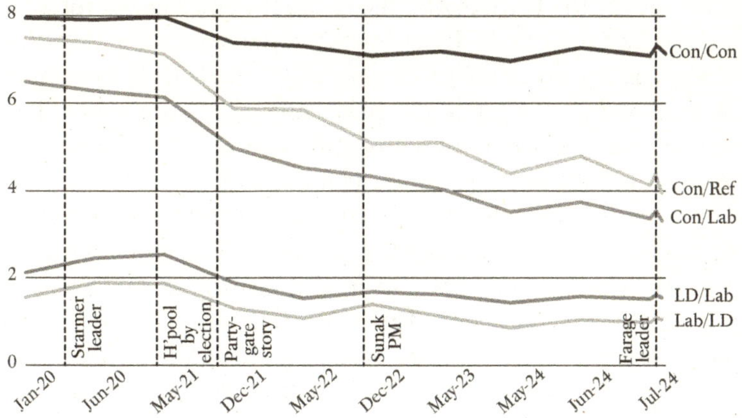

Figure 1 Mean 'like' score for Conservative Party by vote in 2019 and 2024 (0–10 scale)
Source: British Election Study internet panel

The views of those who switched away from the Conservative Party in 2024 began to decline around the time of the 'partygate' scandal. They declined further across the remainder of the parliament. The already low ratings of those who switched between Labour and the Liberal Democrats (in either direction) fell further, both after partygate and, particularly for those who switched from Labour to the Liberal Democrats, across the course of Sunak's leadership.

These very low party ratings among key groups are indicative of negative partisanship,[8] in which dislike of a party motivates voting decisions more than attachment to the party chosen. Almost three in ten voters said that, given the choice to vote against a party, they would vote against the Conservatives. A further quarter said they would vote against Reform UK.

Tactical voting has long been a feature of British electoral behaviour,[9] but the 2024 election provided particularly fertile conditions for it. There was a strong desire to get rid of the Conservatives, alongside a leadership – Starmer as opposed to Corbyn – of the Labour Party that appealed to Liberal Democrat voters and a Liberal Democrat leadership that was no longer directly critical of Labour.

While an intense desire to get rid of the Conservatives was undoubtedly the key factor in the result, the efficiency of votes for Labour and the Liberal Democrats (and therefore the scale of the defeat and the size of the Labour majority) rested on the willingness of their voters to switch to the other party where it mattered. This was in part a reflection of Starmer's leadership. Data collected at the start of the campaign showed that those who had voted Liberal Democrat in 2019 rated Starmer as highly as those who had voted Labour. On a zero to ten scale of 'liking' the Labour leader 2019, Labour voters had an average score of 5.5. 2019 Liberal Democrat voters had an average of 5.4. This was in sharp contrast to the 2019 election, where those who had previously voted Liberal Democrat were far more negative about Corbyn than those who had voted Labour and where the Labour leadership was seen as a block to voters switching between the two parties.[10]

The reasons people gave for their vote immediately after the election give some indication of the scale of tactical voting. Among those who switched from Labour to the Liberal Democrats, more than one in three said their reason for doing so was because they felt their preferred party had no chance in their constituency. Among those switching from the Liberal Democrats to Labour or from the Green Party to Labour, this was around one in four voters. The high levels of tactical voting on the 'left' were much less evident on the 'right'. Only one in 20 voters who switched to Reform UK said they voted that way for 'tactical' reasons. Among those who voted Conservative, less than one in ten said they did so for tactical reasons.

The lowest levels of tactical voting were among those who voted for the Green Party, and particularly those switching *to* Green *from* Labour. Less than 3% of this group gave 'tactical' reasons for their vote. In part, this reflects the electoral reality of the Green Party position. The party was highly focused on its four target seats. Outside of those, it was unlikely that a vote for the Greens would be a good 'tactical' choice. However, this also reflects Labour Party strategy and the nature of party competition between Labour and challengers on its electoral left.

This is an important part of the story of the 2024 election, and equally important for thinking about how Labour's electoral fortunes might change over the course of the current parliament.

LEADERSHIP AND LOSSES ON THE LEFT

One critique of the Labour Party's performance in the two elections under Corbyn's leadership was that while the party deepened its appeal among core groups of supporters, it lost critical votes elsewhere. The geographic distribution of those voters meant that Labour's vote was very inefficient. In 2019 it piled up almost 51,000 votes per seat won.[11] In contrast, the Conservatives' vote in 2019 had been efficiently spread, meaning they needed just 38,300 votes per seat won. The new Labour leadership were keen to undo this, to try to win over voters who had been lost in some parts of the country and to recognise that the party could 'afford' (in terms of seats) to lose some voters in seats where it had large majorities. The strategy, as measured by vote efficiency, was remarkably successful. In the 2024 landslide, Labour needed just 23,622 votes per seat won.[12] This was reflected in reduced majorities in many 'safe' seats as well as gains with relatively small vote shares.

Labour's strategists were keen to cheer the so-called 'hero' voters. These voters were critical to the strategy. They had voted Conservative in 2019, but were open to Labour in 2024, not least because they had voted Labour at some point in the past.[13] Many of them lived in the critical seats in the 'red wall'. But this improved vote 'efficiency' also reflected lost votes, and particularly those lost to candidates on the 'left'. The Green Party may only have gained one seat directly from Labour, but around one in ten Labour voters from 2019 switched to the Green Party in 2024, while an array of Independents and George Galloway's Workers Party, both positioned to Labour's left, also benefited from the party's focus on the 'centre'.

The reasons for this are complex. There was an impact of the war in Gaza, which caused many Muslim voters to turn to the Greens in seats where no Muslim independent candidate stood. There was also some 'late swing', possibly in response to polling showing a large Labour majority was highly likely. But this is not the whole story.

Figure 2 looks at how much those who voted for Labour in 2019 liked the party across the course of the parliament, according to how they voted in 2024. We can see that those who eventually switched to the Green Party became less positive after Starmer became leader, and by the time of the 2021 local elections, moved further away from the party.

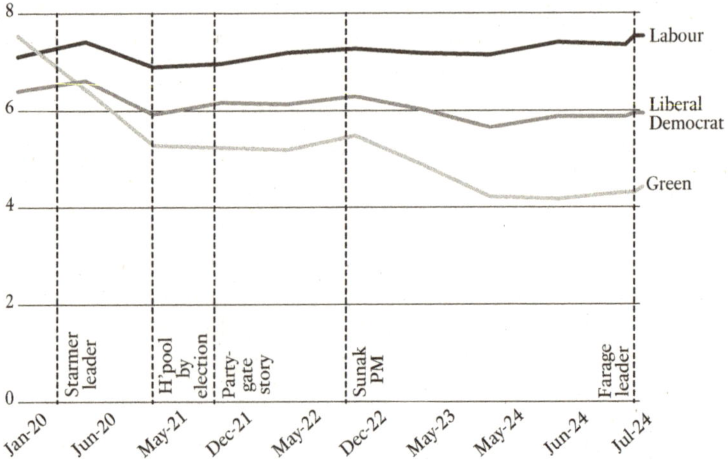

Figure 2   Mean 'like' score for Labour Party among 2019 Labour voters by vote in 2024 (0–10 scale)
Source: British Election Study internet panel

There were further falls in 2023, which may be accounted for, to some extent, by both Labour's post-Corbyn repositioning and the war in Gaza. But for many of those who eventually voted Green in 2024, their issues with the Labour Party began much earlier. While panel data of this kind is excellent for capturing change across the parliament, it is not able to pin down precisely when such change took place, nor what drove it. In the period between June 2020 and May 2021, even while 'normal' politics seemed on hold due to Covid, there were a number of possible factors that could explain this. But key among them was the removal of the Labour whip from Jeremy Corbyn in October 2020.

We can explore this further by looking at how these voters viewed the Labour leadership during this time as well as how they viewed the party.

The Green Party vote share was overwhelmingly drawn from the most liberal and left-leaning political segment. It is worth looking more closely at how this group viewed the Labour Party and the Labour leadership over this period.

Analysis of voters according to their core values is a useful tool for understanding this group of 'liberal-left' voters. Core values are defined using data from the British Election Study and the responses to series of questions designed to measure economic left–right and social liberal–authoritarian values.[14] These have been used in British electoral studies since the late 1980s.

Using these measures, we can define a series of values groups[15] based on the intersection of these two value 'dimensions'. How each of these groups viewed the Labour Party and its leader over the period between the 2019 and 2024 elections is shown in Figure 3.

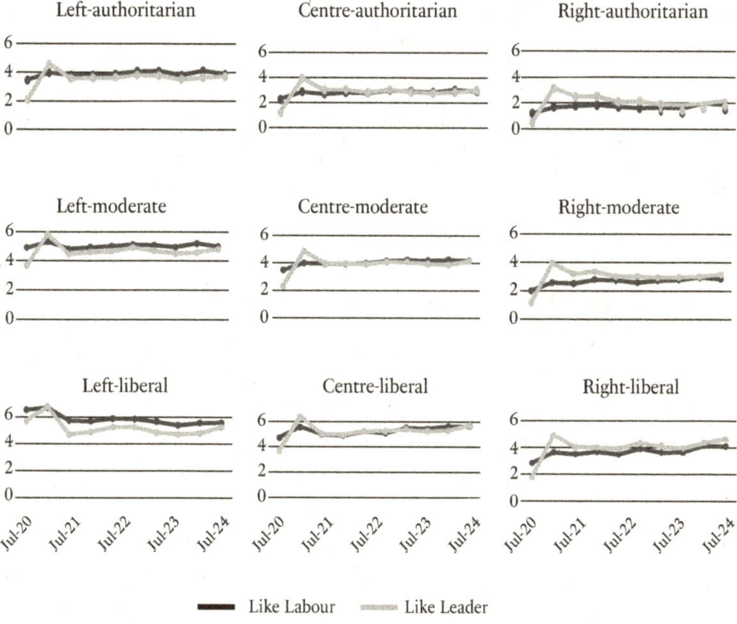

Figure 3   Mean 'like' score for Labour Party and Labour Party leader by values group, 2019–24 (0–6 scale)
Source: British Election Study internet panel

In all groups, the 'like leader' scores jump substantially between the 2019 election and the first post-election wave of the panel in June 2020. This data point represents the change from Corbyn to Starmer as Labour leader, and the initial 'honeymoon' for the new Labour leader. All groups also saw a smaller rise in their 'like party' scores, which then remained flat in most groups across the parliament.

The liberal-left group stand out because they showed a different pattern for both leader and party. While this group had higher initial starting points, being more positive about Corbyn and the party in 2019 than other groups, it also saw a rise in the leader ratings after Starmer's election. In this initial 'honeymoon' period, all groups give Starmer a higher rating than the Labour Party itself. However, a year later, at the time of the local elections in May 2021, this had changed. This was a time when the Conservatives were enjoying a polling bounce, the nation was emerging from the Covid crisis as vaccines became available, and it was before there was public attention on partygate. It was also a time where Starmer himself had indicated that he considered resigning as leader.[16] Yet after the initial 'honeymoon' bump that had receded by May 2021, ratings were remarkably flat. On average, neither Starmer nor the Labour Party were more liked by the public in July 2024, when elected with an historic majority, than when they had been defeated in the 2021 Hartlepool by-election. The critical change was not the Labour Party's rise, but the Conservatives' fall.

For the liberal-left group, however, the average 'like' score for the Labour Party fell a little over the period, and notably, for this group Starmer's ratings remained below those of the party throughout. Whatever the exact reason for this flow of voters from Labour to the Green Party and others, it was never a concern for a party that was trying to reshape the geography and composition of its electoral coalition. Instead, the focus was on winning over the so-called 'hero' voters from the Conservatives in places where their votes were critical to Labour success.

'HERO' VOTERS

The Labour leadership team were focused on changing the inefficient vote of the 2017 and 2019 elections, which was deep in some places, but not wide enough to win across the country, into one which, although it might deliver fewer votes, would deliver more seats.

Labour strategists had identified 'hero' voters, those they could win from the Conservatives, particularly in places where the Conservatives had won relatively recently. The conditions of the second half of the 2019–24 parliament were especially favourable for Labour to improve its position with these voters. Economic insecurity and a cost-of-living crisis ensured voters were focused more on economics and much less on the politics of Brexit, immigration and the culture wars,[17] issues where these voters were more likely to agree with other parties. Labour was unexpectedly aided in this task by the Conservatives. The Truss mini-budget had trashed the Conservative reputation for economic competence. The concern for Labour must be that, if the focus shifts back to Brexit, immigration and the culture wars (as it might well do), while economic insecurity and a cost-of-living crisis continues under the new government, the weaknesses of hero voters' support for the party may be revealed.

At the start of the 2019–24 parliament, dominated by Covid and Britain's exit from the European Union, there were very few voters who said that, having voted Conservative in 2019, they would switch to Labour at the next election. This changed gradually at first. By May 2022, just over 6% of the 2019 Conservative vote intended to vote Labour at a future general election. Between May and December 2022, this voter flow rose from 6% to 10%. It seems likely that having three different Tory prime ministers during this period played a role, but critical too was the mini-budget during Liz Truss' brief time in Number Ten. For voters without a strong connection to the Conservative Party and who were now most concerned about the cost of living, the Labour Party were more appealing – and were deliberately trying to woo them.

However, returning to Figure 3, it suggests that while more voters turned to Labour during this period, this improvement in the party's support did not drive an overall increase in the favourability ratings for the party or its leader. If the large majority won in 2024 was indeed 'loveless', it was not because Labour's love had been lost; it had never been found.

Crucially, the strategy put in place to win over hero voters even at the cost of votes on the left may not have been enough to deliver such a large Labour majority without the return of a challenger to the Conservatives on the right, Reform UK, splitting the right-leaning vote to the advantage of all the left-leaning parties.

THE CHALLENGE FROM THE POPULIST RIGHT

After Nigel Farage's Brexit Party stood down against incumbent Conservative MPs in the 2019 general election, to the Tories huge advantage,[18] and with Brexit 'done', the challenge to the Conservatives on the right of British politics seemed to have been successfully seen off. Farage subsequently stepped down as leader of the Brexit Party. It was formally renamed Reform UK in January 2021, and it had been led by Richard Tice throughout the parliament. For most of this period the party was polling in single figures and was largely ignored by the media and the voters. In the 2021 Hartlepool by-election, Reform UK managed to win just 368 votes, in a seat Tice himself had contested in 2019 when he won more than 10,000 votes.

After Johnson's departure, Labour were not the only beneficiaries of the Conservative woes. Reform UK's recovery saw its standing in the opinion polls rise after the Truss mini-budget and her replacement as prime minister. It rose again in the summer of 2023. The government's Rwanda policy kept immigration on the political agenda. There were many provocative interventions from the Tory right, most notably Suella Braverman, on the subject.[19]

The data suggest that relatively few voters moved directly from a Labour vote in 2019 to voting Reform in 2024.[20] However, the Reform surge did prevent some of those previously Conservative voters who were considering Labour voting for it. The numbers are not large. Many of those who switched from the Conservatives to Reform were openly hostile to Labour (data from BESIP show almost half of Reform voters give Labour a zero on a zero to ten scale of how much they liked the party, while just 7% give a score greater than five), but nonetheless the impact on the Labour vote share overall shouldn't be entirely ignored.

STAYING AT HOME

The pattern of where turnout fell the most suggests that this too was related to the type of contest in a constituency and may reflect the campaign intensity of different parties. The seats where turnout fell the most were those which Labour already held. This could be because people were less motivated to vote where there was no incumbent Conservative to defeat. But it also reflects Labour's strategy to avoid piling up votes in seats with large majorities in 2019. The lowest falls in turnout were seen in seats the Liberal Democrats gained from the Conservatives, and those won by the Green Party. The motivation to unseat the Tory incumbent, or in the case of Brighton Pavilion and Bristol West, for the Green Party to defeat Labour from the left, acted as a boost. What is clear is that there are large numbers of people in all areas who voted in 2019 but not in 2024, and that this has the potential to be an important story in the next election. Will these new 'non-voters' be motivated by a closer contest? And if so, how will they vote? It is a difficult question to answer now, but something to watch closely.

THE NEW POLITICAL MAP

The local political context in which voters were making choices was critical in 2024, and is likely to remain so. The result has left the types of competition even more varied and more marginal. During the campaign, it became clear there was no longer such a thing as a 'safe' Conservative seat,[21] and with increased volatility and smaller margins next time around, all parties may find that at least some large majorities come under threat. The alternative view, of course, is that there are now no 'unwinnable' seats – as the Greens showed by coming from fourth place to win in North Herefordshire.

The political map after the 2024 election reveals new types of contest for Labour. Reform UK is in second place in 89 Labour-held seats, many of which are the so-called 'red wall' seats Labour lost in 2019 and regained in 2024. There are 39 seats where the Green Party is in second place behind Labour, with most of these in London. Fighting off both types of challenges at the same time will bring tensions back to Labour strategy that it put to one side in 2024. However, there may be a little breathing space for Labour, as in many of these contests it holds large majorities. Among the 20 safest seats, there are eight where the Greens are in second place to Labour and seven where Reform UK is.

The traditional battlegrounds remain. Of the 20 most marginal seats after the election, 15 have Labour and the Conservatives in first and second places (see Figure 4). In Scotland, the SNP is in second place in all 37 Labour seats. While much has been made of the new contests Labour faces, small changes in fortunes for the parties hit by the incumbency curse in 2024 would significantly impact Labour's ability to hold on to its majority.

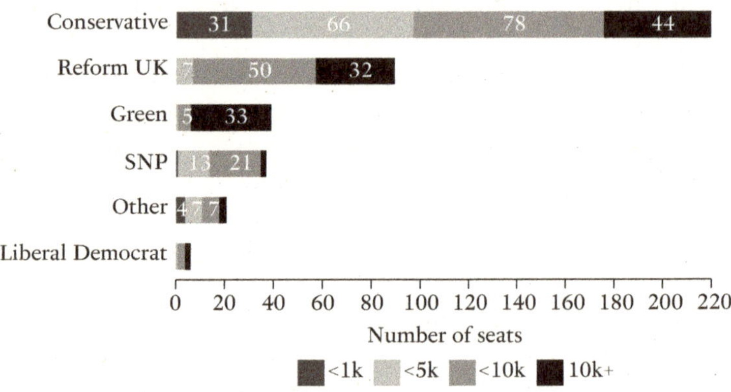

Figure 4   Labour-held seats by second-place party and size of majority

A NEW NORMAL?

Much is unknown about how party competition will evolve before the next general election. Both voters and parties have shown considerable volatility in recent years. It is likely the shape of the challenges Labour faces is largely outside its control as Conservatives and Reform UK battle for pole position on the right. It now seems very unlikely that Reform UK will vacate the field for the Conservatives as Reform UK seeks after 2024 and again in 2025 to continue the momentum gained in 2024 and again in 2025. It is unclear whether any informal arrangement might be made between the parties. There are high levels of distrust on both sides, and some antagonism between different groups of voters. These may make informal pacts less effective.

Having secured a remarkable set of results, the Liberal Democrats face tricky times. Even a small revival of Conservative reputation may cost them seats, while at the same time their success depends to some extent on Labour, liberal ex-Tory and Green voters continuing to vote for them as the party best placed to ensure the Tory loses.

Despite the relatively small vote share won in 2024, the shape of the results might give some cheer to Labour. While there are many more marginal seats overall than previously, those under threat from Reform UK and the Greens are 'safer' than those under threat from the Conservatives. Despite the remarkable level of tactical voting between Labour and the Liberal Democrats, there remains untapped potential for further tactical voting in many places – especially where there may be the threat of a Reform UK win. With the election result echoing that of 2015, a fragmented electoral landscape seems more likely to persist than the sharp reset seen in 2017.

An electoral landscape where all voters find five or more serious options on their ballot papers, and in Scotland and Wales six, is likely to continue to lead to unpredictable outcomes. A growth in the profile and viability of minor parties will increase the unpredictability of results in a number of seats. Couple this with the workings of a first-past-the-post electoral system, and any prospect for easy-to-make foolproof forecasts is at an end. But what is clear is that this landscape will pose challenges for all political parties. Low vote shares and negative leader ratings may be the new normal when parties enjoy the support of only a small group of voters. There are no longer homogenous left and right blocs, and fewer and fewer voters are wearing either the Labour or Tory rosette. Labour's task is to find a way through this new electoral maze.

ENDNOTES

1. Harold Clarke, David Sanders, Marianne Stewart and Paul Whiteley 'Valence Politics and Electoral Choice in Britain, 2010' *Journal of Elections, Public Opinion and Parties* 21/2 (2011) pp. 237–253.
2. Ipsos 'Sharp Improvement in Economic Optimism but Little Benefit for Conservatives' 20 May 2024 www.ipsos.com.
3. John Curtice 'General Election 2024: How Britain Voted' *Political Insight* 15/3 (2024) pp. 9–13.
4. John Burn Murdoch 'Democrats Join 2024's Graveyard of Incumbents' *Financial Times* 7 November 2024 www.ft.com.

5. Marta Miori and Jane Green 'The Most Disproportionate UK Election: How the UK Labour Party Doubled Its Seat Share with a 1.6-Point Increase in Vote Share' *Political Quarterly* 96/1 (2025) pp. 37–64.

6. Ed Fieldhouse, Jane Green, Geoffrey Evans, Jonathan Mellon, Chris Prosser, Jack Bailey, Roosmarijn de Geus, Hermann Schmitt, Cees van der Eijk, James Griffiths and Stuart Perrett 'Wave 29 of the 2019–24 British Election Study Internet Panel' British Election Study July–September 2024 www.britishelectionstudy.com.

7. Unless otherwise stated, all data in this chapter are drawn from the British Election Study internet panel, waves 19–29 www.britishelectionstudy.com.

8. Yphtach Lelkes 'What Do We Mean by Negative Partisanship?' *The Forum* 19/3 (2021) pp. 481–497.

9. Ron Johnston and Charles Pattie 'Tactical Voting at the 2010 British General Election: Rational Behaviour in Local Contexts?' *Environment and Planning A: Economy and Space* 43/6 (2011) pp. 1,323–1,340.

10. Rob Ford, Tim Bale, Will Jennings and Paula Surridge *The British General Election of 2019* Palgrave Macmillan, London 2021.

11. Eloise Uberoi, Carl Baker and Richard Cracknell 'Research Briefing: General Election 2019 Full Results and Analysis' House of Commons Library, London 28 January 2020 www.commonslibrary.parliament.uk.

12. Richard Cracknell, Carl Baker and Louie Pollock 'Research Briefing: General Election 2024 Results' House of Commons Library, London 24 September 2024 www.commonslibrary.parliament.uk.

13. Sam Coates 'Keir Starmer Used His Party Conference Speech to Sharpen His Message and Go Heavy on Patriotism in a Pitch to "Hero Voters"' *Sky News* 27 September 2022 www.news.sky.com.

14. Paula Surridge 'Libertarianism and Authoritarianism' in Maria Grasso and Marco Giugni (eds) *Encyclopaedia of Political Sociology* Edward Elgar Publishing, Cheltenham 2023 pp. 262–267.

15. More detail on the items used and rationale for the values group can be found at www.pollingsnippets.substack.com.

16. Tom Baldwin *Keir Starmer: The Biography* HarperCollins, London 2024.

17. Paula Surridge 'Brexit, British Politics and Values' UK in a Changing Europe 30 January 2021 www.ukandeu.ac.uk.

18. See Rob Ford, Tim Bale, Will Jennings, Paula Surridge 'The British General Election of 2019 and the future of British Politics' 11 December 2021 www.ukandeu.ac.uk.

19. For example, see 'Suella Braverman – 2023 Speech to Conservative Party Conference' 3 October 2023 www.ukpol.co.uk.

20. Adam McDonnell 'How Britain Voted in the 2024 General Election' YouGov 8 July 2024 www.yougov.co.uk.

21. Alain Tolhurst 'Nigel Farage's Election Bid Means There "Are No Safe Tory Seats Anymore"' Politics Home 6 June 2024 www.politicshome.com.

No Direction Home:
The Non-Politics of Starmerism

Jeremy Gilbert

This is a time of febrile uncertainty as to the political direction of the UK, the Labour Party and the world. In the UK, the Labour government's overarching ambition is to signal to the voting public and business community that Labour is serious about its commitment to economic growth: a monomaniacal obsession that has become the only thing resembling a strategy.[1] In early 2025, the government suggested that a new Heathrow runway and a new oilfield in the North Sea would be approved: a set of gestures calculated to incite angry protest from environmentalists. Provoking such resistance may well have been the principal object of the exercise, from the perspective of a government and a Labour leadership that had made antagonising the left into its apparent *raison d'être*.

FROM BLAIR TO STARMER

It's instructive to compare the current situation to that of the previous Labour government during its first few months. Of course, the circumstances were very different. Blair had the full support of his party, the left having been exhausted and defeated not just by internal factional machinations, but by two decades of a losing war against Thatcherism. Starmer, by contrast, deceived and tricked his way into leading Labour in an entirely different direction from that endorsed by most of its members, and a large section of the voting public.[2] Both Blair and Starmer came into office with huge parliamentary majorities, but Starmer's share of the popular vote is ten points lower than Blair's, and only slightly higher than what Labour achieved at the disastrous 2019 election. His parliamentary majority is entirely an effect of the right-wing vote having been split, in an extremely low-turnout election, between the Conservative Party and Reform UK.

The widespread consensus, shared even by commentators who remain politically sympathetic to Starmer, is that he does not have a discernible project for government. Of course, it's easy to exaggerate how far Blair had any such project. He was elected leader primarily because he was seen as the centrist candidate, at a time when there was a broad perception that both the 'radical left' (in 1983) and the 'soft left' (1987, 1992) had been given a fair chance to lead the party to victory but had not been able to. There was always a strong body of opinion on the left according to which the defeat of 1983 can be blamed on the secession of a large section from the right of the party to form the short-lived Social Democratic Party, while the expulsion of sections of the 'hard left', and Neil Kinnock's uninspiring leadership, had only weakened Labour's positions in 1987 and 1992. The consensus among party members in 1992 was that the left had been given plenty of time to prove its case and had failed. This gave Blair considerable ideological leeway.

Over the next few years, several political philosophies associated with a number of centre-left thinkers were touted as the 'Big Idea' informing New Labour thinking. These ranged from the 'communitarianism' of Amitai Etzioni to Will Hutton's 'Stakeholder Capitalism'.[3] In government, Blairism amounted to an ad hoc assemblage of elements: neoliberal macroeconomic and public-sector policy; egalitarian and liberalising tendencies on issues such as same-sex relationships and working mothers; authoritarian policies on crime; welfare policies designed to mitigate the worst social effects of neoliberalism without challenging its fundamental social relations; a foreign policy almost entirely dictated from the White House. In practice, Blairism meant following the economic and political dictates of Washington, Wall Street and the City of London, trying to mitigate against rising social and economic inequality while operating within their strict parameters. Nonetheless, in opposition and then in government, Blair and other New Labour ideologues were able to present this package as consistent with an overall project to 'modernise' Britain, adapting the country and its workforce to the emergent rigours of a global 'knowledge economy'. Coming into office just as the American-led internet boom began to promote real growth, New Labour was able to have its political cake and eat it for almost a decade: delighting powerful interests with a hands-off attitude to financialised capitalism, while expanding opportunities for some constituencies within the education system and labour market.

GOING FOR GROWTH

A sympathetic assessment of the present government would acknowledge that both Starmer and his influential chancellor of the exchequer, Rachel Reeves, have put forward a coherent case for their project to improve Britain's anaemic rates of economic growth. It isn't wrong to say that UK growth has been effectively stagnant for years, and it isn't wrong that – as the Blair experience showed – high levels of growth allow governments to pursue the relatively progressive policies their voters want, without having to challenge powerful interests. Nor is it wrong to say that people want jobs and the levels of public service that can only be funded by a stable and growing tax base. But voters have been making clear for years now – in countless opinion polls as well as the 2017 election – that they want more than that. They want chronic inequalities in wealth and income to be addressed. They want core infrastructure in the energy, transport and postal systems renationalised. They want corporate power curtailed. Apart from some very half-hearted moves to take sections of the rail network back into public ownership, the Starmer government is planning none of this. Meanwhile, entire social sectors – among them universities, social care services, policing and local government – are in conditions of abject crisis, with any proposals brought forward insufficient for their remediation or reform. Those tax increases which have been proposed – notably an increase in employers' national insurance contributions – will not have significant redistributive effects, nor will they tap into the vast pools of wealth that the rich in Britain have accumulated since the 1980s. This all stands in marked contrast to the promises made by Starmer when he stood for election to the party leadership in 2020, offering a programme largely similar to Labour's at the 2017 and 2019 election. Almost all these 'pledges' have now been broken.[4]

The other obvious defence of Starmer's project is that it worked. Even if he did break every promise to his own members, even if his abject hostility to the left, and his embarrassing embrace of casual jingoism (he is almost never pictured without a Union Jack behind him), have not actually won back any significant number of the votes that Labour lost to the Tories in 2019; nonetheless, he achieved a parliamentary landslide for Labour. Labour's parliamentary success can be attributed entirely to the implosion of the Tory vote (see 'A Conservative Meltdown' in this collection), under economic conditions that proved fatal for incumbent governments around the world in 2023 and 2024, as rampant inflation eroded living standards at a faster rate than any of them could mitigate. But arguably, since the 1970s, Labour only won elections when it managed to deter Conservative voters from turning out to vote against it or persuaded them not to vote tactically to block it. Labour's embrace of conservative nationalist rhetoric in 2024 may not have attracted many votes, but it may at least have given right-wing voters permission to punish the Conservatives at the ballot box.

Even if we accept this most generous possible interpretation of the July 2024 election result, it has created a political situation in which any electoral deal between the Tories and Reform (such as the one made between the Conservative and Brexit parties in 2019) could wipe out Labour's majority, while much of the party's natural support base has been alienated by its wooing of ageing conservatives. Labour's apparent lack of direction is necessary because to head too decisively in any direction would be to alienate either Conservative swing voters or (less importantly) its increasingly dissatisfied core vote.

NO DIRECTION

A less sympathetic assessment would put forward several key reasons for the lack of any apparent project. The first is that Starmerism, unlike Blairism, never had a coherent proposition as to how the country should be governed. Starmerism was never an answer to the question 'How could Labour govern?' It was only ever an answer to the question 'How can Corbynism be expunged from the Labour Party?' It was to this end that Starmer, on spurious grounds, oversaw the mass expulsion of Corbyn's supporters and eventually Corbyn himself. Those few elements of Corbyn's policy agenda that Starmer has retained are those necessary to retain the support of delegates from key trade unions (notably Unison and the General and Municipal Workers' Union) on Labour's National Executive Committee (NEC). Without this support, Starmer's apparatchiks in the party bureaucracy would not have been able to proceed with their grotesquely anti-democratic interventions in the selection of parliamentary candidates, in flagrant violation of Starmer's explicit pledge to allow local parties to choose candidates.[5] There is little doubt that without such an intervention, obviously intended to ensure the most compliant possible makeup of the parliamentary party, there would be a few more popular and progressive Labour MPs.

The second key reason is that there simply is no possible project available to a British government that does not involve either allowing life to get worse for a majority of Britons or making a genuine challenge to the privileges of certain powerful social groups. Landlords and property owners cannot enjoy rising rents and asset values forever if housing costs for ordinary people – especially the young – are ever to return to historically normal levels. The utility sector cannot be effectively reformed as long as it is organised to maximise shareholders' profits. The university system cannot be rendered functional for most of its users without shifting the cost burden away from students and graduates onto wealthier taxpayers. But these are all powerful groups that Starmer, as is traditional for right-wing Labour leaders, chooses to appease.

The third key reason concerns the ultimate motivations of Starmer, Reeves, their allies in the party bureaucracy, and the carefully imposed general election candidates who have now become Labour MPs. The nature of politics as a profession has changed since the 1970s. The great age of progressive reform (lasting from the late 19th century to the 1960s) seems long gone now. Globalisation and profound socio-cultural change have made it difficult for national governments to engage in the kind of grand projects that brought the modern welfare state into existence. The tendency of senior politicians to amass fortunes after their political careers has become so well established as to constitute a norm. Under such circumstances, it is only logical to assume that politicians with no particularly cultural or ideological affinity for radical politics or its traditions are likely to calculate – consciously or otherwise – that spending a few years in office without earning the enmity of financial corporations or media conglomerates is more important to their prospects than actually trying to achieve anything of historic importance.

This is where Britain now finds itself. The Starmer government is unpopular because being popular would require it to commit to a project. Almost any such project would necessarily alienate certain powerful institutions. Most members of the government are more concerned to maintain their good relationships with those institutions than they are to win the next election; never mind representing the interest of their constituents. Under these circumstances, is the country simply doomed to perpetual decline?

EXIT STRATEGIES

Of course, no such fate is inevitable. It is possible that Starmer intended to keep his leadership election campaign promises when he made them in 2020, only reversing course once he became convinced that this was necessary to win the election. The fear of being a 'one-term failure' may push him to change course again. Indeed, the government's rhetorical commitment to interventionist corporatism could quite easily be re-framed as a drive to build a true developmental state, complete with a significant programme of price controls and wage rises, and a major drive for green industrial investment. But this is the least likely outcome. The kind of psephological calculation that underpinned Labour's 2024 electoral strategy is likely to lead to a continued emphasis on holding the support of Conservative voters in provincial marginal constituencies; if Green and independent left candidates pick up another few seats in cities and university towns, this is likely to be seen as a price worth paying.

Is any change in Labour's direction possible? Unlike Blair in 1997, Starmer does not have a popular base within the electorate, or even a very strong organisational base among Labour members. The recent successes of right-wing organising networks (Labour First and its front campaign, Labour to Win) in winning delegates to the NEC has only been achieved through a systematic campaign to demoralise mainstream members. This was done through the open rigging of candidate selections and through the leadership's departure from any political programme that most members would endorse. It has caused members either to leave the party[6] or entirely disengage.[7] There would be little resistance to his replacement as Labour leader if he lost the support of key party institutions. Starmer's control of the party since becoming leader has depended partly on the support of key trade union delegations, and that support cannot be expected to last as long as the present situation obtains. Sooner or later, Starmer and his cabinet will run out of concessions they can make to the unions without offending either powerful interests or more neglected sections of the workforce. Were the largest union, Unison, to withdraw its support, it would have significant consequences for Labour's future direction. Despite Labour's current majority, a hung parliament after the next election is possible, with an expanded blocs of Reform MPs but also Green MPs, and a larger 'independent' parliamentary group currently led, to all intents and purposes, by Jeremy Corbyn.

Much British commentary on the possibility of regrouping progressive forces in recent years has focused, understandably, on the questions of organisational form and of whether socialists should continue to organise inside the Labour Party. Perhaps more fundamental, however, is where the potential might lie for coalitions thereof that could underlie any progressive institutional project. To approach this issue, it is helpful to ask three related questions: who is Starmerism for, which forces are the most likely to be mobilised against it, and what progressive coalition might be assembled from them?

WHO WANTS STARMER?

The simplest answer to the first question is: almost nobody. The one effective aim of the Starmer project has been to preserve the jobs and bureaucratic privileges of the network of party and union bureaucrats and elected representatives, who make up most of the 'Labour right'.[8] The unexpected success of Corbynism in 2015–17 threatened their incomes and status. They defended them in the only way they knew; by lying, rigging votes, packing meetings, fraudulently suspending rivals from the party, and colluding with the Conservatives and the press. But to the extent that this specific network represents a wider social layer, it is precisely that professional political and managerial class that came into being during the 1980s and 1990s. Since the global financial crisis of 2008, in many countries this group has been forced to resort to increasingly desperate measures to fend off populist threats from right and left. As Alex Williams and I argued in our book *Hegemony Now*[9] this elite managerial class emerged as part of the process by which global neoliberal hegemony was established. It has served to manage the wider public in the interests of financial and technological capital.

This is not exactly the post-war 'professional and managerial class' described by the Ehrenreichs in the 1970s, which included schoolteachers and social workers, characterised by a patrician ethos of public service.[10] Public sector professionals in recent decades have often been subject to managerial discipline by the neoliberal 'managerial-technocratic-political elite'.[11] As Williams and I suggested,[12] other sets of workers and citizens have been managed largely through the commitment of successive governments since the 1980s to maintaining 'standards of living', even while these were being supported by ever-rising levels of personal and household debt. But after the 2008 global financial crash, the capacity of professional politicians to enable majority populations to enjoy ever-higher levels of private consumption has been severely compromised. Young people in particular have seen real wages fall while rents, prices and property prices rise, seemingly inexorably. It's unsurprising that the people who ran parties and governments in the 1990s and 2000s have faced political challenges from both the left and the right. It's also unsurprising that one of the major effects of the Labour right's interference in the process of candidate selection in 2022–24 was to see many popular local Labour candidates with backgrounds in the public sector, community activism or the labour movement replaced by individuals coming from private-sector management and corporate consultancy backgrounds.[13] Starmerism has amounted to a desperate effort to restore the institutional position of this managerial elite even without the semblance of democratic legitimacy. The fact that this elite no longer has any coherent political or economic project is clear. They are, as

Raymond Williams would have put it, a 'residual'[14] class fraction, clinging to a set of inherited institutional privileges, but lacking the intellectual or political resources that would be required to enact a meaningful historic project, even a reactionary one.

THE EMERGENT FORCES

We only have to glance across the Atlantic to see where this is likely to end. The inability of this residual technocratic class fraction to exercise political hegemony on behalf of Silicon Valley and Wall Street led to the defeat of Kamala Harris in 2024 and immediate genuflections to Trump by most major tech and platform companies. Of course, classically capitalist and petit-bourgeois interest groups – forever in search of lower taxes, lower wages, reduced regulation and unhampered profits – are the Republicans' base. What tipped the balance of the popular vote in Trump's favour in 2024 was a set of constituencies convinced that they would never get anything they wanted from centrist Democrats. In particular, young men on lower incomes, of all ethnicities, are attracted to Trump's vacuous swagger. Many of them have seen more of their contemporaries get rich from speculation on cryptocurrency, which Trump has promised to keep stoking, than have found steady jobs and affordable homes. In the absence of any kind of leadership being allowed to emerge on the left, where else are they to look?

No leadership is being allowed to emerge from the Democrats; in the year Trump was elected, key progressive legislators were removed from office by aggressive, well-funded primary campaigns in support of Democrat centrists.[15] Mass abstention by Democratic voters, disgusted by the party's unwavering support for Israel and its genocidal ambitions, also played a role. Similar sentiments saw a number of independent candidates defeat Labour in July 2024 and come very close to unseating several more, including key Starmer allies Wes Streeting and Shabana Mahmood.

Given the rising popularity of Nigel Farage's Reform UK, there are reasons to expect an outcome to Starmer's term of office no better than Joe Biden's. Either the Conservative Party or Reform or a coalition of the two may form the next government, deploying a comparable rhetoric and policy agenda to Trump's. This might be avoided if Starmer is replaced with a more visionary leader, or if the destabilising impact of both Reform and various leftist electoral initiatives is sufficient to produce a hung parliament. The question is what social forces might come together to render either of these outcomes likely?

The progressive left in Britain has a number of constituencies that will endorse a radical political and economic programme: public-sector workers (both highly qualified professionals and lower-paid workers), poorer unionised workers in the private sector, and a some post-industrial communities (such as former coal-mining villages in South Wales and the North of England). Labour only wins elections when it wins support from large majorities of them, and from significant numbers of non-unionised private-sector employees. There is a difference between graduate professionals and non-graduates. The former tend towards cautious, aspirational liberalism. They have suffered least from decades of neoliberalism, and they have the least motivation to break with their habit of deferring to the managerial elite. The latter, by contrast, tend to disidentify with the cosmopolitan culture of that elite,[16] associating it with their own growing sense of precarity and loss of status, while expressing support for social democracy.

Winning support from either of these constituencies is challenging, but not impossible. The single social group that a progressive political project should find easiest to win over under present circumstances is the well-educated, middle-aged, increasingly disillusioned graduate professional class. The long period during which this group was effectively insulated from the effects of austerity and the financial crisis has finally ended. In recent years, left forces have made little effort to win over this constituency, tending to dismiss them as 'centrist dads' with little incentive to give up their deference to technocratic neoliberalism. Those days are over. Developing a message directed at this group – whose information sources tend to be strictly confined to broadcast news and broadsheet newspapers – is important. The principal aim of such messaging should be to drive a wedge between them and the residual managerial elite.

What of the non-graduate private-sector employees? Arguably the biggest problem for both Labour and political forces to its left is that such voters tend to be hostile to any party they perceive as endorsing liberal immigration policies, while the metropolitan core of the left's own most loyal constituencies tend to be deeply invested in liberal and cosmopolitan positions on immigration and multiculturalism. At the 2017 general election, when the issue of immigration was widely assumed to have been settled by the 2016 Brexit referendum result, Labour was able to hold together this potential voter base, achieving one of the biggest swings in its history,[17] albeit with a vote share that was too inefficiently distributed to dislodge the Conservative government of Theresa May.

Any progressive electoral force seeking to challenge both Starmerism and Farage would have to reproduce that unified voter bloc while deploying the overall progressive vote more efficiently. The latter could be achieved either by a formal coalition between parties of the left and centre – a 'progressive alliance' – or by the kind of sophisticated tactical voting that saw four Green MPs elected for the first time in 2024. But for any such tactic to prove effective, a broader strategy of coalition-building would have to rally Labour's 2017 voter base, preventing a repeat of the 2019 disaster that saw it fatally divided over the issue of Brexit and the free movement of people. Could any strategy deliver that result?

There is a widespread sense right now, across much of the left in both the US and the UK, that a left socio-economic programme can only be popularised if attached to a conservative social agenda. There is no real evidence for this claim. While voters with negative views on immigration will also give broadly negative answers when invited to comment on topics such as 'wokeism',[18] there is little evidence that their opinions on matters such as trans rights are deeply held or of great importance to them; most analyses of the 2017 and 2019 general election results imply that Labour's change of policy on free movement in Europe cost it at least a million votes, from voters who presumably were happy to endorse Labour's otherwise 'libertarian'[19] social politics in 2017.[20] There is less evidence that active homophobia, anti-feminism or racism shape attitudes of any group of voters whose support the left has any chance of winning. There are voters who share those attitudes, but they are never likely to vote Labour, and they are few enough in number for almost any party to form a government without their support.[21] The existence of a significant bloc of voters who seem to want very strict immigration controls alongside a radical socio-economic programme, however, is a persistent problem for the left, with no easy solution.[22] It is rendered even more intractable by the false assumption that every voter who holds such views is just a racist. In fact, this is pernicious conservative ideology that we should neither believe nor reproduce.

I think that a broadly progressive position on immigration – as well as other social issues – could be popularised, provided it was associated with a plausible, radical programme of social and economic reform, the tangible benefits of which were clearly explained to voters. It is a mistake to assume that conservative polit-ical orientations are necessarily the expression of immovable sets of 'cultural values' or psychological dispositions. They are often the expression of a justified political pessimism. When specific social groups – such as white, British, working-class men – regard them-selves as unlikely to benefit materially from any achievable social change, they are very likely to adopt a posture oriented toward the defence of existing privileges, necessarily manifesting as a conserva-tive politics.[23] The task of any radical, progressive movement is to convince this group that a better future is possible, for them as well as for those unlike them.

Finally, what of the coming generations, whose current attitudes and behaviour presumably tell us something about possible futures? Here, perhaps, is the single most obvious ground both for optimism and for extreme caution. On the one hand, the extraordinary collapse of support for the Conservative Party among the under-40s over the past decade has not yet been met by any significant surge in support for Reform among the young. Rhetorical reactions by some commentators to the presence of young people on anti-immi-gration demonstrations in the summer of 2024 were not justified by actual polling.[24] Unfortunately, this is not the only demographic group that votes in the UK; in fact, it is the one least likely to do so. Disillusion with democratic politics is at an all-time high among the under-30s.[25] Young people know they live in a country governed by a political class that, for more than a decade, has shown nothing but contempt for them, their desires and their prospects. The pop-ularity of reactionary icons such as 'manosphere' influencer Andrew Tate suggests that, if no better prospect presents itself, young British men might start to move in the same direction as their American counterparts. It's up to the left and the labour movement to put that better prospect on the table.

From the disillusioned middle classes to the post-industrial 'left-behind', a potential coalition for a radical reform programme waits to be activated by effective leadership and capacious strategy. The challenges faced by any such initiative are evident. So are the opportunities. The obstacles include hostile media, billionaires funding the far right, and a professional political class desperately clinging to its privileges. But each of these can be and has been challenged by progressive forces: on the streets, in communities, in parties and unions, with the innovative use of new media. It's by working across all these fronts that a serious challenge to the far right can be made; and it seems implausible that such a broad-based coalition can operate entirely within any single party or organisation, or entirely outside of Labour. Almost certainly, a wide range of parties, factions and organisational types would have to be involved. Organisational diversity should be seen as a strength.

The greatest potential resource for a progressive fight-back is that most people want a robustly social-democratic reform programme, a comprehensive curtailment of corporate power, a restoration of effective political democracy and an end to the petty tyranny of an increasingly self-serving managerial class.[26] Trump and Farage offer the last of these, without any of the economic or political reforms to make a democratic alternative possible. Our task is to make clear that contradiction, while building a real alternative.

ENDNOTES

1. Aditya Chakrabortty 'Labour's Plan for "Growth" Won't Take Off, but It Will Leave Ordinary People Behind' *The Guardian* 29 January 2025 www.theguardian.com.
2. Patrick Maguire and Gabriel Pogrund *Get In: The Inside Story of Labour under Starmer* Bodley Head, London 2025; Oliver Eagleton *The Starmer Project: A Journey to the Right* Verso, London 2022.
3. Alan Finlayson *Making Sense of New Labour* Lawrence and Wishart, London 2003.
4. Keir Starmer's ten pledges of his 2020 leadership campaign have been usefully archived for historical record by the Campaign for Labour Democracy at www.clpd.org.uk.

5. 'Interview with Michael Crick: "I'm a Blairite but I Won't Vote Labour"' Novara Media YouTube 4 June 2024 www.youtube.com.

6. Daniel Green 'Labour Party Membership Dips below 400,000 for First Time in Almost a Decade' Labour List 23 August 2024 https://labourlist.org/.

7. 'What to Make of Labour's NEC Results?' Labour Hub 19 September 2024 www.labourhub.org.uk.

8. Jeremy Gilbert 'Why Wouldn't They Be Reconciled? Corbyn's Leadership and the Recalcitrance of the Parliamentary Labour Party' *Political Quarterly* (17 June 2021).

9. Jeremy Gilbert and Alex Williams *Hegemony Now: How Big Tech and Wall Street Won the World* Verso, London 2022.

10. Barbara Ehrenreich and John Ehrenreich 'The Professional-Mangerial Class' in Pat Walker (ed.) *Between Labor and Capital* South End Press, Boston 1979.

11. Manuel Castells 'European Cities, the Informational Society, and the Global Economy' *New Left Review* 1/204 (1994) p. 26.

12. Gilbert and Williams *Hegemony Now* pp. 118–127.

13. Katie Neame, Morgan Jones and Tom Belger 'Labour Selections: Parliamentary Candidates So Far for the General Election' Labour List 6 June 2024 www.labourlist.org.

14. Raymond Williams *Marxism and Literature* Oxford University Press, Oxford 1977 pp. 121–127.

15. Edward Helmore 'Jamaal Bowman's Primary Defeat Leaves Progressives Angry at Role of Aipac' *The Guardian* 26 June 2024 www.theguardian.com.

16. Maria Sobolewska and Rob Ford *Brexitland: Identity, Diversity and the Reshaping of British Politics.* Cambridge University Press, Cambridge 2020.

17. Philip Cowley and Dennis Kavanagh *The British General Election of 2017* Palgrave Macmillan, London 2018.

18. John Curtice *One-Dimensional or Two-Dimensional? The Changing Dividing Lines of Britain's Electoral Politics* National Centre for Social Research, London 2024.

19. Ibid.

20. Robert Ford, Tim Bale and Will Jennings *The British General Election of 2019* Palgrave Macmillan, London 2021; Cowley and Kavanagh *The British General Election of 2017.*

21. 'British Social Attitudes 41: Five Years of Unprecedented Challenges' National Centre for Social Research 2024 www.natcen.ac.uk.

22. Jeremy Gilbert 'The Crisis of Cosmopolitanism' Stuart Hall Foundation 15 May 2017 www.stuarthallfoundation.org.

23. Gilbert and Williams *Hegemony Now* pp. 137–170.

24. Voting intention in the United Kingdom 2025 by age, 11 April 2025, www.statista.com.

25. David Batty '"Desperate for Change" – but is UK Gen Z Really Disillusioned with Democracy?' *The Guardian* 6 February 2025 www.theguardian.com.

26. Mark Fisher and Jeremy Gilbert *Reclaim Modernity: Beyond Markets Beyond Machines* Compass, London 2014.

Even Boring People Can Be Dangerous

Gargi Bhattacharyya

I am not persuaded that there is a 'Starmer Symptom'. Quite the opposite – to the extent that the Starmer government is a symptom, it is sadly fitting in its charmlessness. Naming the object implies a charisma and coherence that is just not there. There is a danger that focusing on the Starmer government limits our analytic horizons, and restricts us once more to those British parochialisms that lead to the terrain of exceptionalism.

The British brand of exceptionalism claims that the shape of the world has nothing to do with us (because we are another century's imperium) and that our view is of global importance (because the global landscape is made by the cultural legacy of our previous pre-eminence). Well, maybe not. More useful would be to lift our heads from so insistent a fixation with Britain. And I include myself in this necessity; I find the contours of my education endlessly knocking up against the events of a world in which knowing mainly about Britain can feel like knowing not very much at all.

I try in this chapter to say something about this fractious unravelling space of imperial nostalgia and fantasies of self-sufficiency. This may, despite itself, be a paradigm-changing government, but this will certainly not be through an ability to formulate and enact a coherent 'project'. This is a government blown around, painfully, by a world in which previous levers of influence have all but disappeared.

STARMER(ISM) AS AN OBJECT OF STUDY?

One of the downsides of Stuart Hall's genre-changing naming of Thatcherism[1] is that, since then, we have had to endure a seemingly endless stream of neologisms (Blairism – maybe, Brownism – probably not, Cameronism, Mayism, Johnsonism, Trussism,

Sunakism – hardly) as if each government encapsulates a fully fledged political philosophy and policy approach. We give them too much credit. We also misread the forces that insert political philosophy into statecraft.

Not all governments represent a sea change in state technique or ideological framing. Some do just the opposite. We need to understand this 'symptom', this conjuncture, through a less honorific lens.

Even a passing suggestion that this Starmer government may be the author of its own destiny and direction, let alone that of anyone else, feels like a kind of post-imperial fantasy. However unpleasant and repressive the policies from this particular administration, they are a symptom, not an author, of these times. And they know it – it was the platform on which they stood for election.[2] In an uncharacteristic burst of honesty, albeit couched as a justification for punishment, Labour ran its 2024 election campaign on a ticket of being open about how little could be done. In the first weeks after election, the newly elected prime minister employed a rhetoric of 'coming clean', or 'levelling with' the British public.[3]

The move to an electoral politics where the population is warned off harbouring any hope feels like something new. Of course, the 'management' of particular strands of decline has been a constant since Thatcher's 1979 general election victory. However, not until Starmer have we seen a government say so openly how little could be done. Before the election, still-hopeful commentators from the centre left suggested that under-promising was its own cunning plan, and that when the true radicalism and enervating change for good started happening, it would be all the more effective for being a surprise.

John Kampfner, former editor of the *New Statesman*, observed:

In contrast to Blair, the showman, could the dourer Starmer achieve at least as much during his first term in office? And could he entrench Labour hegemony for at least as long a period as his predecessor did?

...The tactic is simple: Don't rock the boat. Don't challenge the political and economic fundamentals; instead, do what you can at the margins – if necessary, by stealth.

... Starmer struggles to smile in the way Blair did. He doesn't gladden the hearts, and he certainly isn't promising the world. He is a man for his times, one of the few grown-up mainstream politicians still standing. With expectations so low, it will be hard for him to disappoint. Might that present him with an opportunity?'[4]

Commentators (Kampfner's piece was introduced as 'an expert's point of view on a current event') cling on to these childish hopes, despite the painful lack of any evidence to substantiate their analysis. But the consequences of an electoralism where the claim is not that we can do anything different or better or in addition to the other lot, but only that we can be *not* them, is something even many on the centre left have found too hard to accept. If there were policies to be discerned, these were matters of continuity; the only promise was to enact these policies, policies presented as inevitable and unarguable, more efficiently than their original authors. It is a form of electoralism that presents the content of statecraft as non-negotiable, as if there are no choices, only imperatives.

It is a dangerous game. Although there has been something instructive about the abandonment of the pretence of electoral choice or electoral anything, the predictable outcome has been rapid and vocal (further) disillusionment.[5]

For some years, we have seen embedded anti-politics strains within the business of electoralism. Sometimes this is expressed as an attempt at inoculation, as in the Boris Johnson's 2019 general election campaign to 'Get Brexit Done'. He inserted anti-politics into the submerged narrative of the campaign. This served to prepare the electorate to expect dastardly Eurocrats to scupper the will of the British people. And as a result, Johnson, at least for a while, pre-empted doubts about the competence of his government. Sometimes anti-politics is a strand in the misleading rhetoric of populism, which we have seen Nigel Farage master so decisively. In the face of the non-impact of electoral non-choices, it should surprise no one to see people (quite a lot of people) look around for some way to kick against politics as usual.

In this very dangerous context, what might come of running a government that denies the power of government? While the Labour Party may be programmed, through painful experience, to approach politics with the view that the core objective is to avoid blame, it has become quite difficult for many (inside, outside, alongside) to understand why it then bothers at all. Whatever sympathy we have from witnessing the legacy of monstering by the press of Westminster politicians and the associated media pile-on for being seen to break electoral promises, it is hard to comprehend a political project in which the bulk of the party's energies are devoted to not being caught out. Even the most bend-over-backwards attempt at an empathetic reading cannot avoid, surely, some doubt over the loss of the core mission of politics (not only to 'get elected', but to wish and plan to do something).

So my approach to racism and the Starmer government is informed by this overarching concern: how do we understand the political gestures of a government doing its best to embody a post-politics/anti-politics administrative entity?

It is clear that race is one of the few topics cleared as suitable for public pronouncement. We have seen a new level of shamelessness as Labour ministers attempt to hide behind mythologies of race and ugly uses of racism. The response should not simply be to berate a Labour government for deploying racism – not least because there is nothing new about that. As Sivanandan wrote in another century: 'What Enoch Powell says today, the Conservative Party says tomorrow, and the Labour Party legislates on the day after.'[6]

The point is not to regret the moral failure of the Starmer government's racism – tactical and/or continuity racisms have been central aspects of Labour governments throughout the post-war period. It is more useful to consider what work governmental performances of racism fulfil now, and what we can learn from understanding the shifting techniques of state racisms.

This shift in technique is worth noting. It is a mode of normalising the racialisation of all political dilemmas, as a means of silencing and excluding other considerations. Once in office, Rachel Reeves, chancellor of the exchequer, framed the 'black hole' in the public finances as stemming from the costs of so-called 'asylum hotels'.[7] This was an allegation made legitimate by the analysis of the Institute of Fiscal Studies, which pointed to the difficulties arising from repeated under-estimating of budgetary needs for costs which government (of all parties) did not wish to acknowledge.[8] The trailing of Reeves' speech in the *Telegraph*, leading with the trigger words 'asylum hotel', was designed to confirm that every fiscal challenge could be traced back to the spectre of immigration.

There has been a repetition of more obvious and established modes of race-baiting. Framed as a response to the rise of Reform, in February 2025 the government launched a series of ads celebrating the 'success' of deportation plans,[9] messaging that has continued non-stop ever since. It is a shameless and outrageous political approach, but for Labour there is nothing new about this tactic. In 2002, in order to gain political capital from the spectacularisation of state racism in action, David Blunkett, then home secretary, invited journalists to film the deportation of Roma families.[10] Pretending that the excesses of Starmer's displays of state racism are not a continuity of the messaging and actions of previous Labour (and Tory) governments risks perpetuating the myth of British fair play, where each excess of state violence is considered an anomaly requiring moral outrage, but forestalling analysis.

My point is not that Labour is more than happy to be racist. That would hardly merit a chapter of anything, however brief. Instead, my suggestion is that we note the change in technique in both the reframing of all issues as questions of race and nation (entitlement, borders, sovereignty, industry, services) and the take-up of techniques honed by anti-politics vehicles. The latter is notable for the abandonment of a focus on clear and unambiguous political messaging. On the contrary, and learning from the dynamics of online culture, we see a move toward communications designed to contain multiple and contradictory messaging.

An apparently trivial but technically significant example is how Wes Streeting, minister for health, responded to President Trump's bonfire of diversity, equality and inclusion (DEI) practices.[11] Streeting pandered to his anti-equality interviewer with claims of misguided 'anti-whiteness' while simultaneously arguing that DEI initiatives had a place in a health service where staff and patient experiences were marred by racism. This ensured that the soundbite and the headline worked to position him as another 'sensible/ Trump-like' voice against the imposition of equality requirements. This approach to media work disrupts much of the content analysis-led approaches that have been adopted by the left. After the intensive training around messaging during the Blair years, we now see a move toward apparent incoherence. It no longer matters whether the interview or piece makes sense; disciplined messaging in the manner of the 1990s no longer fits the media dynamics of the 2020s. Instead, 'messaging' becomes the collation of a series of moments/soundbites/phrases designed to be recirculated for different audiences and able, through this dispersal into non-narrative, to appear to reflect and chime with quite contradictory political positions and demands.

This, terrifyingly, may be the clearest 'symptom' of the political approach being employed by the Starmer government.

The manner of messaging no longer requires consistency of message. If anything, including contradictory elements within the same 'message' appears to have become part of the technique now adopted. The über-racist aspects can be shared via social media, creating an aura of extremism on a par with that of Reform or other perceived contenders from the right. The softening contradictions within the narrative mean it is not clear who is addressed here, apart perhaps from the remaining party workers and members who have not yet caught up with the programme.

Labour is no longer merely 'responding' to Reform and Tommy Robinson. It is setting out a policy pathway beyond that demanded even by these bad-faith actors. This is an escalation of race-baiting led by a Labour government, as it ventures onto a terrain that is both unlawful and an attempt to out-right all comers, in the process adopting a posture that reminds me of my childhood, when no one denied being racist. They only quibbled about where such racism might lead (mass deportation – yes, of course, what else could save Britain? Death camps – how dare you, who won the war?). But there is something about the combination of gestural racism as a core aspect (sometimes the only aspect) of mainstream political performance, alongside a mumbling disavowal of the power of the state, that merits attention. What is it to say, 'Nothing can be done, but look at these sub-humans, how much we hate them?'

POST-HEGEMONY

Despite this descent into racist populism, we are living through a period where Labour's primary message to the electorate seems to be, 'Who cares what you think?' Labour's general election non-campaign relied on an electoral system where voters had nowhere else to go: 'If you don't vote for us, the other lot get back in.' The catalogue of non-promises and lowered expectations encouraged voters to hope for nothing, except perhaps that things would not become worse. The electorate understood that their role was to make do, to take the least-worst option and to batten down for more bad times ahead.

There is a political performance, but we the voters are not the intended audience. Everything is a gesture of reassurance to 'the markets', perhaps more pointedly, to an international financial class split from any productive forces.[12] Unlike an earlier centrist Labour government, this is not really a performance designed to entice investment. Whereas Blair had the sense to claim that the deregulation of the labour market was to attract jobs, the 2024 Labour government pretends to nothing except perhaps a hope to guide the turbulence of the next phase of crashing decline. Kinder commentators framed this as a sensible move away from short-termism, something recognised as much needed in UK economic planning.[13] However, for the public the message has been clear. Times are tough, they are going to get tougher, do not expect anything but more pain.

Is this is the post-hegemony that the political class have longed for? Peter Thomas summarises the debates about 'post-hegemony' as:

> temporal post-hegemony where previous hegemonic practices have been superseded; foundational post-hegemony where subaltern critiques of hegemonic power reveal the uneven and ineffectual reach of hegemonic projects from above; expansive post-hegemony signalling an expansion of the realm of politics beyond the hegemonic and counterhegemonic.[14]

Some hope this means a politics that forgoes hard political power in favour of the everyday, the technical and the consensual. Other readings embrace the possibility of bypassing a need for popular consent altogether.[15] There seems to be less belief in the ability of formal political process to address any concern than I have seen in my lifetime. The implied pacification of post-hegemony is in play. Consent is no longer an apt framing of what is demanded from the populace. These political tactics seem designed to create a sense of despondent resignation – not exactly consent as we have understood it, but a form of pacification nevertheless.

It hurts to admit it, but this tactic of lowering expectations and diminishing hope has been effective. We can chart the bumpy landscape of UK electoral politics from 2008 as a series of experiments in inculcating consent-as-resignation as opposed to consent-as-agreement.

The monstering of Corbyn rarely argued that his 2017 manifesto's ideas were the wrong thing to do. It sought to persuade people that such ideas were unworkable, unachievable and, for reasons only hinted at, dangerous because of the hopes that might be ignited but not fulfilled.

This is a point worth returning to. The electoral pledge rests on the promise that political process can do something. Starmer's Labour has tried, in part, to present itself as the competent alternative to the Tories. This involves reframing Tory policies as failures of operation, not as wrongheaded or damaging in themselves. The only promise was to say, 'We will do these things, but much more effectively than those clowns. But we do not disagree that this is what must and should be done.'

Contrast this to what Aditya Chakrabortty, having read Labour's 2024 *Change* manifesto,[16] surmised:

> the great missed opportunity of this moment: that the public is ready for change of a kind that is simply not on offer. That a political system prizes continuity and stability over reform and fairness. That a Labour leader should boast of how much he has changed his party, so that it will not change the country.[17]

This government believes (whatever malign motivations may run alongside this sincere belief) that statecraft cannot transform everyday lives. I think it also believes that statecraft can do nothing to prevent further damage to the life experiences of most people.

LET'S ZOOM OUT

Of course, understanding the conjuncture requires zooming out from the UK. This is always true, but I am not trying to make a facile out-lefting point about internationalism. Let us assume we all understand that part.

The project of cultural studies can be understood as an account of hegemonic strategies within spaces of declining global status and influence. I wonder whether this explains the different path taken in US cultural studies, notably far more celebratory and enamoured of the *pleasures* of the popular than British trajectories. The analytic repertoire that arises from the collective and collaborative experimentation of British cultural studies revolved around the conundrums thrown up by an imperial power in decline. While re-reading *Policing the Crisis*, I was struck by how explicitly this context is referenced. It does it with even greater clarity in the second edition, which seeks to place the project in its time.[18]

After so many re-runs of the fantasy that the UK is a world power and must learn only to wield its power effectively and for 'good' for all to be right in the world, it is hard to remember that until very recently (albeit decades not months), the peripheralisation of the UK and the absolute unchallenged ascendance of the US did not seem assured or unsurprising.

I don't think many doubt the diminishment of the UK's international status and influence now. There were a few squeaks of protest at election time, but in the main there is an acceptance that other powers shape our national destiny.

This sense of government being at best imperfectly equipped to manage the institutions of the nation has been around since 1973 – who knows, maybe since Suez '56? But something has escalated in the admission of the limits of government. Or in the performative declaration of limited power.

WHAT ABOUT THE RACISM?

How, then, should we understand the strange and insistent racism of Labour's 2024 election 'campaign'?

Those active in the theatre of electoral politics in the UK have, for some time, been engaged in a kind of political game of chicken – all sides egging each other on to adopt increasingly extreme and bizarre positions and policies.

The point of these performances is not to focus on the persecution of any particular group. It is to carry on the active demonstration of racialised repression, because to let up is to show weakness (it is imagined). Unlike some previous UK politicians, this cabinet does not (necessarily) trade in race science; there may even be one or two black best friends to call upon. It may believe that it is entitled to rule, but the claims of the white man's burden have receded in the mix. When people are targeted by the violence of the racist state, these techniques are formulated not on the assumption that such people are intrinsically inferior. The assumption is that they are expendable.

However, since 2024 something has shifted in what is speakable in national politics. After the performative gestures in the wake of Black Lives Matter, some of us believed that the overt race-baiting would need to be muted, if only for public relations purposes. Yet 2024 was an election which saw various highly dangerous resurrections of apparently old-style racism. Most obviously, the ongoing demonisation of migrants continued and grew. More surprisingly, targeted appeals to anti-blackness appeared to stem from some kind of intentional communications strategy. In a campaign where the Labour Party core strategy was to say as little as possible, and certainly nothing about policy, the gestural anti-blackness stood out. It is difficult to understand the treatment of Diane Abbott, including her long suspension and the apparent attempts to make it impossible for her to stand for election, except as a performance designed to be appreciated by an imagined audience of racist swing voters.[19] This was not a smooth display of forensic competence from Starmer. It was a matter that ate public attention and distracted from the party's policy message. However, this reading, I realise, relies on the assumption that the party *had* a policy message. And now, with some discomfort at my previous credulity, I think it more likely that the theatre of racist gesture and non-policy was the electoral gambit in play.

The question remains: why ramp up the theatrical racism (with theatre here combining inflammatory announcements and practices of direct cruelty and violence)?

Starmer, infamously, has argued for the right of Israel to conduct crimes against humanity and has denied that the carnage in Palestine constitutes a genocide.[20] In an escalation of racist rhetoric far beyond previous governments of any stripe, Starmer vowed from the dispatch box to 'close the loopholes' that enabled a judge to grant a family from Gaza the right to family reunion in the UK under the terms of a scheme initiated for Ukrainians.[21] As has been pointed out, the use of parliamentary privilege to threaten the independence of the judiciary, with this threat couched as an appeal to popular racism, is very dangerous terrain.[22]

The Starmer government has moved from covert forms of racism, albeit punctuated with an insistent repetition of some of the same extremist slogans of the previous government such as 'stop the boats', to what we now see as a different order of all-out racist attack.

It is true that some of this is orchestrated, or at least amplified, from beyond the UK. There was a brief period of agitation after Elon Musk decided that the UK had failed to address the alleged issue of Pakistani grooming gangs. In the period that followed, there was an unhinged media debate and speculation was rife, including from the shadow home secretary, leading to the secretary of state for the Home Department, Yvette Cooper, pledging that something will be done. The allegation of the grooming gang has served as a recruitment tool for followers of Tommy Robinson and associated groups.[23]

Yet now we see a government adamant that no aspiration of the population can be met and that the state can do little to nothing. The only exception is to amplify acts of state racism presented as extensions of the popular will. If such promises of racist excess fall short, the underlying anti-politics of the non-claims of government can be recirculated – hating experts, hating lawyers, hating due process, hating refugees, hating Muslims, hating black people. This is a government that presents itself as embodying the inadequacy of the state, and therefore relies on a repeated whipping up of hatred as an energy that substitutes for consent.

I curse them with the core of my being.

ENDNOTES

1. See Stuart Hall 'The Great Moving Right Show' *Marxism Today* (January 1979) www.banmarchive.org.uk; see also Stuart Hall and Martin Jacques (eds) *The Politics of Thatcherism* Lawrence and Wishart, London 1983.

2. See Wes Streeting 'False Hope Is Worse Than No Hope. Labour Won't Make Promises It Can't Keep' *The Guardian* 9 July 2024 www.theguardian.com.

3. See Elizabeth Piper 'Starmer Signals Pain and Unpopular Decisions to fix Britain' Reuters 27 August 2024 www.reuters.com.

4. John Kampfner 'Keir Starmer Is Tony Blair, Minus the Optimism' *Foreign Policy* (3 July 2024) www.foreignpolicy.com.

5. See, for example, Noah Keate 'UK's Keir Starmer Suffers Historic Drop in Approval Ratings' *Politico* 29 October 2024 www.politico.eu and Duncan Clark 'Net Approval Rating of the Government of the United Kingdom from July 3, 2022 to February 16, 2025, by Government' Statista 19 February 2025 www.statista.com.

6. Cited by Virou Srilangarajah in 'We Are Here Because You Were With Us: Remembering A. Sivanandan (1923–2018)' *Ceasefire* (4 February 2018) www.ceasefiremagazine.co.uk.

7. Ben Riley-Smith 'Rachel Reeves Will Blame Asylum Hotel Bill for Black Hole in Public Finances' *The Telegraph* 26 July 2024 www.telegraph.co.uk.

8. Max Warner and Ben Zaranko 'Home Office Budgeting and Asylum Overspends' Institute for Fiscal Studies 29 August 2024.

9. Kiran Stacey 'Labour Launches Ads in Reform-Style Branding to Boast about Deportations' *The Guardian* 6 February 2025 www.theguardian.com.

10. 'UK: Deportation Filmed to Show Enforcement' Statewatch 1 August 2002 www.statewatch.org.

11. Tobi Thomas 'NHS Diversity Practices Hindered by Misguided Approaches, Says Streeting' *The Guardian* 4 February 2025 www.theguardian.com.

12. See, for example, William Schomberg and David Milliken 'UK's Reeves under Pressure after Financial Markets Rout' Reuters 9 January 2025 www.reuters.com.

13. Nathan Critch, Andy Westwood and Dave Richards 'Five Ways the Budget Shows Rachel Reeves Is Thinking Long-Term More Than the Tories Ever Did' The Conversation 1 November 2024 www.theconversation.com.

14. See Peter Thomas 'After (Post) Hegemony' *Contemporary Political Theory* 20/3 (2021) pp. 318–340.

15. For a discussion of bypassing consent as a technique of statecraft, see Gargi Bhattacharyya *Crisis, Austerity and Everyday Life: Living in a Time of Diminishing Expectations* Palgrave Macmillan, London 2015.

16. *Change Labour Party Manifesto 2024* Labour Party 13 June 2024 www.labour.org.uk.

17. Aditya Chakrabortty 'Drill Into the Policy, Ignore the Puffery: This Is a Starmer Manifesto More Than a Labour One' *The Guardian* 15 June 2024 www.theguardian.com.

18. Stuart Hall, Chas Critcher, Tony Jefferson, John Clarke and Brian Roberts *Policing the Crisis: Mugging, the State, and Law and Order* (2nd edn) Palgrave Macmillan, London 2013.

19. Albert Toth 'Timeline of Diane Abbott's Suspension: From Her Comments on Racism to Labour Election Ban' 30 May 2024 www.independent.co.uk.

20. Mehmet Solmaz 'British Premier Tells UK Parliament There's No Genocide in Gaza' *Gündem Gazetesi* 13 November 2024 www.aa.com.tr.

21. Becky Morton 'PM Pledges to Close Loophole That Let Gazans Settle in UK' *BBC News* 12 February 2025 www.bbc.co.uk.

22. Dominic Casciani 'Judge "Deeply Troubled" by PMQs Exchange on Gazans Settling in UK' *BBC News* 18 February 2025 www.bbc.co.uk.

23. Alex Oaten 'Tommy Robinson the Martyr – How the Far Right Builds Its Victim Narrative' The Conversation 13 June 2018 www.theconversation.com.

Son of a Toolmaker

Joe Kennedy

Nobody needs to be told that Keir Starmer's father was a 'tool-maker'. At a conservative count, he's brought it up around 40 times[1] in speeches, party political broadcasts and softball interviews. Nor do they need to be told that he enjoys watching Arsenal and playing football. These biographical claims have become so familiar that they have produced something of an industry in mocking and contesting them, and even outright rejection of their truthfulness, which creates common ground between Corbynism's online rump and the populist right. Starmer's father owned the factory, we're told, and he can't tell his old-fashioned wingers from his modern wide forwards. All of it, this line of thought proceeds, comes down to a pantomime of authenticity, a sustained but limited and disingenuous effort by Starmer to distance himself from the alleged haughty metropolitan radicalism of the last Arsenal-supporting Labour leader, who was frequently berated not only in the *Sun* but also, and perhaps much more frequently, in the *Guardian* for his inability to speak to the 'left-behind' of Brexitland. For some, it would seem that a priority of the contemporary left comes down to exposing the spuriousness of the 'toolmaker' narrative, in the hope that managing to do so brings about the collapse of the whole project of the Labour right and its centrist adjutants to reclaim, and maintain, control of the party.

It is easy to see the temptation. Part of it, obviously, amounts to rage in the face of British media's selectiveness and swaggering hypocrisy. Starmer is most of what Corbyn was hung out to dry for, and much, much more, but his positions are so usefully consonant with the post-Thatcher, post-Blair mainstream that he's given licence to present himself as the epitome of bootstrap-pulling. The truth doesn't really matter here – the BBC is unlikely to run an exposé on someone who is ideologically completely of a piece with it – and nor should it, because whether Starmer is 'really working-class' is far less interesting than what it means to insist so forcefully on him being presented as such.

Authentocracy[2] is an attempt to diagnose and describe a growing tendency within the British political and journalistic establishment – here defined, inexhaustively, as the Labour right and centre, moderate Tories, the BBC, *The Times* and the *Guardian* – to leverage claims about class against the left. 'Authentocracy' was, when the theory first appeared in 2018, the rearguard action of Blairism, or Blairo-Cameronism, a desperate attempt to fend off an insurgent egalitarian politics by portraying it as out-of-touch with the hopes and needs of those outside the immediate line of sight of a London-based socialist cadre. There were spiteful op-eds full of snarky remarks such as '[If] Corbyn is to be rebranded as a populist by his inner circle, there has to be a feel for the way people actually speak.'[3] These were bolstered by narrowly polled data collected by political scientists who were hardly disinterested and by journalists doing a watered-down form of regional reporting on how 'Labour [is] losing its heartlands.'[4] Ideologically, the function was to conceal Blairism's role in widening the economic gulf between the capital and, among others, the post-industrial parts of northern and midland England and Wales and the coastal towns and arable flatlands of the east. For the purposes of the authentocratic narrative, these 'left-behind' parts of Britain were homogenised in an image of honest-grafting cultural conservatism with 'legitimate concerns' about various forms of social change, but particularly those associated with immigration. What the centre promised to do was to address these anxieties sympathetically on the cultural level; this promise somehow negated the need to confess any culpability for ongoing material disparities.

What authentocracy ended up doing was pre-fabricating a narrative which could be weaponised by the centrists' other enemies, the Johnsonian Conservatives and those to their right. Indeed, some prominent voices from Labour's authentocratic wing – think of John Woodcock, Ian Austin and John Mann, once MPs for Barrow and Furness, Dudley North and Bassetlaw respectively – were rewarded for their hamstringing of Corbynism with seats in the House of Lords in the period following the 2019 general election. The version of Brexit the centrists dreaded, or affected to dread, came to pass, and it became entirely unsurprising for the right-wing government to float policy on the basis that the latte-drinkers wouldn't like it, and that this dislike in fact somehow *legitimised* a policy. Furthermore, Johnsonian policy increasingly came to be shaped by forces even further right than the Johnson government itself: Nigel Farage, the increasingly feral gutter press and Tommy Robinson, and online conspiracism inspired by and more or less contiguous with paranoiac pro-Trump Americanisms such as QAnon. With the 2019 defeat of Corbyn's Labour, and in that moment's aftermath, these wildcard entities were able to shape the mainstream by invoking what the 'real' people of the North and Midlands either did or did not want. In doing so, they pursued a rhetorical path first trodden by so-called moderates in the period of Corbyn's leadership of Labour. Ironically, the accusations of out-of-touchness levelled by Labour's centre-right against Corbynism in the 2015–19 period are now what they struggle, vainly, to defend themselves against now those accusations come from the right.

THE GRITTY AND THE STARTLING

After several years of many of those who critiqued the idea of authentocracy suggesting it was merely an over-theorised allegation that continuity Blairites were pretending they lived on a diet of chips and tea, and with a 'son of a toolmaker' making himself at home at Number Ten, now feels like a good time to revisit the idea and its explanatory power.

Authentocracy is a medium-term outcome of a perceived lack of realism, seriousness, integrity and, of course, authenticity in the culture and aesthetics predominant at the end of the 1990s and at the beginning of the succeeding decade. It emerged in part out of attempts to correct this. These were laudable, but came ultimately to represent a debased version of realism insofar as it inverted the fundamental mission of realism to depict the world truthfully by putting up a clichéd idea of reality to fortify another kind of truth-claim about how the world *should* be. Prescription, in other words, was presented as description. Authentocracy styles itself as laying bare the real, but actually does nothing more than serve up what has been conventionalised in advance as 'realistic', as evidence of an iconoclasm so heroic it simply must be politically trustworthy.

Authentocrats want to seem as if they have news for you, and they want you to be grateful for it.

What seems to me to have been overlooked or minimised in discussions about authentocracy was the idea's interest in how the political currency authenticity seemed to acquire in the mid-2010s mapped onto a prefigurative resurgence of realism in film, television and literature. The shift to 'grittiness' can be seen in James Bond films beginning with *Casino Royale* (2006), in Scandinavian and then British crime shows, and in the fantasy series *Game of Thrones*. In retrospect, *Authentocrats* read this swing in favour of the abrasive and unflinching as simply superstructural and ideological, as if directors and screenwriters were being ventriloquised by the needs of a political formation determined to preserve the neoliberal economic settlement by means of forfeiting the social liberalisations of the late 1990s. In such a view, 'reality' is 'realistically' portrayed as harsh and unpleasant to service the needs of those who must take 'difficult economic decisions'. Yet such an analysis now looks too mechanistic, or even, in the old language of intra-Marxist name-calling, 'vulgar'. A number of the catalytic texts for the realist turn of the 2000s – perhaps most significantly the American police procedural *The Wire* – were at least conceived at the height of Clinton-Blair anything-goes optimism, too early even to be accused of doing the ideological work *Casino Royale* performed of offering trauma as a justification for ripping up the human rights rulebook during the War on Terror.

The aesthetic shift I'm thinking about here deserves to be understood as relatively autonomous of political need. Doing so requires an acknowledgement that quirk, self-reflexivity, silliness and the non-sequiturial had saturated Anglo-American culture even before 9/11 to the degree that the scales simply had to tip: ironic fun, largely of the forced kind, was oversupplied, and had come to be perceived as grating flippancy. The problem was that the latter often persisted in the absence of the former, an afterlife which perhaps can have more grossly materialist causes attributed to it. Not all of the new realism could have the networks' and broadcasters' faith invested in it in the way *The Wire* clearly did, and such commercial anxieties meant that realism became a matter of defining certain easily recognisable tropes of 'the real': humourlessness, violence, regional accents, grey skies, industrial and post-industrial settings. If high-achieving realism (such as *The Wire*) lived up to an understanding of the mode as a holistic depiction of a place in a time which grasped its knotty intra-dependencies, the more churned-out kind depended on bullying its audience into feeling surprised that anybody would bother being 'realistic' at all after the nominal end of history.

It was Raymond Williams who noted with justified scepticism that:

> a common adjective used with 'realism' [is] 'startling' and ... within the mainstream of 'ordinary, contemporary, everyday reality', a particular current of attention to the unpleasant, the exposed, the sordid [can] be distinguished.[5]

This was an attempt to separate a cheap and ill-gotten realism which depends upon shock about 'going there' from the real thing, which might well be 'startling', but which is never defined exclusively by its being so. Genuine realism sits at a busy intersection of the dynamic and the diagrammatic in its desire to capture how capitalist society is simultaneously highly differentiated and more or less coherent. It is a structure which consists not only of entities and their relationships with one another, but of the parallax by which those relationships alter according to where one is standing. Such a realism can only ever be all-seeing to the degree that it represents the limitedness of every other perspective which it encloses and represents. Second-rate realism, on the other hand, positions itself as the legislator of its audience's naivety, awarding itself the privilege of 'startling' its reader or viewer with whatever the public apparently don't want to think about.

If there is a confusion between these realisms, it is arguably because disenchantment was so often thematised in the 19th-century realist novel. This might be seen on the catastrophic level of Gustave Flaubert's Emma Bovary, who, as most summaries go, dies because life won't fit her romantic aspirations for it; we might also perceive it in quieter and ultimately compensated form through George Eliot's Dorothea Brooke, whose marriage to a man she intellectually idealises collapses on her recognition he is an underachieving bore. However, both *Madame Bovary* and *Middlemarch* situate their characters' collapsing idealisations (as, for that matter, does *The Wire* with Jimmy McNulty and Stringer Bell) as contingent outcomes of a series of societal computations which it is the novel's real job to gauge. It is possible to misinterpret what these narratives are doing as merely rubbing our faces in the mud – 'startling' us into a recognition of the gap between the ideal and the real – on a kind of need-to-know basis. Furthermore, this possibility is increased by the fact that the brute force of what Williams calls 'the exposed' has become confused for realism itself in the time that has elapsed since the 19th-century novel's sophisticated efforts to map social complexity.

Since authentocracy was first theorised, the 'startling' has become even more entrenched, both culturally and politically. Take, for example, the wild success of the West Yorkshire-set detective show *Happy Valley*, which is full of unlikely plot events and is as procedurally implausible as any other work in the genre, but which is nevertheless praised for its 'poignant realness'.[6] Its 'realness', I would argue, leans very heavily on *signs of the real* such as rain-battered council housing, flat vowels and violent crime. While all of these things exist, none of them are more real – or, for that matter, more authentic – than, say, the tea-drinking vicars, clipped accents and elaborate, greedy killings in a cosy and 'unrealistic' programme such as *Midsummer Murders*. They are merely more startling. Likewise, in the political sphere, it is ubiquitous that an interview with an up-and-coming MP will make clear which football team they support, the implicit commandment being that we should be both surprised and grateful to have representatives who are 'like us' even if our concrete personal preferences are for cricket, or opera, or stamp-collecting. Were it not so universal, this would be nothing new, but the point is that authentocracy, having emerged out of a more or less ideologically neutral aesthetic 25 years ago, is now simply how the nation talks to itself.

STRUCTURES OF FEELING AND THE SINGLE ENTENDRE

Raymond Williams' discussions of what he called 'structures of feeling' are helpful here for considering how particular artistic and narrative practices are not, or at least not always, directly ideological at first, but become so over time. New structures of feeling are unmoored affective responses to historical change which are unsettled and ambiguous, and involve the emergence of aesthetics that are – at least briefly – promiscuous, although a hegemonic ideology will typically press them into service in the end.[7] In the specific case of the turn-of-the-millennium move towards grittiness, a motive cause in the form of anxieties about the very desirability of a future committed entirely to post-historical leisure, to *unseriousness*, perhaps, might be detected.

A pre-emptive version of this troubled, guilty notion that a comfort characterised by limitless no-stakes irony is in fact no comfort at all can be found in the American novelist David Foster Wallace's influential 1993 essay 'E Unibus Pluram: Television and US Fiction', which wondered whether the writers of the near future might once again gamble on 'single-entendre values'[8] in a reinvigorated search for unrefracted and precise truth. Similarly, the late 1990s in Britain were not just the age of riotous irony – often wielded for deniability's sake, as in the case of lad mags such as *Loaded* – but of complaining about the pernicious ubiquity of irony and looking for alternatives to it. One example of this can be found in the painters Billy Childish and Charles Thomson's Stuckist Manifesto of 1999, which had as its first principle 'Stuckism is the quest for authenticity [...]. By removing the mask of cleverness and admitting where we are, the Stuckist allows him/herself uncensored expression.'[9] A year later came the manifesto of the New Puritans in fiction-writing, which declared a commitment to 'textual simplicity' and foreswore 'all devices of voice: rhetoric, authorial asides'.[10] Though less declarative, it is interesting to remember how the cartoonish zaniness of Britpop gave way to the heartfelt expressivism of The Verve's 1997 album *Urban Hymns* or even Blur's eponymous release of the same year.

A belief in authenticity and simplicity, or the rejection of irony in favour of acoustic guitars or single entendres, do not necessarily lead us towards realism, but realism obviously offered one of the most well-signposted routes out of the endlessly proliferating self-reference of 1990s media. *The Wire* was a natural counterpoint to Quentin Tarantino: for all its multi-facetedness and narrative layering, it was ultimately a depiction of Baltimore, a real place, rather than a knowing depiction of already-existing depictions. Likewise, the succession of Daniel Craig's Bond from Pierce Brosnan's centred the portrayal of a traumatised character after Brosnan's winking theatricalisation of the franchise's essential pointlessness in the post-Cold War era. Come the early 2000s, the pop-cultural tone in both the UK and the United States was a confusion of 90s ironies, which still remains in the form of so-bad-it's-good music and gameshows, authenticity-seeking portrayals of the unfettered human such as *Big Brother*, and the re-emergence of dramatic realism, whether laudable or clichéd.

The point at which growing hostility to irony and a tentative embrace of realism became harnessed properly by ideology – the convergence of an emergent aesthetics with hegemonic imperatives – was the War on Terror, with its attendant rhetoric of realpolitik and 'difficult choices'. In Britain, Blairism had initially mapped itself onto the festivity of the End of History, meaning that the new prime minister was differentiated from the rock stars he socialised with, Oasis in particular, only by a job title: often, he was presented as little more than a legislator of the inevitable and infinite fun he would release by his removal of the usefully grey, cartoonishly suburban John Major. After 2001 and 9/11, however, Blair was reimagined as a maker of difficult decisions, the Iraq War in particular, and as the person who took responsibility on the basis of a heightened sense of what was and was not 'realistic' when nobody else would or could. Realism in an aesthetic sense need not correlate with an ideologically defined notion of what political realism is. Indeed, one can find very many historical cases in which it occupies a critical and counter-hegemonic stance: Dickens' *Hard Times* or Emile Zola's 1885 mining novel *Germinal* or indeed Raymond Williams' own fiction. But in the 'startling' mode Williams identifies, it has at least formal similarities with the idea of the 'hard choice'. Nobody likes to be told that it's a shitty world out there, but somebody's got to do it.

KEIR STARMER AS INTERMEDIATE REALIST

How does Keir Starmer slot into the authentocracy thesis? How does he symptomise it? For starters, he fits the profile of the kind of culture supplement-reading Gen-X urban professional we might imagine at some point in the mid-2000s reading with interest in the *Guardian* about the refreshing grittiness of a new crime drama. Before he was focus-grouped into a corner,[11] Starmer was happy to declare that his favourite novel was *A Disaffection* by the Glaswegian author James Kelman, a realist so startling that one of the judges walked off the panel when he won the Booker Prize in 1994 for another novel, *How Late It Was, How Late*. Much of Starmer's rhetoric is about responsibility and duty, about what he wishes he didn't have to do but in fact must, about the stark fact of the nation's emptied pockets and a rising tide of geopolitical threat. These are the urgent and difficult choices Starmer will make us confront despite our understandable reluctance: we are not to be cosseted.

And this, surely, is where the toolmaking and the *Happy Valley*-esque pebbledash semi and the evenings watching the Gooners and playing five-a-side come in. How could somebody with this catalogue of earthy experience be any less than well fitted to discern the knock of reality from the cooing of idealism? When he talks about his toolmaking father, it is designed, in precisely Williams' use of the word, to startle us: we are meant to react with some shock, not only that someone at the apex of British professional life might come from such callused beginnings, but that toolmakers exist at all! It's often taken for granted that the audience for Starmer's recollections are the working-class voters of Austin's Dudley and Woodcock's Barrow and Mann's Bassetlaw constituencies, those lost to the Tories in the cataclysm of the 2019 general election. But the team around the now-prime minister are not psephologically idiotic, and will have been able privately to anticipate what did in fact happen in July 2024, which is that many to most of these enthused-about 'hero' voters either stayed with the Tories or shifted even further rightwards to Farage and Reform UK. Where 2024 Labour acquired votes was among the more-or-less liberal middle classes who, in 2019, had either indulged Johnson with one more chance to be a one-nation conservative or rejected Corbyn's project for its perceived Euroscepticism or Euro-apathy. This constituency was surely perceived as vital behind the scenes, so what explains a rhetoric apparently designed specifically to appeal to the so-called 'left behind' or, even more euphemistically, the 'traditional working class'?

The answer must surely be that the 'toolmaker' talk was aimed at the voters who Starmer actually *was* able to impress. Authentocracy is not a pitch for recognition from the working class, but a strategy which seeks consent from the middle classes who want to be assured that a prospective leader is serious about the task facing them. This consent is won not through promises – Labour's 2024 manifesto is utterly bereft of specific strategies resembling anything like betterment – but through a shock effect which embarrasses its audience into submission. Few want to be the person seen to be idealistic or out-of-touch, which is what 'startling' realism – whether that's a detective drama set on a windswept housing estate or a senior politician brandishing their proletarian credentials – is designed to induce in those it confronts.

This realism is so dependent on formulated effects that it shouldn't really be considered realism at all. In an essay on *The Wire*, Frederic Jameson demonstrates how that show threw its own complex realism or thick description into relief by depicting what he calls the 'intermediate' realism of the detectives it depicts. The detectives, Jameson writes, cannot apprehend the 'ultimate structure' of the reality of drug-dealing in Baltimore – its all-encompassing 'source, refinement, transportation, sales network, and bulk or wholesale distribution'[12] – because they encounter it only narrowly in the form of street dealing, thus confusing the part for the whole. We can borrow this coinage to think about how authentocracy uses the part (the toolmaker father, the football fandom) not as a way of getting back to the whole (class as a social relation within a complicated series of social relations), but as the ultimate confirmation which somehow proves beyond doubt that Starmer is as 'realistic' as a politician and Knight of the Realm can be.

Thus, instead of being used as the starting point for an approach to politics, class is reduced to a cipher for suitability. We might ask why it is that being the son of a toolmaker should have the power to startle in the 21st century, and also about the role of Labour in this failure of egalitarian politics that Starmerism looks likely to perpetuate. Against this, we might also listen out for any rustles of a structure of feeling which can help serve to expose and oppose this increasingly decrepit aesthetic of authenticity our son of a toolmaker has come to represent.

ENDNOTES

1. See mydadwasatoolmaker.uk for an attempt at an itemised list, although the site's author acknowledges that there are 'probably countless other instances'.

2. Joe Kennedy *Authentocrats: Culture, Politics and the New Seriousness* Repeater, Alresford 2018.

3. Suzanne Moore 'Labour's Corbyn Reboot Shows Exactly Why He Needs to Go' *The Guardian* 11 January 2017 www.theguardian.com.

4. See, for example, John Harris' piece called just that, which begins with the non-more-representative line 'By the time I got to Stoke-on-Trent, it was obvious' *New Statesman* 22 September 2016 www.newstatesman.com.

5. Raymond Williams 'Realism and the Contemporary Novel' in David Lodge (ed.) *Twentieth Century Literary Criticism: A Reader* Longman, Harlow 1972 p. 582.

6. See 'The 100 Best TV Shows of the 21st Century' *The Guardian* 16 September 2019 www.theguardian.com.

7. See, for example, Raymond Williams *Marxism and Literature* Oxford University Press, Oxford 1977 pp. 128–135.

8. David Foster Wallace 'E Unibus Pluram: Television and U.S. Fiction' *Review of Contemporary Fiction* 13/2 (1993) p. 19.

9. See 'Stuckism' Stuckism International 26 August 1999 www.stuckism. com.

10. See Nicholas Blincoe and Matt Thorne 'The Pledge' in Nicholas Blincoe and Matt Thorne (eds) *All Hail the New Puritans* Fourth Estate, London 2001 pp. vii–xvii.

11. For more on Starmer's pivot from 'Kafka fan to atlas enthusiast', see Finn McRedmond 'Labour's Anti-Intellectual Moment' *New Statesman* 24 July 2024 www.newstatesman.com.

12. Frederic Jameson 'Realism and Utopia in *The Wire*' *Criticism* 52/3 (2010) p. 361.

THE FALLOUT

Time to Reshuffle the Labour Left

Neal Lawson

Countries follow broad patterns in terms of the ebb and flow from left to right and back. But they can be electorally out of sync. Labour won its 'loveless landslide' in the context of a systemic crisis of social democracy which has seen election losses and governing failures by the centre-left the world over. Unless it changes course, Labour's victory, rather than correcting that crisis, looks in danger of merely confirming it. But only in the context of the historic, global and UK crisis of a politics that attempts to combine the social with the democratic can we understand what, if any, future Labour has and what Starmerism is or might become.

Social democracy has been in crisis since the late 1970s. If we re-read Eric Hobsbawm's 'The Forward March of Labour Halted',[1] we learn that the demise of the working class as an effective political force began in the late 1940s when jobs shifted from blue- to white-collar. But it wasn't only a class that social democrats lost in this switch, but a method. Industrialisation didn't just gift social democrats a homogenous electoral base, but a culture of Fordism and labourism. This was the method and the nature by which social democracy was to govern with machine-like control. The factory gave social democrats a voting bloc and a centralised and linear system to govern the state and deliver public services. And it gave Labour a creed wedded to tribalism, the Union, the state and limited deals to reform capital.

In the face of the dual threat of mass trade unionism and Soviet communism, the capitalist class agreed to an accommodation with post-war welfarism and the need for full employment. But even at its moment of creation, this 'golden age' of social democracy was running out of steam. Come the end of the 20th century, stripped of both class and culture, in the wake of the fall of the Berlin Wall and the rise of globalised capitalism that could source cheap labour from across the planet, and therefore a moment of supreme weakness, social democrats felt they had no option but to accommodate themselves not just to capitalism, but to the neoliberal strain of it, the goal of which was the eradication of the possibility that a society could be both social and democratic. The best they could do was a doomed attempt to humanise something that was out to destroy them. So the tailspin of decline began.

Today, as we scan the social democratic landscape, we witness a wasteland. Nowhere across the globe is any vaguely social democratic party leading ideologically, culturally or programmatically. What we see are temporary upticks in electoral performance, as momentarily voters tire of the right or the populist right, and swing back to social democrats as the only available alternative. But the swing is temporary because the cultural and political weaknesses of social democratic parties mean they struggle to govern successfully. They can't make society more equal, or deal within the pressures of the poly-crisis world we face. So the electoral dice is thrown again in an attempt to address the deep insecurities people feel. But the dice are now loaded in favour of the populist right, who have few if any answers, but thrive in the chaos of economic and democratic breakdown.

Recent social democratic electoral successes have all fizzled out: witness the German SPD, the Australian Labor Party and Biden's Democrats. All were hailed as turning points back to the centre-left; all are struggling or are already defeated. In Spain, the Social Democrats cling on to office, but only via a contentious deal with Catalan separatists. Almost everywhere else it is the right, and increasingly the populist right, who are in the ascendant who thrive in the chaos as the power of democracy gives way to the power of billionaires who are lauded and who hold increasing political sway.

It is not as if the new post-2008 left fared better. If anything, their decline has been even more dramatic, most spectacularly in the case of Syriza in Greece, which ran the country from 2015 to 2019 and which tends now to poll below 10%. In Spain, Podemos, which for a while shared office with the social democrats, struggles to hit even 5% in the polls.

THE CRISIS OF LABOUR

Over the last quarter century, the UK has experienced a series of social democratic spasms. Since 1979, the ideas and practice of what we knew back then as Thatcherism and now call neoliberalism have become deeply embedded. The plundering of the commons, in the shape of council house and nationalised industries sales, the commercialisation of the NHS and comprehensive schooling, the crushing of working-class solidarity, not least through the 1984–85 defeat of the miners, and rampant turbo-consumption meant that what Margaret Thatcher had said seemed to be true: 'there is no alternative'. Or at least no alternative that could fundamentally challenge neoliberal hegemony.

The first reaction to the crisis of social democracy was New Labour. Stuart Hall nailed Blairism with his description of it as a 'double shuffle'[2] as it took one social democratic step forward, via the minimum wage or initiatives like Sure Start, but two neoliberal steps back in the form of deregulation of the city or the denigration of those on social security as shirkers. Of course, it did some good in terms of public service investment, but all under conditions subservient to neoliberalism, to produce consumers not citizens, paid for not by higher taxes but through complex public-private initiatives that benefited global capital. Gordon Brown's desire to be more social democratic came at the tail end of a long period in office. It was too late, and lacked the awareness or forces to break with neoliberal orthodoxy.

A more concerted attempt to head in a social democratic direction came with Ed Miliband and then Jeremy Corbyn. Miliband was prepared to critique both his New Labour inheritance and predatory capitalism, but without a strong enough political base in either the party or the country, he lost his direction and morphed into the odd mix of New and 'Blue Labour'[3] that was crushed in the 2015 general election. This defeat, to everyone's surprise, gave rise to Corbynism. As a putative left populist, Corbyn rode the wave of widespread dissatisfaction with austerity and democratic decline.[4] But the old left surfer struggled to embrace the energy of very new social waves. He eschewed the basic requirements of pluralism and professionalism needed to run a modern political party and election campaign.[5]

Like its other left populist counterparts across Europe,[6] and Bernie Sanders' challenges for the Democrats' presidential nomination in the USA, Corbynism has largely come and gone without leaving a trace. For Corbyn, we shall have to wait and see whether his winning Islington North in 2024 changes that.

ENTER THE SOFT LEFT

This is the 'long shadow' context within which Starmerism must be viewed. It is a context of profound weakness and defensiveness. It is increasingly evident that 'Starmerism' is defined by a rather brilliant short-term ability to achieve a particular goal, namely the leadership of Labour, and then thanks to the abject performance of the Tories under Johnson-Truss-Sunak, to win office. But in both cases, the methods used to secure electoral victory limited the possibility of long-term political transformation. First, Starmer turned on the left in the party, and then accommodated with the forces and arguments of the establishment in such a way that he won a record haul of seats, but built a cage that imprisons the potential of what his victory could achieve.

So far, so gloomy. Is it social democracy's fate to be half-life blips in a frightening landslide toward a populist right future? Where can hope come from, and can it latch on to the Starmer project?

To find out, it is necessary to explore the history and potential of the tradition within and around Labour called the 'soft left'. Historically, the term 'soft left' only made sense in the context of the 'hard left'. The differences are clouded in the mists of time, and stem from personality, tactical and strategic differences going back decades. The roots lie in the left splitting over Tony Benn's 1981 deputy leadership bid, which some saw as heroic, but which others saw as futile. Fuelled by the intellectual engine *of Marxism Today*, powered by the Labour Coordinating Committee (LCC),[7] and represented in parliament by the likes of Robin Cook and Clare Short, the soft left developed a politics attuned to both electoral necessity and modern forms of democratic and economic transformation. In particular, the soft left represented a different style of politics, more plural and sensitive to the rule that means always shape ends, so that how we achieve social democracy is determined by how we behave on the journey toward it. In this, the soft left was correct, but it made itself vulnerable because it was less prepared to act in ways counter to these plural democratic instincts in order to win Labour's internal factional battles. While the soft left sought to reconcile means and ends, the hard left and the hard right in the party were busy doing whatever it took to win.

Any balanced account of the soft left will register pluses and minuses. Some argue it helped save Labour in the 1980s following the 1983 and 1987 general election defeats. Others argue it opened the party to its eventual accommodation with neoliberalism.[8] While such a historic analysis would be of value, what matters now is what soft left thinking and practice can offer Labour and wider progressives for the future.

An important essay, 'Whither the Soft Left?',[9] by John Denham, a Labour minister under Tony Blair, for *Renewal*, the journal of social democracy, outlines the key features of what constitutes this soft left. According to Denham, there are three:

1. How do we understand the evolution of the capitalist economy nationally and globally, and what does this mean for efforts to create an economy that works for the common good?
2. How do we understand the nature of the state, and what does this mean for the way in which power should be exercised in contemporary society?
3. How do we understand the changing electorate and civil society, and what does this mean for politics of power and the possibility of radical economic and social change?[10]

If social democracy is to have anything to offer the future of our country, then it must be in mining these three key areas, but in ways that address the fundamental weaknesses of social democracy, namely the absence of agency and a method. It must do so in the context of a resurgent populist right, the climate emergency and economic crisis, the AI revolution and geo-political upheaval. We cannot simply reinvent, even if we wanted to, the soft left of the 1980s. Indeed, the very term 'soft left', with all its outdated factional references, needs to be junked. So what might be the contours of a post-2024 strategic left?[11]

A New Economy

The idea that social democrats can simply manage neoliberalism more effectively and more humanely is clearly untenable. If one key purpose of neoliberalism is the eradication of the possibility of alternatives to it, then it is precisely on the creation and curation of economic alternatives to neoliberal structures and cultures that the left must focus. At a macro level, this must entail new ways of generating sufficient investment resources to ensure both social stability and the transition beyond carbon. At a micro level, it requires different forms of ownership and control of enterprises, in which democratic and participatory employee control and engagement is key.[12] More generally, the strategic left must focus on economic innovation and creativity, not just distributional issues, if it is to win the hearts, minds and active support of a broad base of citizens.[13]

A New State and Democracy

The British state and the democracy that underpins it are incapable of delivering the social and economic transformation our country needs. In the absence of a progressive alliance[14] between Labour, the Liberal Democrats and Greens, the first-past-the-post electoral system requires Labour to win over disaffected Tories. It can only achieve this with the promise not to change anything of significance.[15] Once in office, Labour finds a system that is over-centralised and over-controlling and led by Treasury orthodoxy. In the age of Fordism, this worked for Labour, most famously in 1945, and to some extent for Harold Wilson's 'white heat of technology' in 1964–70, but now? In the chaotic, complex and dispersed world of the 21st century, this old empire state isn't fit for purpose.

The top-down control of the two main parties means many lack a political home, such as one-nation Tories, red-greens, green-reds and potentially the strategic left. While electoral reform is key to unlocking a system now dominated by rich party donors, media moguls and a few swing voters in a few swing seats, this should only be seen as a precursor to dispersing power much more widely and deeply, not just through devolution, but by establishing different methods by which citizens can negotiate and shape the future, not least through citizens' assemblies, juries, referendums and other democratic practices, which takes us beyond mere representation. Meanwhile, public services need to be reimagined as sites of co-production between workers and users. Deepening democracy as an everyday practice must become the central goal of any transformative left government.

A NEW CLASS AND A NEW METHOD?

Can a new class or combination of classes be moulded effectively from this analysis of a different approach to the economy and the state? Labour was always an amalgam of interests between the working class and the progressive middle class. This combination must be re-engineered. An abiding sense of modernity was a hallmark of Labour successes in 1945, 1964 and 1997. But New Labour took its grasp of modernity, in its neoliberal and hyper-globalised form, too far. The very self-definition of Labour as 'new' was meant in part to show it was no longer old. Old Labour, by which was meant working-class labour, was viewed pejoratively. It was presumed by Blairite strategists that the working class had nowhere to go electorally and socially, and had to accept a fate which meant keeping up with the demands of a globalised economy and becoming middle-class, or be left behind. If there is to be a new class alliance, then aspects of the Blue Labour agenda[16] and the recognition and acceptance of at least some level of cultural conservatism in working-class culture and lives is important. But as necessary as stitching together such cross-class alliances will be, it's unlikely to be sufficient.

The bigger and more pressing question is how to bend the zeitgeist to the values of social democracy, without accommodating to neoliberalism. If the golden age of social democracy was forged by the technology and culture of the factory, then any new political venture based on a future that is both social and democratic will be shaped by the sentiment and dynamics more akin to how we use our smartphones. Given we no longer live in an industrial society, but in a networked society, a Kodak political movement won't work in an Instagram moment.

Critically, though, social democracy lost its industrial roots and foundations in the nation state but maintained them internally – as technocrats and tribalists who deliver the 'good society' to and for a grateful people. This is evident in the way that both the hard left and especially now the hard right attempt to control and dominate the party in their own factional interests. But this controlling methodology no longer works, and new methods rooted in active economic and social citizenship must be forged. Out of the fragments of the existing working class, the precariat, the post-material, the array of networked citizens and social and economic entrepreneurs, a new historic bloc must be forged to embody, champion and sustain a reinvention of the left project. By definition, this will not be homogenous, but plural. To date, there have been few signs that social democracy can be sufficiently separated from its technocratic and tribal culture. But the cultural leap to pluralism means letting go is essential if a renewed and modern social democracy is to have a future.

WHAT COULD HAPPEN?

There are two theories of change available. The first is Milton Friedman's 'in a crisis politicians look for the ideas laying around them'.[17] The second is courtesy of Buckminster Fuller, who said, 'You never change things by fighting the existing reality. To change something, build a new model that makes the existing model obsolete.'[18] Both strategies have their place, but only taken together do they offer a new broad and deep strategic left the possibility of meaningful influence.

Since the mid-1990s, there have been two moments when it seemed the soft left might have a more decisive influence on Labour. In 2007, Jon Cruddas launched a bid for Labour's deputy leadership and came close. In 2020, Clive Lewis went for the Labour leadership on a promise that he would 'transform to win'. He failed to get on the ballot paper, squeezed by the false promise of Starmerism and the continuity Corbynism of Rebecca Long-Bailey.[19] But the embryonic policy programme and political culture they both embodied was in clear contrast to Brown or the cynical foundations that Starmer used to win – and then rejected so quickly.

Both Cruddas and Lewis failed because, from the early 2000s, and despite their opposition to the Iraq War led by Cook and Short, the soft left lacked the power base and organisational capacity to win. This was especially the case when Blairism set the tone by insisting on total leadership domination of the party. A tone applied more ruthlessly by Starmer and his chief of staff, Morgan McSweeney, and their enforcers in local Labour parties and the Labour to Win faction. But it was also because, as a 'soft' or plural left, refusing a win-at-all-costs approach, it rejected a ruthless and cynical politics, sticking instead to the belief that means shape ends. Does this inevitably mean doing the right thing, but at the cost of failing to achieve 'change' (to coin a phrase), or getting organised to counter the direction in which Starmer is taking both Labour and his government? It's a paradox that must be lived with, but as Paul Thompson, when chair of the LCC, said to a Trotskyite heckler, 'We might be the soft left, but we're not that soft.'

Which leaves us with two questions.

First, can a post-general election strategic left renew and invent itself in ways that are meaningful?

Second, where and how does this impact on Starmer, or any successor as leader, and the Labour Party itself?

Let's presume the answer to the first question is yes, and that there is enough here, in the Denham essay and more widely in the soft-left ecosystem of academics, think tanks, publications, campaign organisations, grassroots members and progressive alliance allies, for its renewal. Let's accept that Compass, the softening of the hard left, the Tribune Group, Open Labour, the social democratic journal *Renewal* and more can build a more effective base and make up for what Cruddas and Lewis lacked. Then what?

The downside of whatever Starmerism is is its fluidity and detachment from any ideology. But at one and the same time, the upside is *precisely* its fluidity and detachment from ideology. Starmer has been a Corbynite, represented Corbynism without Corbyn, an anti-Corbynite, and even a fan of Mrs Thatcher. If he can change, then he can change again. We know from his casting off of key members of staff that he's ruthless. He came to full-time politics late in the day; he was only elected a Labour MP in 2015, and had little previous experience as a Labour activist. Within just five years, he was Labour leader, and within nine, prime minister. Yet he has a strong emotional attachment to Labour. One can disagree with the outcomes and consequences, but he has worked to win back the party rather than set up a rival as the Blairites were planning post-Brexit, and has a commitment to the working class and the role of the state to be deployed on its behalf. The platform Starmer stood on to win the Labour leadership in 2020 wasn't far off what is needed now. It embraced necessary social, economic and environmental policies, decisively ditched any hint of antisemitism, and looked to professionalise the party. Somewhere this is still all part of Starmer's DNA – if he, and we, can only rediscover it. Finally, the belief in the centrality of human rights runs right through him, and could come to define his premiership, if he'll let it.

A progressive Starmer pivot to reach out to a new strategic left is unlikely, but it shouldn't be ruled out. While the soft left seems weak, the analysis outlined above and by John Denham is the kind of policy package the country needs for its transformation – and for the party to stand a chance of re-election. There are now a record number of progressive MPs in the House of Commons. They were put there by an alliance in the country that voted for the candidate best placed to beat the Tory incumbent. It is this progressive bloc which is now learning that 'not being the Tories' is insufficient. There is a growing demand for more radical solutions, and there is a loose network in the country that could be open to the search for a new political direction: the more modern trade unions, community organisers and activists, social entrepreneurs, a growing ethical and transformational business culture, public sector workers and the care economy, progressive NGOs and campaign organisations, not least those working to stop climate chaos, and those angry about injustice and desperate for lasting peace in the Middle East and elsewhere.

Across this spectrum, there is an emergent 'systems consciousness'. This is the idea that meaningful change will only come about via the structural and cultural transformation of our key social, democratic and economic institutions, and not just through a wish list of isolated demands. So-called 'non-reformist reforms' are necessary, and could command widespread support for what has been called a 'pragmatic left'.[20]

The left needs to take a leaf out of Thatcher's playbook when she said 'the economy is the goal; the means is to change the soul'.[21] The left should look to build institutions and incentives which reward and grow the groups and behaviours which reflect the values of solidarity, equality and co-operation.

Historically, the soft left has been committed to extra-parliamentary activity, but given the increasing limits of parliamentary-led change, that commitment must be deepened. A civil society broad left must co-exist alongside a parliamentary road to socialism. In more recent times, this combination of parliamentary and extra-parliamentary activity has been called '45° Change', the diagonal meeting point of emerging horizontal forces and the more established vertical institutions of the state.[22] Colin Crouch, a leading intellectual of the soft left, in his seminal book *Post-Democracy* described what that left strategy must do:

> First, stay alert to the potentialities of new movements which may at first seem difficult to understand, because they may be the bearers of democracy's future vitality.
>
> Second, work through the lobbies of established and new cause organisations, because post-democratic politics works through lobbies. Even if the causes supported by egalitarians are always weaker there than those of the large corporations, they are weaker still if they stay out of the lobby.
>
> Third, work, critically and conditionally, through parties, because none of their post-democratic substitutes can replace their potential capacity for carrying through egalitarian policies.[23]

Thus, a fundamental issue of strategy and values can't be ducked by a wider strategic left, namely the question of cross-party working or progressive alliances. Back in 2011 Compass, the think tank and campaigning organisation which grew out of the soft left LCC, made the decision[24] to operate beyond just Labour and welcomed people from other parties who shared its 'good society' vision.[25] The decision was both moral and strategic. How in good faith could Compass include those in Labour not committed to a future that was much more equal, sustainable and democratic, while excluding those in other parties that were? And it foresaw a future of political fragmentation and the breakdown of the two-party system, which would demand cross-party working. Of course, Labour now holds a huge parliamentary majority, but only with 34% of the vote, while the Tories only secured 24%. This in a system designed explicitly to prop up the dominance of two parties. The strategic left should see the opportunity of a more fragmented electoral landscape and the appeal of a more plural approach to political transformation.

The conversion of the Labour Party membership and trade unions to proportional representation is key. It implies an acceptance of democratic justice and therefore cross-party pluralism. Any strategic left ecosystem which sees Greens, Liberal Democrats and Scottish and Welsh nationalists as enemies will be electorally, politically and morally weaker than it could be and needs to be.

John Denham wrote in his *Renewal* essay that 'Labour's soft left is now more obvious in its absence than its presence.'[26] And on a Compass podcast, ITV Deputy Political Editor Anushka Asthana, speaking about her book *Taken as Red*, said that one telling critique of the soft left is that it 'backs whoever the leader is': Brown, Miliband, Corbyn and now Starmer.[27] This speaks to the historic strength and the weakness of the soft left, willingly playing a necessary interface but subservient role between the hard left and the right of the party. This sense of pluralism militates against its own interests in reconfiguring the balance of inner-party power, but it has helped stop the factional destruction of the party. Or at least it has, to date. The onslaught of the hard right against both the hard and soft left could see Labour trying to fly with just one wing. But the culture of pluralism is the only method by which the left and social democrats can have any have influence on a future that can no longer be controlled, only negotiated.

Whether a strategic left can invent itself, first intellectually and strategically, and then organisationally, remains to be seen. Ending the historic but now unnecessary division between the hard and soft left is one important starting point. Whether Starmer or his successor are meaningful influenced by such a renewal remains unknown. But one thing is certain: a future for a country that isn't built around the goals of equality and sustainability, via cultures and structures of deep democracy and pluralism, will be a future that belongs to the populist right.

ENDNOTES

1. Eric Hobsbawm *The Forward March of Labour Halted* Verso, London 1981.

2. Stuart Hall 'New Labour's Double-Shuffle' *Soundings* 2003/24 (2002) pp. 319–335.

3. See Ian Geary and Adrian Pabst (eds) *Blue Labour: Forging a New Politics* I.B. Tauris, London 2015.

4. See Neal Lawson 'I Voted for Jeremy Corbyn Today – and Here's Why' *New Statesman* 19 August 2015.

5. Ibid.

6. See Marina Prentoulis *Left Populism in Europe: Lessons from Jeremy Corbyn to Podemos* Pluto Press, London 2021.

7. I was a member of the executive committee of the LCC during the late 1980s and early 1990s.

8. For a contemporary account from this latter position, see Mike Marqusee and Richard Heffernan *Defeat from the Jaws of Victory: Inside Kinnock's Labour Party* Verso, London 1992.

9. John Denham 'Whither the Soft Left' *Renewal* 32/1 (2024) pp. 22–31.

10. Ibid. p. 23.

11. For a more detailed exposition of these ideas, see *The New Settlement* Compass September 2024 www.compassonline.org.uk.

12. See Stir to Action, which leads the debate on new forms of economic ownership: www.stirtoaction.com.

13. See Roberto Unger *The Knowledge Economy* Verso, London 2019.

14. See Neal Lawson *All You Need to Know about a Progressive Alliance* Compass June 2021 www.compassonline.org.uk.

15. See Matthew Sowemimo, Neal Lawson and Lena Swedlow *Thin Ice: Why the UK's Progressive Majority Could Stop Labour's Landslide Melting Away* Compass December 2024 www.compassonline.org.uk.

16. For an updated version of Blue Labour politics, see Jonathan Rutherford 'Labour Must Beware the Lure of Progressivism' *New Statesman* 3 June 2024.

17. Milton Friedman *Capitalism and Freedom* University of Chicago Press, Chicago 1982 p. xiv.

18. Originally quoted in Mike Vance and Diane Deacon *Think Out of the Box* Career Press, Franklin Lakes 1995 p. 138.

19. See Clive Lewis *Transform to Win* Compass 2020 www.compassonline.org. uk.

20. See Neal Lawson 'The Left Wing of the Possible' *Renewal* (8 February 2024) www.renewal.org.uk.

21. See Margaret Thatcher 'Economics Are the Method: The Object Is to Change the Soul' Margaret Thatcher Foundation 3 May 1981 www. margaretthatcher.org.

22. Neal Lawson *45° Change: Transforming Society from Above and Below* Compass February 2019 www.compassonline.org.uk.

23. Colin Crouch *Post-Democracy* Polity Press, Cambridge 2004 p. 122. A 2012 explanatory and updated text by Colin Crouch, 'Coping with Post-Democracy', is available free to download from www.fabians.org.uk, and a further 2019 update, 'Post-Democracy and Populism' *The Political Quarterly* 90/S1 pp. 124–137, is also free to download from https://pure.mpg.de/.

24. I am currently the Executive Director of Compass www.compassonline.org.uk.

25. See Ruth Lister *Towards a Good Society* Compass April 2020 www.compassonline.org.uk.

26. Denham 'Whither the Soft Left' p. 24.

27. See the podcast Anushka Asthana 'The Year of Elections – 2024 Round-Up Episode' 10 December 2024 www.compassonline.org.uk.

A Conservative Meltdown

Phil Burton-Cartledge

The 2024 general election was a catastrophe for the Conservative Party: 230 seats fell in all directions – mostly to Labour, but to the Liberal Democrats too. The party took 59 seats from the Tories. Scraps were picked over by Reform, which took five from the Conservatives, and the Greens, which won two. The party's sole consolation was Leicester East, which they won from Labour. This was the worst result for the Tories since the passing of the 1832 Reform Act, and their popular vote of 6.8 million (23.7%) was the lowest since Stanley Baldwin led them into the December 1923 general election. They found itself at the centre of a strong anti-Tory mood, with challenges from all over the political spectrum prising their coalition of voters apart.

After their triumph in 2019, it seems incredible that the Conservatives should be laid low. It had appeared that the so-called 'red wall' – the band of old industrial constituencies in the Midlands and North of England – had been permanently lost to Labour. Working-class seats that had loyally returned Labour MPs since the party had become a national force in 1918, and which had been victimised by the austerity programme of the preceding decade, fell to the blue tide. There was talk of Boris Johnson leading the Tories into the 2030s, and much concern that the 'working class' had abandoned its traditional party for social conservatism and the vapours of Johnson's Brexit boosterism. It is tempting to say, with the benefit of hindsight, and considering his well-documented character and predilections, that it was inevitable that Johnson would blow up his party and sink his government. For the problems besetting the Tories were visible, if one was prepared to look at them.

THE LONG-TERM DECLINE OF THE TORIES[1]

The conjunctural factors that had a role in the Tories' electoral collapse have received a lot of attention from political commentators, such as in Tim Bale's work on the recent history of the Conservatives[2] and the 2021 collection edited by Bale and others that looked at the Tories' electoral performance at the 2019 general election.[3] Comparatively few have considered longer-term shifts in Britain's political economy and what that means for party loyalties and voting behaviour. Some of the work that has appears at odds with political realities. For example, a decade ago, James Tilly and Geoffrey Evans forecast the 'conservatisation' of the electorate as demographic ageing conditioned the outlooks and preferences of voters – to the advantage of the Conservatives.[4] More recently, a couple of influential studies by Stephen Farrall and colleagues argued that younger people, who are typically associated with socially liberal values, were found to harbour Thatcherite and authoritarian attitudes to social security and crime.[5] The actual voting data suggests otherwise. This cohort's commitment to the Tories was conspicuously absent in the general election. Just 5% of 18–24-year-olds supported the Conservatives, with only 8% supporting their extreme right-wing rivals in Reform UK.[6]

To make sense of what happened, it is necessary to examine the composition of the Tory voter coalitions the party assembled in 2017 and 2019 and to understand what drives the political consequences of ageing. The base of mass conservatism during this period has rested on the Tories hegemonising older people, and particularly the retired. This has two components: the first being conditions consciousness, social location has the biggest impact on how one views the world, perceives one's interests, and draws political conclusions about them. This is as true for retired people as anyone else. And it is significant because an important political divergence rests on the difference between being retired and being in work: that is, the experience of retirement is increasingly analogous to the structural location ascribed to small business owners.

Overwhelmingly dependent on their own labour for an 'independent' livelihood, the petit bourgeoisie fear bigger businesses' ability to use economies of scale to cartelise markets and to drive out smaller competitors. Small businesses may also have employees, which bring with them wage demands, motivational issues and varying degrees of reliability. Both present existential dangers to the small proprietor. The political consequence of this is a predisposition to an authoritarian politics. Living with such ontological angst creates a desire for certainty, which successions of populist, extreme right-wing, and outright fascist political movements and parties offer – at least rhetorically. Hence the heavy emphasis they place on symbols of certainty. In this country, these are the flag, the military and nostalgia for a better, imperial, yesterday.

This is relevant to understanding mass conservatism in Britain because being a pensioner means having a relatively fixed income. One cannot simply re-enter the workforce to make good a financial crisis, so one is at the mercy of events. Additionally, old age becomes an experience of growing health concerns and frailty, which exacerbates a feeling of ontological angst. In other words, pensioners are caught between economic and physical realities beyond their control, and like the petit bourgeoisie, this predisposes them toward a politics of certainty. This location is close to petit-bourgeois anxiety, and similarly predisposes one toward a politics of certainty. Therefore, right-wing parties have disproportionate successes mobilising the support of older people by affecting an antipathy toward things that epitomise undesirable and, in some ways, 'unknowable' change, such as immigration, shifts in popular culture, feckless youth, green mitigations and the growing acceptance of previously stigmatised minorities.

This is aggravated when one owns property. If the police baton charges at Orgreave and Wapping were the Tory stick to bring the labour movement to heel in the 1980s, Thatcher's Right to Buy was the carrot. Selling off council-owned houses at discount rates, plus the modest house prices and equally modest deposits of the 1970s and 1980s, brought millions more into home ownership, and the consequences were conservatising. Home ownership individuates, because each owner has a material interest in the value appreciation of an asset. It disciplines, because servicing the mortgage/debt makes industrial action that much more financially difficult. Over the decades, those who availed themselves of council house sell-offs and mortgages have tended to keep hold of their properties, treating them as handsome nest eggs that could be handed down to their children or grandchildren. Some have joined the growing ranks of petit-bourgeois landlords. Once David Cameron came to office, the Tory policy platform catered to these interests and dispositions.

Pensioners have been protected from the immediate consequences of austerity. The cuts to public services they disproportionately depend on – above all, the NHS – have been presented as natural pressures as opposed to deliberate under-funding. Meanwhile, 14 years of not building enough houses to meet demand has protected asset price inflation. Combine this with tax cuts and increases to the state pension, the pulling at the nostalgic heart strings of an independent Britain bestriding the world stage, and lashing out at trans people and immigrants, perceived as harbingers of unwelcome (if not dangerous) social change, cemented an aged voter coalition that is also disproportionately likely to turn out and vote.

The problem the Tories have with making older people the basis of their voter coalition is its time-limited character. 'The pensioner' as a social location is a weaker right-wing authoritarian disposition than owning property, and the story of Britain since the mid-1990s has been a contraction in housing supply. Fewer homes were built, and the diminishing of council housing has led to the surging growth of the private rented sector. With asset prices inflating ahead of real wages, millions were and are locked out of acquiring property until much later in the life course. It means that couples aren't starting their families until later, if at all. This has continued under the last five prime ministers. Related to this were the everyday class politics of the Tories in office. Holding down wages, defending landlords, encouraging precarity, attacking the public sector, despoiling the environment, victimising minorities – this has been the lot of working age people and young people for 14 years. Their record is unlikely to convert many of this layer into Tory voters, even if millions of them do get on the housing ladder. As the Conservative support passes away, it is not replaced like-for-like by younger layers. In assembling the coalition that won them huge votes in 2017 and 2019, they've undermined the basis for renewal and thus for sustaining their ability to win in the longer term.

Then there are values. These too are time-limited. The Tories' coalition tends toward social conservatism, but the younger one is, the more socially liberal one is likely to be. This is not the result of left-wing teachers and liberal institutions, but a consequence of class cohorts. Following the work of Hardt and Negri,[7] what have become increasingly dominant in advanced capitalist societies since the World War Two have been immaterial labour and the advent of socialised workers. Displacing the industrial worker as the hegemonic working-class figure, its object is the production of care, knowledge, services and subjectivities – the production of the social relations capitalism needs to reproduce itself as a social system. Therefore, as the generations have passed through the changed character of work, the traits selected by it – tolerance, sociability, networking, care – have come to the fore of popular consciousness. One might expect not only increased levels of social tolerance across the board, but as new generations are born into an increasingly socially liberal culture, the tendency for younger people to be more tolerant of and open to difference than older generations. Not only is the Conservative base in long-term decline, so is the material root for social conservatism. It is arguable that the political dominance of the Tory press, what Tim Bale has often called 'the party in the media', has helped slow this process. But this is only effective in so far as people continue to buy and read its titles. It is perhaps something more than a coincidence that there are parallel declines in the Conservative Party and the reach of the Tory press's political content. It follows that when the Tories victimise people, play divide and rule, and cultivate the prejudices of their base, this serves only to drive a wedge between themselves and the bulk of the population. The efficacy of this kind of politics, no matter how much it is amplified by their media support, is time-limited.

The Tories have little inkling of this crisis in their support. Of the last three Conservative prime ministers, it was only Boris Johnson who showed a dim awareness that the Tories had to build a new coalition. Having assembled a large support base that, if anything, was consolidated during the initial period of the Covid pandemic, his understanding was that Brexit had to be hitched to a programme of Tory modernisation – his famed levelling-up schemes. This made some sense. Getting house-building going again, with jobs created in public works, infrastructure schemes, green industry plans, and the chimerical promise of the free ports programme had the potential to win over layers of working-age people through bricks laid and opportunities made. However, much of this was derailed by Covid, and he did not push it, and allowed Rishi Sunak – a figure who did not have a base in the wider party until Johnson elevated him to Number Eleven – to undermine, procrastinate, and effectively veto these efforts. Johnson also demonstrated that these were rhetorical feints, considering how little effort he spent on driving them through in the face of cabinet opposition. When the 'partygate' scandal came, his authority suffered a significant blow. While this was not fatal, what cut short Johnson's tenure was the Chris Pincher scandal. There were several complaints about unwanted sexual touching against Pincher, a key Johnson ally who had been appointed the party's chief whip. Johnson denied he knew anything about them, despite having previously described him as 'Pincher by name, pincher by nature'. After a week of sending ministers to repeat what were obvious lies in media interviews, the party had had enough. The health secretary, Sajid Javid, and Rishi Sunak resigned, and were followed by a parade of ministers and junior ministers. Effectively, the majority of the parliamentary Conservative Party went on strike and in an unlikely display of solidarity and collective action, forced Johnson from office.

It was evident that Liz Truss was a disaster waiting to happen thanks to the gaffes made over the course of the Tory leadership contest. These included floating a scheme that would introduce regionalised pay for public servants, with the aim of lowering salaries for those outside of London and the South East. Her famed 'mini-budget' was typical of the approach she had paraded in front of the Tory Party faithful. Nevertheless, while Truss did not address the long-term problems of the party, an argument could be made that stimulating a boom was Truss's strategy to turn around the political fortunes of her ailing party. It was unfortunate for her that reality has never accorded with the Tory view that low taxes lead to a ramping up of investment, and the resulting economic chaos eviscerated the Conservatives' standing in the polls. But it could not rebuild the crumbling coalition of ageing homeowners, especially not in the way it was presented.

Rishi Sunak's strategy was concerned with re-establishing some sort of political stability and hoping that he would appeal to 2019 Tory voters by going hard on immigration and declaring a so-called 'war on woke'. But unlike Johnson and Truss, Sunak tried to get by with offering nothing substantial. In this, he was true to his performance as chancellor. He was opposed to levelling-up because of a commitment to Tory small-statism, a political strategy designed to defund and wind down public services in such a way as to delegitimise them by rendering them dysfunctional. As a result, political demands for more funding would be undercut by the services' baleful performance, so the Tories would be better able to manage political pressure to fix them – especially so since they regard people dependent on them as not being the sorts of people ever likely to vote Conservative. On top of this, the capital sunk into the Rwanda scheme – the effort to deport asylum seekers to the central African country – was meant to create a wedge issue the Tories were hoping would mobilise Brexit supporters. Johnson was able to demonstrate in the initial period of his premiership that he was serious about leaving the EU by proroguing parliament, expelling remain oppositionists on his party's benches and running close to flouting the law. Sunak was hoping a similar gambit with Rwanda would win him plaudits.

The scandals that brought down Boris Johnson were not an inevitability, nor was the acute crisis of the Liz Truss mini-budget, nor the complacent negligence of Rishi Sunak's turn in charge. However, their collective refusal to address the material base of Tory decline only consolidated support for the broad left of centre among working-age people, driving Tory numbers within this social cohort to historic lows, and alienating a swathe of softer support won previously. Does the election of Kemi Badenoch as the new leader change any of this?

TORY OPTIMISM

While the party leadership election contest was broadly between the 'centre' of the party and the various flavours of the right, any real debate over why the Tories collapsed was almost entirely absent. For the right, represented by the victorious Badenoch, Robert Jenrick and Priti Patel, the party lost because it did not deliver on its promises – above all, to limit immigration. For the 'centrists' consisting of Mel Stride, Tom Tugendhat and James Cleverly, it was a range of issues apart from immigration, and a lack of party unity.

The final round of voting among MPs selected Badenoch and Jenrick to go to the membership, and showed that two-thirds of the

121-strong parliamentary party believed that moving more to the right was the answer to Tory woes. Taken on its own terms, and despite the crisis gripping the reproduction of the Tory voter coalition, there is a logic behind doubling down on the programme that brought cataclysm to the party. While it is likely to seal the Conservatives off permanently from their softer vote that turned to Labour and, particularly the Liberal Democrats, courting Reform and right-wing voters is not 'mad'. As Nigel Farage's campaign was decisive for the loss of dozens of Tory seats, it is simple arithmetic to add Reform's support to the Conservative vote and realise that, united, the right received more votes than those won by Labour.

However, to achieve this means overcoming a number of difficulties specific to Badenoch's leadership. Winning by 56% to 44% among the membership meant she had the narrowest victory since the Tories moved to their present method of electing leaders in 2001. There are problems with the composition of her parliamentary party. In the final round of leadership nomination voting, only 42 MPs chose her; 41 went for Jenrick, and 39 for James Cleverly. In the first round, she came second with just 22 supporters – about a sixth of the selectorate. The latter figure suggests she has a very small base of genuine and convinced supporters, which might cause her problems when her leadership encounters severe political challenges. The second problem is that one-third of the parliamentary party went for Cleverly. The main figures associated with the 'centrist' wing, such as Jeremy Hunt and Cleverly himself, ruled themselves out of taking a front-bench position. This exacerbates the problem of having too few MPs to fill all the shadow roles. Going too hard on culture war issues or making unwise remarks leaves her operation vulnerable to resignations and makes disciplining recalcitrant MPs difficult. Crucially, even if Badenoch was minded to undertake revamping the Tory party's strategy and addressing the long-term problems of its declining electoral coalition, there is not enough support in the parliamentary party for it.

This might not be necessary ahead of the next general election in 2029. If Starmer's 'mission-driven' government is not able to fix public services, boost living standards and provide the feel-good factor, there is a possibility that the Tories could just edge a majority, or at least be the biggest party in a hung parliament.

But this scenario depends on how the Tories deal with the inroads Reform made into their support. It has already become clear from the party's interventions that tacking further right is the strategy of the Tory leadership. Whether that is successful and/or makes some sort of electoral pact arrangement with Farage more likely depends a great deal on the political ups and downs of the coming years. What the Tories have in their favour is Labour's willingness to talk a tough game on immigration and asylum. Sunak had his Rwanda scheme, but Starmer is quite enthusiastic about a similar arrangement with Albania, and has held meetings to this effect with Giorgia Meloni, Italy's far-right prime minister. This is an opening for both the Tories and Reform. They can easily outbid Labour on this. The more the government tries to reduce immigration, the greater the likelihood of it demobilising its remaining left/liberal support – for very little political gain.

For the Tories to capitalise on this requires a certain amount of deft politicking, flexible thinking and being dependent on the actions of their opponents. Neither Badenoch's leadership nor the parliamentary party at large appear to have the skillset this requires. And if they find it difficult to navigate this landscape, then how can they address the party's long-term decline, a crisis that has not stopped just because they catastrophically lost a general election?[8]

Just five years on from the 2019 victory that was supposed to see the Tories dominate the 2020s, the party found itself broken, its coalition eviscerated and split. In the aftermath, the preferred way back is clinging to the policy platform and the talking points that produced the party's worst ever defeat. If recovery means copying the extreme right and going cap in hand to them for some sort of non-aggression arrangement, this suggests there hasn't ever been a worse time to be a Conservative.

ENDNOTES

1. For a fuller explanation of the argument here, see Phil Burton-Cartledge *The Party's Over: The Rise and Fall of the Conservatives from Thatcher to Sunak* Verso, London 2023.
2. Tim Bale *The Conservative Party after Brexit: Turmoil and Transformation* Polity Press, Cambridge 2023.

3. Robert Ford, Tim Bale, Will Jennings and Paula Surridge *The British General Election of 2019* Palgrave Macmillan, London 2021.

4. James Tilley and Geoffrey Evans 'Ageing and Generational Effects on Value Change: Combining Cross-Generational and Panel Data to Estimate APC Effects' *Electoral Studies* 33 (2014) pp. 19–27.

5. See Maria Teresa Grasso, Stephen Farrall, Emily Gray, Colin Hay and Will Jennings 'Thatcher's Children, Blair's Babies, Political Socialisation and Trickle-Down Value Change: An Age, Period and Cohort Analysis' *British Journal of Political Science* 49 (2017) pp. 17–36 and Stephen Farrall, Emily Gray, Phil Mike Jones and Colin Hay 'Losing the Discursive Battle but Winning the Ideological War: Who Holds Thatcherite Values Now?' *Political Studies* 70/3 (2022) pp. 757–779.

6. Richard Cracknell and Carl Baker 'General Election 2024: Results and Analysis' House of Commons Library, London 2024.

7. Michael Hardt and Antonio Negri *Empire* Harvard University Press, London 2000. For what this might mean for British politics, see Phil Burton-Cartledge 'The Problems of Starmerism' *Political Quarterly* 92/2 (2021) pp. 193–201.

8. For an early account of these difficulties, see Nina Lloyd 'Badenoch: No Quick Fix for the Tory Party' *London Evening Standard* 23 December 2024 www.standard.co.uk.

The Resistible Rise of Reform UK

Joe Mulhall[1]

With 4.1 million votes – 14.3% of the total – Reform UK's 2024 general election result represents the largest ever vote share for a far-right party at a UK general election, beating Nigel Farage's former vehicle the UK Independence Party (UKIP) and the efforts of more extreme far-right parties such as the British National Party (BNP) and National Front (NF). Reform came second in 98 constituencies, 89 of which were won by Labour. Most of these were in the North East, Midlands and South Wales. Reform gained more than 20% of the vote in a further 148 seats.[2] Nigel Farage scored a convincing win in Clacton, taking 46.2% of the vote and winning a majority of 8,405 over the Conservative incumbent. This was a swing of 45.1% from the Conservatives to Reform, the largest in the country.[3] Reform's sole incumbent MP, Tory defector Lee Anderson, received a commanding 42.8% of the vote to defeat the Labour candidate in Ashfield, although with a slightly smaller vote share and majority compared to 2019, when he stood as a Tory. Meanwhile, Richard Tice and Rupert Lowe, the former Brexit Party MEP, won their seats of Boston and Skegness and Great Yarmouth, although both with lower majorities of 2,010 and 1,426 respectively. Perhaps the most surprising result was James McMurdock, who beat Labour with a majority of just 98 votes in Basildon South and East Thurrock.

The speed and scale of this political earthquake is hard to comprehend. Writing in 2022, the journalist Michael Crick noted that while Farage was 'one of the most important politicians in modern British history', he had 'never been elected to the House of Commons, never served as a government minister and will almost certainly never achieve either role'.[4] This begs the question: what changed that made Farage's election possible? His previous vehicle, the Brexit Party, had effectively been 'mothballed' after failing to win a single seat at the general election in 2019. In January 2021, the party re-registered as Reform UK, and just three months later

Farage handed the leadership to Tice. Farage announced that he was standing down from frontline politics, saying: 'There's an awful lot more to do, but for me, after nearly 30 years ... that's enough of active politics.'[5] Lucrative media appointments on LBC and GB News followed, during which time he sought out new post-Brexit crusades that would afford him continued relevance. These included the dangers of Chinese communism, the supposed 'woke' indoctrination of children in schools, opposition to Black Lives Matter and Covid-19 lockdown measures, and a spell on the reality TV show *I'm a Celebrity*.

It was the issue of cross-Channel migration by boats that gained him most traction. My fellow Hope not Hate researcher David Lawrence describes Farage's focus: 'While no stranger to anti-immigrant politics, Farage now targeted a supposed "invasion" of small boat crossings with a new degree of alarmism.'[6] He produced emotive video content, some of which was filmed aboard boats in the Channel and on the cliffs over Dover. These enraged and delighted his viewers in equal measure. 'This issue more than any other helped turn Farage into a broadcast video reporter,'[7] explains Michael Crick. With Farage enjoying the riches and influence that came from his slot on GB News, and keeping one eye on the forthcoming US presidential race, it seemed unlikely he would return to frontline politics in the UK. Speaking in May 2024, he said that while he would campaign for Reform UK, it was 'not the right time' to stand as an MP.[8] His decision was less than final.

On 3 June he dramatically returned, resuming leadership of Reform and announcing he would stand for election in Clacton. It was immediately clear to all observers that his decision would change the election. 'Nigel Farage's return means turbulence for the Tories,'[9] read a BBC headline, while *Politico* called it 'Sunak's worst nightmare'.[10] Farage himself vowed to 'lead [a] political revolt to topple the Tories'.[11] Reform duly surged in the polls, and on 14 June the party overtook the Conservative Party for the first time.[12] Polling of Reform voters by the anti-fascist organisation Hope not Hate suggested that while half of Reform voters had already decided to back the party when the election was first called, a further 25% were persuaded when Farage announced his return. The remaining quarter decided in the final few days of the campaign.[13] Come election night, it was clear that Farage and Reform were to pick up their first MPs. Few predicted it would be as many as five.

Since the election, there have been high-profile defections from the Conservative Party which have further increased Reform's impact and reach. Most notable are former MPs Marco Longhi, Dame Andrea Jenkyns and Aidan Burley. There was also the major Tory funder Nick Candy and the founder of the highly influential Conservative Home website Tim Montgomerie.

FERTILE GROUND

Though Reform's success shocked the British political establishment, it shouldn't have come as much of a surprise. Over the past decade, there has been a troubling rise in far-right politics around the world. Far-right parties have won elections and entered parliamentary chambers with alarming regularity, with electoral victories for Donald Trump in the US, Jair Bolsonaro in Brazil, Narendra Modi in India and more. Across Europe, Hungary, Poland, Italy, Austria, Sweden, France, Germany and Spain – among others – have seen growing success by the electoral far right. Of course, the far right is a broad spectrum, with notable diversity among the parties sharing the label. Some, such as the Sweden Democrats, Brothers of Italy and France's National Rally, emerged out of explicitly fascist movements in the post-war period and only found electoral success after prolonged periods of moderation. Others lack fascistic roots and have emerged more recently. While their histories vary significantly and significant differences remain, they share common traits, most notably hostile opposition to immigration, immigrants, Islam and Muslims, the left and, increasingly, the ill-defined concept of 'wokeness'.

The UK has often been regarded as something of an exception.[14] It has, however, witnessed a similar growth in far-right politics, though perhaps less obviously. The UK's first-past-the-post electoral system results in much more ideological diversity within the major political parties, as opposed to much of Europe, where proportional systems tend to create narrower and more ideologically coherent parties. It is for this reason that Farage has long supported proportional representation. That said, Reform's growing success means that come the next general election, it might be in a position to break through more significantly, even within the existing system. This remains a huge task, and one that no party has managed in recent Westminster elections. In 2015, the SNP came closest, winning 56 Westminster seats, all of them Scottish constituencies. Following the 2016 EU referendum and the subsequent collapse of UKIP, the rise of radical right politics in the UK occurred largely within the ruling Conservative Party and the media, rather than as a distinct party alternative – until Reform.

Since 2019, the right of the Conservative Party has radicalised to a point where elements of its platform are almost indistinguishable from European far-right parties. This rightward shift was, in part, driven by a fear of Farage and his various political vehicles occupying the political space to the right to the Tories. Professor Tim Bale noted:

> Owing to their desperate, decade-long desire to defeat (or at least contain) the insurgency on its flank led by Nigel Farage, the Conservatives are in severe danger of transforming themselves from a mainstream centre-right outfit into an ersatz radical right wing populist party. [...] True, the Tories have long flirted with radical right-wing populism; but they now appear to have swallowed it whole.[15]

Unsurprisingly, as we have seen elsewhere in Europe, the tactic has proved counterproductive. Quite aside from the moral imperative not to adopt far-right policies, this tactic merely serves to legitimise and raise the salience of far-right politics and policies. The Conservative Party's adoption of irresponsible and inflammatory language around issues such as immigration has exacerbated societal anger and prejudice which, in turn, Reform has been able to exploit.

In addition to the Conservative Party, the UK has seen the emergence of an increasingly influential radical right ecosystem, comprised of think tanks, conferences, academics and media outlets, which has laid the groundwork for Reform's rapid growth. Most prominent is GB News, an increasingly influential media outlet for far-right opinion that regularly pushes radical right and conspiratorial narratives. 'While viewpoints vary across its programmes, a number of

GB News's most high-profile presenters use the platform to promote harmful conspiracy theories and socially divisive, hyper-partisan political narratives,' says Gregory Davis from Hope not Hate.[16] In 2021, at least ten people employed by GB News were closely linked to Farage, leading to its founding chairman Andrew Neil to dub the channel a 'UKIP tribute band'.[17] The channel continues to employ and provide a platform for Reform supporters, most notably the radical right academic Matthew Goodwin. Goodwin was once a respected political scientist publishing work that was critical of the far right.[18] However, in recent years he has dramatically radicalised, becoming one of the most notable promoters of radical right politics in Britain via his personal Substack,[19] and more recently via his own show on GB News. Beyond GB News, there is a growing roster of columnists at publications such as the *Daily Telegraph* and the *Spectator* magazine who advance Reform-esque politics and who elevate Farage and his party.

There is also a group of think tanks and a burgeoning calendar of conferences that have advanced radical right politics in Britain. This was perhaps best illustrated by the National Conservatism Conference in May 2023. Organised by the US-based Edmund Burke Foundation, the event was one of a series of conferences around the world that have hosted high-profile far-right politicians, including Viktor Orbán and Giorgia Meloni. Much of the rhetoric emanating from the stage was indistinguishable from the sort of conspiratorial and reactionary speeches found at traditional far-right meetings. Speakers warned about transgenderism, wokeism, cancel culture, neo-Marxism and globalists, as well as the end of 'our' way of life. Another group operating on the fringes of the Conservative Party is the New Culture Forum (NCF). Set up by former UKIP London Assembly member Peter Whittle, it claims to challenge 'the cultural orthodoxies dominant in the media, academia, education, and wider British culture'.[20] The NCF functions from 55 Tufton Street in London, described by the BBC as 'the other black door shaping British politics'.[21] Among the many organisations that operate from there and advance far-right policies are the Tax Payers' Alliance and the Global Warming Policy Foundation. It is the former home of many others, including Vote Leave and Brexit Central. Restore Trust, the supposed 'anti-woke' group which attempted to take control of the National Trust, operated from this building, as did Net Zero Watch and the right-wing Institute of Economic Affairs.

In addition, Reform has benefited from the toxification of X (formerly Twitter) under Elon Musk's ownership. While social media has always posed a problem, X, with its lax moderation policies, poor enforcement and embrace of formerly banned extremists, has become a safe place for extreme politics to flourish.

Together, this ecosystem has contributed to the fertile climate which Reform exploited so successfully at the general election.

FAR-RIGHT?

Reform's representation in parliament poses new dangers. Chief among them is the 'legitimacy' it bestows on the group in the eyes of the media and public. As has been the case elsewhere, when far-right parties win seats, there can be a tendency to wrongly presume it will blunt their radicalism, or even worse, that parliamentary representation is 'proof' that the party is not extreme, racist or far-right. Much of the post-election media coverage of Reform has refrained from calling the party far-right, in favour of an ever-expanding set of euphemisms and vague terminology. The party has variously been described as 'right-wing populist' or 'classically right wing', merely 'populist', or increasingly, the never-defined term 'hard right'. Meanwhile, Farage himself is described as everything from a 'bog-standard Essex Man Thatcherite'[22] to a 'a renegade nationalist conservative'.[23]

In March 2024, apparently after being contacted by lawyers acting for then-leader Richard Tice, the BBC issued a correction and apologised to Reform for applying the term 'far-right' to the party. Tice claimed he was 'also in touch with other news organisations' for using the term, which he claimed was 'defamatory and libellous'.[24] Politicians rejecting the label is nothing new. Many of those who fit into accepted definitions of 'far-right' feign outrage when accurately described as such. Many Reform voters and activists sincerely believe that they are not extreme or fringe, but are rather ordinary, normal exemplars of 'the people'. For some campaigners, the terms 'far-right' and 'fascist' are mistakenly interchangeable, creating an inaccurate expectation that the label should only be applied to swastika-waving skinheads and Third Reich apologists. Despite having attracted its fair share of these sorts of extremists,[25] Reform itself is not fascist. Reform is more moderate than earlier far-right parties such as the BNP and NF, and it lacks a history of explicit fascist or Nazi sympathies. It has also made efforts to distance itself from more violent figures such as Stephen Yaxley-Lennon (a.k.a. Tommy Robinson), although here the difference is more stylistic and tactical rather than ideological.

Reform is less extreme, but it still fits comfortably within academic definitions of 'far-right'. While some, such as Tim Bale, have argued that describing Reform as such 'is unhelpful' because the 'term causes too visceral a reaction and at the same time is too broad to be meaningful', it remains important to do so.[26] Some have described Reform as 'national populist', others merely as 'populist'. While the party is indeed populist, it isn't a sufficient label to explain its politics. In the words of Cas Mudde, the leading political scientist in the field: 'Reform UK is far right! That is not an opinion, that is a fact!'[27]

To understand why it is correct to label Reform as 'far-right', it is helpful to grasp that it is an umbrella term and not a monolith, which is why academics and practitioners split it further into its constituent parts. The historians David Renton and Neil Davidson essentially divide the right of the political spectrum into conservatives, the non-fascist far right and fascists.[28] In these definitions, Reform sits comfortably in the 'non-fascist far-right' category. Similarly, Mudde divides the term far-right into the 'radical right' and the 'extreme far right'. The latter 'rejects the essence of democracy, that is, popular sovereignty and majority rule', while the radical right 'accepts the essence of democracy, but opposes fundamental elements of liberal democracy'.[29] This applies to Farage and Reform, given its rejection of key elements of liberal democracy. Perhaps the best example is Farage's own history of racism, xenophobia and misogyny and his calls for Britain to leave the European Convention on Human Rights.[30]

Reform generally accepts democracy, but Farage has a track record of seeking to undermine institutions and the wider democratic process. Like his close ally Donald Trump, Farage has regularly disputed or questioned election defeats, including Oldham in

2015,[31] Peterborough in 2019[32] and Rochdale in 2024.[33] Another key element of far-right politics is a belief that the nation is in decay or crisis and radical action is required to halt or reverse it, often at the hands of a strong leader. The 'nation', however defined, usually includes an in-group that perceive themselves to be under threat and an outgroup/enemy. For Reform, this outgroup is currently asylum seekers, Muslims and Islam more generally. Farage and Reform should correctly be categorised as part of the radical right element of the wider far right.

Reform is also a populist party, which Mudde defines as:

a (thin) ideology that considers society to be ultimately separated into two homogeneous and antagonistic groups, the pure people and the corrupt elite, and which argues that politics should be an expression of the *volonté générale* (general will) of the people.[34]

Despite being a millionaire, Farage has always been adept at presenting himself and his parties as defenders of 'the people' against the 'corrupt elite'. It is clear that Reform and Farage can and should be called populist radical right, or more simply 'far-right'.

REFORM SUPPORTERS

The nature of Reform becomes clearer when exploring the views of the party's voters. In August 2024, Hope not Hate commissioned a poll of 4,088 Reform voters with a view to understanding who they were and what motivated their support for the party.[35] Though there were predictable commonalities, the results presented a more nuanced and complex view of what motivated people to support the party. Interestingly, there is a notable fault line dividing two broad blocks of Reform voters. Those earning less than £30,000 a year were more economically left-leaning. Those earning over £50,000 a year were more libertarian and 'small government' in their outlook. Reform's policy platform is more aligned to the views of their higher-income supporters than those on lower incomes, among whom there is support for policies such as bringing railways under public ownership and improving workers' rights.

Unsurprisingly, it is attitudes towards immigration, Islam and multiculturalism that unite Reform voters most. A remarkable 81% believe that immigration into Britain has been bad for the country, compared to 54% of the British public overall. Just 5% think that the arrival of immigrants has changed their local community for the better, whereas 54% think it has been changed for the worse. Unlike much of the general public, who selected the 'cost of living' as one of their three most important issues at the moment, 55% of Reform voters picked 'immigration and asylum'. Similarly, their attitudes towards multiculturalism are stark: 84% believe that multicultural society is not working, and 89% believe that there is increasing tension between different groups living in Britain. The polling also illuminated Reform voters' views on societal racism, with just 1.7% strongly agreeing with the idea that Britain is institutionally racist, and a mere 4.6% strongly agreeing that Black and Asian people face discrimination in their everyday lives. A large section of Reform voters hold an ethnocentric view of identity and Britishness. Almost two-thirds believe that ethnicity is a key component of being considered British.

Another area of widespread agreement, and a key driver of support for the party, is anger at a perceived sense of national decline. At 95%, the view that Britain is in decline was near universal amongst Reform voters. Most telling is that when asked why they believed this to be the case, just over 60% pointed toward immigration, while 48% blamed the government's supposed interest in appeasing minorities instead of focusing on the majority community. In order to reverse national decline, twice as many Reform supporters chose stopping all new immigration in preference to any economic solution.

In line with support for other far-right parties in Europe, Reform voters overwhelmingly hold negative views about the political system and the politicians who run it: 84% think the political system is broken, while 92% believe that 'politicians don't listen to people like me'. It is worth noting that among the wider public, 71% think the political system is broken, and 69% think politicians do not listen to them. On this issue, Reform voters are not massively out of step with the rest of society, something that should be worrying to mainstream political parties.

There is a clear correlation between economic pessimism and support for far-right alternatives. Among Reform voters, almost 80% were pessimistic about the future, with only 21% being optimistic. People across the country are rightly angry at the state of the nation and their lives in it, making a defence of the status quo untenable. If political parties continue to fail to meet the material needs of the population, ever more people will likely turn toward Reform.

These insights into Reform voters suggest that the most productive tactic to stop Reform's growth is, in the words of Hope not Hate's founder Nick Lowles, to 'identify softer Reform voters, for whom concerns about immigration might stem from economic insecurity and pessimism.'[36] The polling clearly shows that Reform supporters are not a monolithic bloc, but rather:

> They, like supporters of every other party, are motivated by a number of pull and push factors. Understanding these motivations could allow us to split the Reform coalition and peel some supporters away by engaging with, and addressing, some of the underlying issues that have drawn them to Nigel Farage's party in the first place.[37]

Reform's opponents therefore need to identify the fault lines that divide soft supporters from Farage and Reform's stated policies and beliefs, rather than seeking to convince 'hardcore' Reform supporters about the benefits of immigration.

WORSE TO COME?

One troubling aspect of Reform's success at the general election is that it was achieved with very little party infrastructure. Reform is not a traditional political party, but a limited company. During the election, this 'non-party' lacked a significant activist base and had very few functioning branches. Yet despite this lack of a professional ground game consisting of organised activists targeting constituencies informed with data insights, it still came away with over 14% of the vote.

Immediately following the election, the party claimed that it would democratise and build a formidable ground operation. Just five months later, Reform's Chairman Zia Yusuf was able credibly to claim:

> On the day of the General Election Reform UK had zero branches, we now have over 400 Reform branches across the country. And we know how important that is. [...] That's what we are focused on. That the ground campaigning capabilities that in this party were largely non-existent, despite extraordinary enthusiasm, and the processes and the systems and the technology just didn't exist, that is what we are assembling now.[38]

Farage added that the party's membership had surpassed 100,000, bringing with it a significant injection of money. And soon after, Reform boasted of having more members than the Conservative Party. The party aim is to replace the Conservative Party as a national contender at the 2029 general election. It seems certain that Reform will be a much more professional and resourced challenger to its mainstream political competitors, Labour as well as the Tories, over the coming years. Even if Reform fails to replace the Conservatives by 2029, it poses an enormous risk to the Tories. On the Tory right there are mutterings about the advantages of a pact or merger. This is unlikely, but it seems certain there will be a gravitational pull rightward.

Labour also faces a difficult task in dealing with this new threat. Some in the party see Reform as a problem purely for the Conservatives, one that may even prove positive for Labour. Others, however, often in seats where Reform finished second to Labour, are calling for a shift to the right on certain issues, most notably immigration, to head off its threat. Both positions are counterproductive. If the government seeks to occupy Reform's space with ever more right-wing rhetoric on immigration and asylum seekers, this will only serve to legitimise Reform's politics, increase the salience of its issues and boost its electoral success. But if the party ignores Reform, or sees it as a problem just for the Conservative party and fails to meet the material needs of the communities Reform is targeting, Labour, and the country, will wake up to a nasty surprise at the 2029 general election. Only by providing social advancement and national hope, in direct contrast to Reform's opportunistic politics, will Labour be able to see off this far-right threat.

The question is, what should Labour do? Most importantly, campaigns to oppose Reform must be locally led and focused. People around the UK understandably want change, and for many, Reform offers them that. While many racists and far-right extremists vote or even work for the party, writing off all Reform voters in this way will be counterproductive. The key to combating the group is to engage with and peel away the angry, disenfranchised and fearful people who wrongly see Reform as an answer to their problems. This is a lesson that the anti-fascist organisation Hope not Hate learnt over many years when campaigning against the British National Party. Of course, there are differences. Reform is far less overtly extreme than the BNP; supporting it comes with much less social stigma. Combating Reform will require going well beyond pointing out the extremism within the party. While the campaign will still need to be locally focused and rooted in the affected communities, the messaging will often have to be different. Correctly identifying the BNP's Nazi core was effective because it was true; trying to do the same to Reform won't work because it isn't. The key tactic will be exposing the fault lines, often sizable, between many of Reform's policies and the actual politics of many of the people they are targeting, especially when it comes to local and economic issues.

Importantly, this struggle won't be about protests, but rather about long-term work within communities. A broad anti-fascist and anti-racist movement will be central. However, there is a limit to what can be achieved if Labour fails to do the same. The stark reality is that with the cost-of-living crisis still raging and Labour's support beyond the huge parliamentary majority thin and narrow, the divisive and opportunistic politics offered by Farage and Reform have not reached their ceiling. We can't say we weren't warned. Nor can we say there is nothing to be done. There is plenty, and it's urgent.

ENDNOTES

1. Additional research by David Lawrence, Gregory Davis and Nick Lowles.
2. Iona Stewart '2024 General Election: Performance of Reform and the Greens' House of Commons Library, London 16 August 2024 https://commonslibrary.parliament.uk/.

3. 'General Election Analysis: Reform Wins Highest Ever Far-Right Vote but Few Seats' Hope not Hate 9 July 2024 www.hopenothate.org.uk.

4. Michael Crick *One Party after Another: The Disruptive Life of Nigel Farage* Simon and Schuster, London 2023 p. 2.

5. Ibid. p. 533.

6. Joe Mulhall (ed.) *Reform: What You Need to Know* Hope not Hate, London 2024 www.hopenothate.org.uk.

7. Crick *One Party after Another* p. 523.

8. 'Nigel Farage Won't Stand in UK Election So He Can Help US Campaign' *Sky News* 23 May 2024 www.news.sky.com.

9. 'Nigel Farage's Return Means Turbulence for the Tories' *BBC News* 3 June 2024 www.bbc.co.uk.

10. 'Nigel Farage Comeback Is Sunak's Worst Nightmare' *Politico* 4 June 2024 www.politico.eu.

11. 'Nigel Farage: I Will Lead Political Revolt to Topple the Tories' *The Telegraph* 3 June 2024 www.telegraph.co.uk.

12. 'Reform UK Overtakes PM Sunak's Conservatives in Opinion Poll' *Reuters* 4 June 2024 www.reuters.com.

13. Mulhall (ed.) *Reform* p. 28.

14. Janan Ganesh 'Britain Is Europe's Haven from the Hard Right' *Financial Times* 3 August 2023 www.ft.com.

15. Tim Bale, in Nick Lowles and Joe Mulhall *Turning Right: The Dangerous Transformation of the Conservative Party* Hope not Hate, London 2023 p. 24.

16. 'The Threat of Reform UK' Hope not Hate 24 September 2024 www.hopenothate.org.uk.

17. Crick *One Party after Another* p. 542.

18. See Mathew Goodwin *New British Fascism: Rise of the British National Party* Routledge, Abingdon 2011 and Robert Ford and Matthew Goodwin *Revolt on the Right: Explaining Support for the Radical Right in Britain* Routledge, Abingdon 2014.

19. See Matt Goodwin www.mattgoodwin.org.

20. See The New Culture Forum www.newcultureforum.org.uk.

21. '55 Tufton Street: The Other Black Door Shaping British Politics' *BBC News* 26 September 2022 www.bbc.co.uk.

22. Stephen Daisley 'Nigel Farage Is Not the Future' *The Spectator* 2 July 2024 www.spectator.co.uk.

23. Jason Cowley 'The Seismic Radicalism of Nigel Farage' *New Statesman* 5 June24 www.newstatesman.com.

24. Tim Bale 'It's a Mistake to Call Reform UK "Far-Right"' LSE British Policy and Politics Blog 21 March 24 www.blog.lse.ac.uk.

25. 'More Hateful Reform Candidates Exposed' Hope not Hate 3 April 2024 www.hopenothate.org.uk.

26. Bale 'It's a Mistake to Call Reform UK "Far-Right"'.

27. Tweet quoted by www.hopenothate.org.uk 24 September 2024.

28. David Renton *The New Authoritarians: Convergence on the Right* Pluto Press, London 2019 p. 13.

29. Cas Mudde *The Far Right Today* Polity Press, Cambridge 2019 p. 7.

30. 'Who Is Nigel Farage?' Hope not Hate www.hopenothate.org.uk.

31. 'Labour Sweep to Victory in Oldham By-Election' *ITV News* 4 December 2015 www.itv.com.

32. James Tapsfield '"Another Rotten Borough": Nigel Farage Lashes Out after Observers Warn Labour's By-Election Win in Peterborough Was "Like Corrupt Kazakhstan" as Police Probe Five Cases of "Malpractice"' *Daily Mail* 16 June 2024 www.dailymail.com.

33. Ben Chapman '"Sectarian Politics Is Here to Stay" – Nigel Farage Issues Chilling Warning after "Ugly" Victory for Galloway: "Votes on Religious Lines"' *GB News* 1 March 2024 www.gbnews.com.

34. Mudde *The Far Right Today* pp. 7–8.

35. The poll of 4,088 Reform UK voters was conducted by Find Out Now between 19 and 28 August 2024. Find Out Now is a member of the British Polling Council and Market Research Society, and abides by their rules.

36. Nick Lowles in Mulhall (ed.) *Reform* p. 32.

37. Ibid.

38. Transcribed from live feed.

Making the Case for an Independent Left

Hilary Wainwright

As I walked away from the Highbury ward committee room of Jeremy Corbyn's 2024 general election campaign in Islington North, I did not dare imagine that he had won. It was not only superstition. It was what I thought then was a sober assessment of the power of the Labour machine. The kitchen that served as a committee room in Highbury was packed with young activists from across the country – including a coachload from South Wales, spurred into action by news that Peter Mandelson was canvassing for Labour against Corbyn. There were also local Labour Party stalwarts, fearless of their certain expulsion, including those who lived with my friend Lynne Segal.

Lynne joined the Labour Party when Corbyn became Islington North's Labour candidate in 1983. I only joined in 2015 when Corbyn was elected leader – until then, I was convinced by Ralph Miliband's analysis that the Labour Party's commitment to parliamentarism and the British State[1] rendered it incapable of being a means to achieve socialism.[2] I became a member of the Wick branch of Hackney South and Shoreditch Constituency Labour Party while continuing my independent campaigning and work with *Red Pepper*. Four years later, the openings associated with Corbyn's victory in Labour's leadership elections were closed by those with vested interests in Britain's undemocratic parliamentary system. These were exactly the forces inside the Parliamentary Labour Party, the British state and the media that Miliband had so deftly analysed. Consequently, I resigned, after publicly supporting the Green candidate to be mayor of Hackney, largely because of her open support for the rights of Palestinians and for a ceasefire, about which the Labour mayoral candidate was not even willing to talk.

I continued to campaign locally through extra-parliamentary movements against, for instance, NHS privatisation. I was not alone: these local campaigns were strengthened by activists I'd met in the local Labour Party, but who were radicalised by what they had witnessed and who were now going to challenge a system they better understood, from outside.

It was ex-Labour radical independent socialists like these who gave the Islington North election campaign committee room its buzz. The buzz was hopeful, especially after an unannounced visit from the candidate, distributing white rosettes for us to wear as we reminded our voters to put their X against 'Jeremy Corbyn Independent' on the ballot paper rather than against the Labour candidate, as was custom of most of them. Canvass returns showed that support for Corbyn was high, but awareness that he was standing as an independent was low. No one to whom I talked could assuage my profound sense of mission impossible.

I was wrong. To my great pleasure, Jeremy Corbyn, Independent won with a 7,000 majority. Four other independents were also elected that night. All were gains from Labour. There were also four Greens, one a hold – Siân Berry retaining Caroline Lucas' seat – one a gain from Labour and two from the Tories.

Does any or all of this amount to the emergence of an organised independent left to go 'beyond the fragments'? [3]

THE RED-GREEN THREAD OF PARTICIPATORY DEMOCRACY AND POPULAR CAPACITY

Since my first political engagement in the mid-1960s as an anarcho-syndicalist Young Liberal, I understood socialism as a socialisation of the economy, not through a centralised state commanding every sphere of economic activity, but rather through a co-ordination of worker-controlled or co-operative enterprise supported by state institutions administered through popular participation. My involvement with the women's liberation movement deepened my understanding of the potential of participatory democracy as a basis of this socialisation from below. The experience of feminist consciousness-raising groups led me to base the ideal of participatory democracy on a more inclusive understanding of knowledge. This experience provided grounds for an understanding of knowledge that included tacit and practical knowledge arising from emotion and experience, rather than restricting legitimate knowledge to that which is codified, scientific and understood through an overview[4] to be aggregated and imposed from above.

The need to understand the limits and possibilities of participatory democracy through experiments and observation as much as through theoretical explorations became my driving passion. Historical and international developments and practical engagements fed and expanded the passion: the student and popular revolts of 1968 – on a global scale – the women's liberation movement, the 1970s movement for workers' control actively encouraged by Tony Benn, becoming an economic adviser to the Greater London Council (GLC) and helping to create and co-ordinate its Popular Planning Unit,[5] and learning from experiences of participatory budgeting in Brazil.[6]

PRACTICAL KNOWLEDGE AND THE CHALLENGE TO THE FREE-MARKET RIGHT

Margaret Thatcher's abolition of the Greater London Council in 1986 was part of a more general counter-revolution against the state as the leading economic actor, both with and against the market. Symbolically, the office once occupied by the Popular Planning Unit on Westminster Bridge became the sales office for expensive apartments in what had been a GLC building.

This domestic then global dominance of market political economy led me to probe more deeply into the politics of knowledge, especially of tacit or practical knowledge. I read Frederick von Hayek, the foremost theorist and promoter of the free market against the social engineering state, and I reflected on my experience and observation of the sharing of tacit knowledge. I realised that tacit knowledge, in contrast with codified or 'scientific knowledge', was fundamental to any effective challenge to the dominance of the free market. For Hayek, the concept and reality of tacit knowledge, understood as essentially a characteristic of individuals, most notably entrepreneurs on the alert for market opportunities, was the foundation of the possibility of an economic order based on the spontaneous and haphazard co-ordination of individual entre-preneurs and consumers. My observation of the various forms of knowledge, shared and developed through social movements and participatory democracy, led me to conclude that the possibility of socialising tacit and practical knowledge could be the basis of an economy based on democratic co-ordination between co-operative and worker self-managed enterprises?

The possibility of a Corbyn-led government, seemed, all too briefly, to hold out the opportunity to begin to test these possibil-ities of popular planning and participatory public administration at a national level. The possibility galvanised my energy to bring together all I'd learned, both about the practicalities and potential of participatory democracy. I wrote *A New Politics from the Left*.[7] It turned out to be seriously over-optimistic, and underestimated the extent to which Corbyn's electoral success in 2017 acted as a warning for the Labour establishment of their worst nightmare, Prime Minister Corbyn. Earlier, in 2017, Peter Mandelson was already boasting of how he worked:

> every single day in some small ways to bring forward the end of his tenure in office. Something, however small it maybe be – an e-mail, a phone call or a meeting I convene – every day I try to do something to save the Labour Party from his leadership.[8]

In the end, the politics of New Labour (manipulative, elitist and driven by a Cold War venom against the very existence of the left) won out. In contrast, Corbyn's politics, while understanding the importance, however limited, of electoral politics, never included tribal party loyalty.

LABOUR'S HISTORIC MONOPOLY

Labour's monopoly of working-class representation has historically been sustained by the first-past-the-post electoral system and the institutional links between trade unions and the party. These have underpinned the dominant position of Labour's parliamentary leadership and the presumption it could take for granted a mass working-class vote.

The other side of this is that a majority of working-class voters historically, especially since 1945, have assumed that voting Labour is part of being working-class. Given this passive electoral commitment, the Labour Party has needed those votes to be concertedly 'knocked up' on election day. In the past, this was the work of constituency party activists, whose permanent presence in enormous number across the party as 'Labour on the doorstep' has been taken for granted.

DEMOCRATIC MYTHOLOGY

Some constituency members, left, right and in between, however, tended to see themselves not as doorstep fodder, but as activists. In 1963, the political scientist and cabinet minister Richard Crossman analysed how these expectations could co-exist:

> These militants tended to be 'extremists'; a constitution was needed which maintained their enthusiasm by apparently creating a full party democracy while excluding them from effective power. Hence the concession in principle of sovereign powers to the delegates at the Annual Conferences, and the removal in practice of most of this sovereignty through the trade union block vote on the one hand, and the complete independence of the Parliamentary Labour Party on the other.[9]

In the early 1980s, this version of Labour Party democracy was no longer convincing broad swathes of the membership. Constituency activists led by Tony Benn sought to enhance the power of party conference and give constituency parties the right to reselect their MPs.[10] These campaigns were generally defeated or undermined, and many activists turned their energies to extra-parliamentary campaigns, a trend exacerbated by Thatcher's emasculation of local government, and then accelerated by Blair's support of the Iraq War, and most recently, Labour's betrayal of Gaza.

Nevertheless, a significant number of Labour left-wingers believed life outside the party to be politically futile. The Labour left retained a significant base, often in combination with those who were active in these extra-parliamentary movements. In 2015, this left was sufficiently strong for Jeremy Corbyn to win the leadership. Under his leadership, many of these extra-parliamentary activists rejoined the party alongside an entirely new post-2010 'generation left', only to be driven out once more under Keir Starmer and his chief aide Morgan McSweeney, whose ruthless apparatus finally ditched all pretence of Labour being a 'broad church'.

The party's machine for discipline and central control clearly remains in good shape. Starmer is, after all, essentially a manager, a technocrat of order and control. My frequent forays into Islington North in the weeks running up to the 2024 general election convinced me that where there is an independent, or sometimes Green, challenge to Labour, the Labour electoral machine can no longer depend on turning out local constituency party members at election time in sufficient numbers to be certain of victory.

STARMER'S PROJECT FOR GOVERNMENT

Starmer is determined to crush the left. But he cannot be adequately understood simply as 'Blair Mark 2'. Deference to the financial markets is an important continuity, but Starmer's stress (however rhetorical) on returning the party to the working class and to the old partnership with Labour indicates that his project is not a return to the aspirational – even evangelical – market individualism of Blair. Starmerism involves a half-hearted reinvention of Labourism in the era of neoliberal political economy.

Labourism, the political idea that the Labour Party is the political means of advancing the interests of the working class as a subordinate but organised and recognised class, was built into the 1906 origins of the party, the Labour Representation Committee. It takes various forms, but an understanding of the working class as *subordinate* is common to all: subordinate in the economy through the unions organising in the workplace without challenging managerial prerogatives; subordinate in the polity to provide for stability and a recognition of the rights of trade unions in the employment contract without challenging the dominant order – be it managerial prerogative, the state and with it the power of the City and the Atlantic alliance. In this context and through changing the party rules to ensure future political stability (so that no left-wing candidate can feasibly make it on to the ballot to be a future Labour leader[11]), Starmer's 'achievement' has been, in fact, not so much to return the Labour Party to the working class as to make the Labour Party safe for the establishment.

TRANSFORMATIVE TRADITIONS

There has always been a tension in Labourism, however, with the idea of the working class as a *transformative* class. An idea of transformation, as distinct from mere amelioration, is incipient in the day-to-day militancy necessary to defend collective bargaining and maintain and improve living standards, including against Labour governments, and especially in the context of a rampant free-market political economy. At crucial moments, this militancy has overcome the constraining divide at the heart of Labourism between 'the industrial' and 'the political'.

The Clydeside shop stewards' movement on the eve of World War One was an early example of politicised industrial action, and the shop-floor strength that was able to thrive during the 1950s leading to the politicised occupations of the late 1960s and 1970s.

In 1974, Tony Benn was made secretary of state for industry in Harold Wilson's government. Benn's appointment held out the possibility of a democratic version of public ownership based on transforming the relations between labour and capital. 'Worker control with management participation', as the shop stewards of Swan Hunter Shipyard on Tyneside put it in their proposed model for the soon-to-be nationalised shipbuilding industry.[12]

Jeremy Corbyn attempted, with many limitations, to bring this tradition to the leadership of the Labour Party. However the institutions of Labourism, reinforced by those of the parliamentary and media establishment, proved too strong for a political insurgency that lacked, after 50 years of free-market politics, a materially strong and well-organised trade union movement at its base. Jeremy Corbyn's own radically democratic and collaborative political instincts inclined toward transformative self-organisation 'from below' rather than the benevolent 'from above' parliamentarist paternalism of the historic Labour left. The unexpected success in winning the leadership led his supporters to repeat the institutional tactics of inner-party mobilisation (plus a few public rallies) that had won the leadership. This was the template followed by Momentum to offer its support, which did not sufficiently organise new, more resilient, extra-parliamentary sources of counter-power. The Corbyn leadership team was put on the defensive from day one by the parliamentary Labour right, and therefore deprived of the intellectual space to think beyond and outside the usual methods of doing politics in the party.

Despite this, the transformative politics that Corbyn stood for as leader was not a politics which itself was especially tied to the party. When he led Labour to the shattering defeat in 2019 and many of his supporters left or were driven out of the party, they did not walk away from political activism. And they were there in their thousands on the streets of Islington North in 2024, supporting Corbyn as an independent candidate.

Are Corbyn and his fellow Independents a one-off?

SHORTCUTS

The left in the UK has a fatal attraction to shortcuts. In 1906, the left-wing Independent Labour Party (ILP) joined the Labour Party because it believed that the Labour Representation Committee, the trade union-dominated committee that founded the Labour Party, would provide socialists with a captive audience – the organised working class – and thereby a shortcut to socialism. The ILP abandoned its independent organisation, and, interestingly, its support for a proportional electoral system and for a republic, and became part of the Labour Party, and with it first-past-the-post, monarchy and the House of Lords as part of the package. It proved to be one of the longest shortcuts in history. It also turned out to be a circuitous journey on which many would-be socialist travellers lost their way.

From the late 1990s onward, following successive Labour leaderships effectively accepting the monetarist consensus and providing craven support for US wars in the Middle East, a radical left, flush from the rapid growth of extra-parliamentary opposition, believed that the declaration of a new political party could be a shortcut to socialism. The assumption was that, similarly to the ILP, popular base-building was not the problem: a mass movement was there, waiting. What was missing, the thinking went, was a leader and an organisation. Enter first, in 1996, Arthur Scargill and the Socialist Labour Party (SLP). In 2000, Ken Livingstone stood for London mayor, and won, as an Independent. Four years later, he was re-elected, back in the fold, as Labour mayor. Meanwhile the short-lived Socialist Alliance split and dissolved, with the various far-left parties involved unable to get on with each other, or anyone else. Out of the fallout emerged George Galloway's Respect Party and his winning the Bethnal Green and Bow seat at the 2005 general election. He lost his seat in the 2010 General Election, but returned to parliament when he, representing Respect, won Bradford West in a 2012 by-election. Only to lose it the 2015 General Election. In the same general election, the SLP polled under 0.1% of the vote. A year later, Respect was dissolved. There have been other efforts. Under proportional representation in 2003, six Scottish Socialist members of the Scottish Parliament were elected. Since 2007, there have been none. Galloway won Rochdale with his new Workers Party in a February 2024 by-election, only for his victory once more to be followed by defeat as soon as he faced his voters again, this time just five months later in the July 2024 General Election.

Any realistic debate, then, about forming another left-wing political party in the UK today must survey the graveyard of failed parties that in living memory have been the hopes of so many entirely sincere activists.

GOING BOTTOM-UP INDEPENDENT

The outline of a very different process to these previous ones is driven by local activists. Mainly ex-Labour councillors, motivated by the material hardship of their constituents and unable in all conscience to remain in the Labour Party or abide by the Labour whip on councils, formed organised groupings of independents. These included the Hackney Independent Socialists, the Southport Community Independents, Ilford Independents, Camden Community Alliance, Chingford Independents, Broxtowe Independents, Tyneside-based Majority and the Islington Independents. They take a long view. Most of them had left, been suspended or expelled by

Labour because of issues with the party leadership's lack of account-ability to and connection with working or would-be working people. The priority of these new groupings has been building effective and accountable local organisations. Deeply aware of the extent of disengagement from politics, they see themselves as creating new foundations based on local assemblies of various kinds.

Local assemblies are already taking place, with independent left councillors there to ensure community needs are given represen-tation. They are unlike many Labour councillors, who simply see their role as councillor as a stepping-stone to bigger things. There is talk also of creating community alliances and providing training for community action[13] rather than simply rushing from one election campaign to another. In Islington, Jeremy Corbyn and his team are likewise rejecting this failed model and are concentrating on building community forums in different neighbourhoods. And he, of all people, knows from experience that victory as an independent depends on a base of popular, community – not party – support built up through community action.

FEMINISM AND A REJECTION
OF INSTRUMENTAL POLITICS

It is striking that women have a leadership role in many of these local initiatives. Certainly, feminism and the experience of the women's liberation movement influence my doubts about pre-exist-ing models. In 1979, fellow socialist feminists Sheila Rowbotham, Lynne Segal and I wrote the pamphlet *Beyond the Fragments: Feminism and the Making of Socialism*, which became the book of the same name.

Sheila describes her impetus behind our writing together:

Having taken part for several years in an innovative politics which had sought to make space for individual expression, I had come to see how specific movements might carry wider implications for social change. I thought how we had organised as feminists could be relevant to others by contributing differing approaches to con-testing capitalism.[14]

This was an impetus Lynne and I shared.

Today's generation of socialist feminists will write their own insights, but back then, in the wake of Thatcher's landslide election, we highlighted two:

1. The means of resistance shapes the result.
2. Don't let the goal become the be-all and end-all, to which everything is instrumentally subordinated, regardless of how people's energy and capacity might be burnt out or in the process and/or their voices silenced.

As women, we were organising a movement while simultaneously being responsible for caring for the young and the very old. An instrumental approach to politics (where the ends justifies the means) tends to create a tempo that overrides such caring obligations and pressures. As feminists, we sought, by contrast, to create a movement which prefigured the kind of society we were working toward – a society in which care and collaboration were fundamental. The movement we created, with difficulty sometimes, was one in which care for the vulnerable was integral to the tempo and priorities of its organisation.

AGAINST THE GRAIN

The language of 'people-driven politics' and 'building from below' slips easily off the tongue. But the work of building such people power from below and doing so in a manner that prefigures the changes we are working for is tough. The difficulties lie not simply in the fact that the daily realities of people's lives mean the basics of survival – housing, health and a source of livelihood – are precarious. People-driven politics is also working against the grain of the inherited institutions through which people are organised, if they are organised at all. These institutions have been shaped by the centralised, parliamentarist state which their Labour representatives signed up to. This involves a trade union movement that resists taking on 'political issues' – responsibility for these has instead been abrogated to the Labour Party. And those local community organisations which do exist have often become a vehicle via which councils explain themselves to residents, rather than a means by which citizens call councils to account.

OLD HABITS DIE HARD

The extent – likely to grow – to which local splits led by councillors from Labour will create favourable conditions for an independent politics from below to thrive depends on the extent they are liberated from Labour's top-down institutional culture. Institutional habits die hard, as the inability of Momentum to change Labour's organisational culture or build an independent radical politics, both in and against the party, demonstrated.

TAKING OUR TIME

It will need time and the concerted attention of all independent actors, whether alternative media,[15] critically engaged left-wing campaigners, strategic thinking[16] and researchers, councillors and radical trade unionists. It will be necessary to nurture the variety of forms these emergent popular initiatives take so that they develop, through horizontal links as much as national initiatives, into a genuinely independent political organisation with a powerful, transformative popular base. This requires a certain discipline and abstinence on the part of those whose only understanding of an independent left worthy of the name is a national political party. Here, the last word can usefully be a statement by Jeremy Corbyn soon after his victory as an Independent. He said in the *Guardian*:

> To create a new, centralised party, based around the personality of one person, is to put the cart before the horse. Remember that only once strength is built from below can we challenge those at the top.[17]

ENDNOTES

1. Ralph Miliband *Parliamentary Socialism* Merlin Press, London 1964.
2. I spell this out in Hilary Wainwright *Labour A Tale of Two Parties* Chatto and Windus, London 1989.
3. Sheila Rowbotham, Lynne Segal and Hilary Wainwright *Beyond the Fragments: Feminism and the Making of Socialism* Merlin Press, London 1980.
4. I explained the importance of this understanding of the plurality of politically relevant forms of knowledge through a critique of Hayek, who uses

an exclusively individualist understanding of tacit knowledge to justify the free market, in Hilary Wainwright *Arguments for a New Left; Answering the Free Market Right* Blackwell, Oxford 1994. But I anticipated some of the implications of this for the relevance of insights feminism for the making of socialism in *Beyond the Fragments*.

5. See Maureen Mackintosh and Hilary Wainwright (eds) *A Taste of Power: The Politics of Local Economics* Verso, London 1987.

6. See Hilary Wainwright *Reclaim the State: Experiments in Popular Democracy* Verso, London 2003.

7. Hilary Wainwright. *A New Politics from the Left* Polity Press, Cambridge 2017.

8. Rowena Mason and Jessica Eglot 'Peter Mandelson: I Try to Undermine Jeremy Corbyn Every Single Day' *The Guardian* 21 February 2017 www. theguardian.com.

9. Richard Crossman, introduction to Walter Bagehot *The English Constitution* Fontana, London 1963.

10. For an updated version of this effort toward Labour Party democracy, see David Osland *How to Select or Reselect Your MP* Spokesman Books, Nottingham 2016.

11. We summarise the process by which this rule change took place in Michael Calderbank and Hilary Wainwright 'Losing Momentum: Strategic Dilemmas Facing Socialists in Britain' in Greg Albo and Stephen Mayer (eds) *Openings and Closures: Socialist Strategy at a Crossroads* Merlin Press, London 2025.

12. See Hilary Wainwright 'Tony Benn Really Was Dangerous – to the Establishment' Open Democracy 18 March 2014 www.opendemocracy.net.

13. One model is Acorn, the community union which, from housing to public transport, uses local and collective action as the basis for its campaigns. See www.acorntheunion.org.uk.

14. Sheila Rowbotham *Reasons to Rebel: My Memories of the 1980s* Merlin Press, London 2024 p. 3.

15. See, for example, the magazine *Red Pepper* (www.redpepper.org.uk) and the multi-media online platform Novara Media (www.novaramedia.com).

16. For an early version of such thinking, see James Schneider *Our Bloc: How We Win* Verso, London 2022.

17. Jeremy Corbyn 'People-Power Led to My Re-Election. It Is the Start of a New Politics' *The Guardian* 12 July 2024 www.theguardian.com.

CHANGE, STABILITY, CONTRADICTIONS

How to Transform
an Unequal Britain

Danny Dorling

When Keir Starmer became prime minister, he promised 'change', and this promise was beefed up in his 2024 Christmas message with his six promises:[1]

1. 'More money in the pockets of working people' – This could be interpreted as more than the future rise for the middle-class, hence lowering income inequalities. It could be interpreted as more than inflation, so increasing living standards. It was not clear.

2. 'Building 1.5 million homes and fast-tracking planning decisions on at least 150 major infrastructure projects' – No change from his previous promise of the '40 new hospitals' kind, but it might become an actual change. It's a promise to speed up decisions to make the decisions of whether something may be allowed.

3. 'Treating 92% of NHS patients within 18 weeks' – It is worth comparing this to the ambition of the 1945 Labour government: creating an entire National Health Service from scratch out of the then mess of charity and private healthcare existing provision.

4. 'Recruiting 13,000 more police officers, special constables and Police Community Support Officers in neighbourhood roles' – This is a very technocratic solution to the breakdown of community cohesion and the disorder this can generate. It amounts to more people walking around in a variety of uniforms, some of them on our streets.

5. 'Making sure three-quarters of five-year-olds are school-ready' – Why not all of them? Or why not school at age six, as elsewhere in Europe? And there is very little detail on how struggling

families with children under age five will actually be helped, including helped to have hope.

6. '95% clean power by 2030' – This is the promise the far right attack the most. As Nigel Farage said at the time: 'I think net zero is going to be an absolute catastrophe, electorally, for Labour.'[2] Starmer could have said 'affordable clean power'.

Contrast the above list to what Labour succeeded in enacting in 1945 after the 1942 Beveridge Report, in which Beveridge was clear that the minimum benefits he proposed 'should be given as of right and without means test, so that individuals may build freely upon it' and that 'no means test of any kind can be applied to the benefits of the scheme'.[3] Or contrast it to the list that Gordon Brown produced in his Leader's Speech to Labour Party Conference in 2009:

> If anyone says that to fight doesn't get you anywhere, that politics can't make a difference, that all parties are the same, then look what we've achieved together since 1997: the winter fuel allowance, the shortest waiting times in history, crime down by a third, the creation of Surestart, the Cancer Guarantee, record results in schools, more students than ever, the Disability Discrimination Act, devolution, civil partnerships, peace in Northern Ireland, the social chapter, half a million children out of poverty, maternity pay, paternity leave, child benefit at record levels, the minimum wage, the ban on cluster bombs, the cancelling of debt, the trebling of aid, the first ever Climate Change Act; that's the Britain we've been building together, that's the change we choose.[4]

A cynic replies: A winter fuel allowance would not be required in a country with a decent social security system. We wait months, years even, for hospital appointments when our health service was once the best in the world. University student numbers increase. University management can profit by taking more, and never mind the declining quality of education provided in return, or the mounting student debt. Half a million children can be taken out of poverty, but by such a small margin that neither they nor their families notice the difference.

Gordon Brown claimed, in much the same way that Keir Starmer and Rachel Reeves now do, that almost all good only comes from economic growth:

> Growth is progress. Growth is what has given the world the tablet you're reading this book on, the medicines by your bedside, the economic breakthroughs that have lifted billions out of poverty.[5]

That claim of Brown's appeared in *Permacrisis: A Plan to Fix a Fractured World*, a book he authored alongside Mohammad El-Erian (chief economic adviser at Allianz, the corporate parent of the Pacific Investment Management Company) and Michael Spence (who in 1999 joined Oak Hill Capital Partners, a private equity firm headquartered in New York City with more than $19 billion of committed capital). Brown and his co-authors, of course, were wilfully missing out what is achieved when 'growth' is not the aim (by those not driven by profit). A former Labour chancellor of the exche-

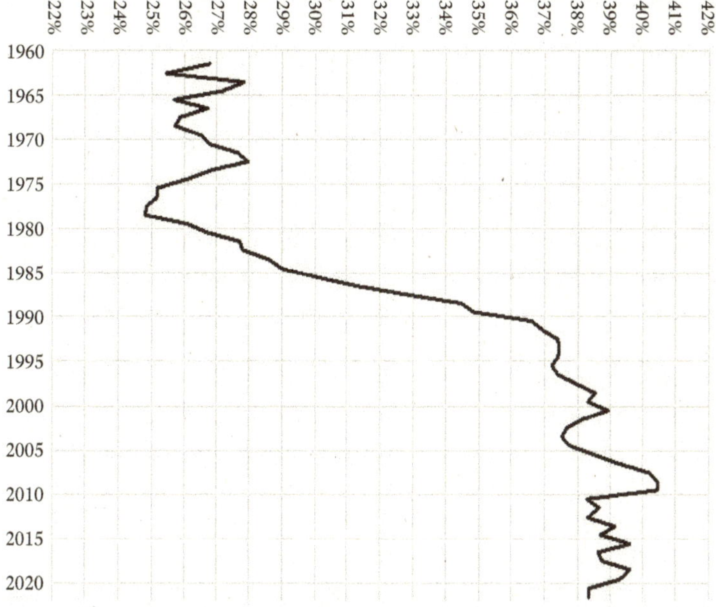

Figure 1   Gini coefficient of income inequality after housing costs, UK, 1960–2021 (0–100%)

quer and prime minister whose politics were so often positioned as 'Brownite' rather than full-on modernising 'Blairite' really shouldn't need reminding by their book's reviewer:

> They assume the development of a tablet computer is due to economics rather than developments in universities and other state-funded bodies which created the micro-components that enable a computer to be transmuted into tablet form. Computers, and electricity before that, were not products of 'the market' but technological inventions that have been marketised.[6]

If Keir Starmer wants to aim for a target that is far easier to achieve than he may realise, he should say he wants to reduce economic inequalities by a greater amount than either of his immediate forebears as Labour prime ministers, Blair and Callaghan, managed (see Figure 1).[7] But to do so means breaking with their, and his, fixation on a model of economic growth that contributes next to nothing toward such a reduction. More often than not, it does the reverse.

AN UNEQUAL BRITAIN

> [Income] inequality harms us all and lies at the root of our escalating environmental, health and social crises. ... greater income inequality is particularly bad for the climate ... nations with high levels of equality have the greatest focus on reducing carbon emissions, while the richest 10% of the population are responsible for more than half of all global emissions. ... [income] inequality impacts every aspect of society, including our economy, ... the UK's record on child poverty in recent years is not an aberration, but what is expected in a country this unequal.
>
> (Richard Wilkinson and Kate Pickett[8])

Economic income inequality is the driver of more social ills than any other single factor. Income inequality is far more damaging than wealth inequality. This may be because in countries with low income inequality and high wealth inequality, the wealthy mainly simply store their wealth or invest it, but take less of it as a dividend or an income, and are less profligate.

The difference between income and wealth is often misunderstood. Income is the flow of money – how much we receive in a year, in many cases from employment, in other cases from a mix of employment and social security payments, and in a smaller number of cases solely from social security payment or as payments from the interest on wealth. The latter tend to be two extremes, but neither case are they actually employed. Thus, it is not possible to think that somewhere a trickle down of taxation from growing wealth will help greatly. For a country to function well, people need to live more similar lives to each other, and that is only possible when we all have similar incomes.

LEARNING THE RIGHT LESSONS

The lower harm caused by inequality in wealth can be seen by several European countries having a good social outcome: low income inequality but high wealth inequality. This may be because inequalities in wealth are less important if the wealthy are not permitted to dominate society. In European countries with high wealth inequality but low income inequality, the wealthy are, in effect, being held in check. In particular, their income from wealth is more likely to be taxed. The strongest evidence that they are held in check is that they fail to get the politicians the wealthy would usually prefer into power, and as a result, rates of taxation remain strong, public services are well funded and income inequalities are kept low.

Norway, Sweden, Iceland, Finland and Denmark form a set of countries with relatively high wealth inequality but low income inequality. However, there are now five countries within the EU which have lower income inequality than the Nordic countries (Slovak Republic, Slovenia, Belgium, Czech Republic and Poland), and another five (Luxembourg, Croatia, the Netherlands, France and Germany) with income inequalities almost as low as the Nordic five.[9] Right across Europe, these countries of varying political makeup enjoy remarkably high income *equality*. All are dramatically more equitable than the UK; in most of these 15 European countries, income inequality continues to fall.

The UK is an exception. It is very different to most of mainland Europe now. This is not just because of the fact that the UK is the most economically unequal state in Europe, on a par with Bulgaria when income inequality is the measure used. The UK is now also a state becoming poorer – and becoming poorer faster than any other state in Europe. A few years ago, we learnt that the poorest fifth of people living in the UK were now poorer than most of the poorest fifth of people living in post-1989 Eastern Europe.

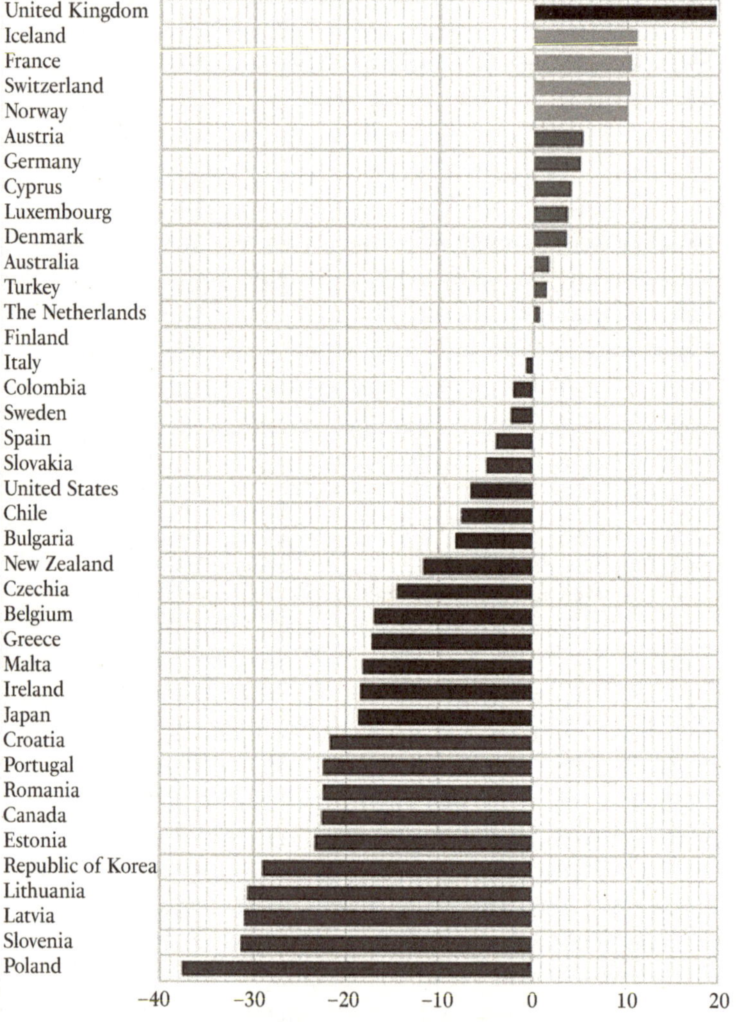

Figure 2 Changes in child poverty rate, 2012–14 to 2019–21 (%)

In 2022, the International Monetary Fund pointed out that Estonia and the UK were the two countries in Europe where living costs for the poorest 20% of households were set to rise by about twice as much as those for the wealthiest.[10] Also in 2022, John Burn-Murdoch wrote in the *Financial Times*: 'On present trends, the average Slovenian household will be better off than its British counterpart by 2024.'[11] And in 2023, Stephanie Flanders, head of Bloomberg Economics, explained that in the UK, 'the poorest fifth of the population are now much poorer than [in] most of the poorest countries in central and eastern Europe'.[12] The UK is now a peripheral, poor European country where life for most people has been becoming worse since 2008 and especially so for children. Figure 2 shows the very latest changes in one United Nations (UN) measure of the rate of poverty in children in the UK. The rate has risen by more than in any other country the UN examined between 2012 and 2021.

It is worth reiterating that the graph in Figure 2 shows the rate of change in child poverty in all the countries the UN compared.[13] The UK stands out. It is worse when we realise that the countries just below it in the graph (Iceland, France, Switzerland and Norway) started the period the graph covers with much lower rates of child poverty, so their increases of around 10% are an increase after having achieved a much better base low level of child poverty. Table 1 shows that, even after the rise, Iceland still has the sixth lowest rate of all UN countries. France still is lower than the UK (but only just), Switzerland is much lower, and Norway the fifth lowest of all.

It is not just that life has become worse for most working-class people, or most part-time workers, or for the unemployed. It has been becoming worse for most people overall. Take civil servants, for example. Senior civil servants have seen their real rate of pay fall by 25% since 2008; for junior civil servants, it fell by 12%. Child poverty will have risen by more among the children of junior civil servants despite the smaller fall, as more of them are near the poverty line. If civil servants do not live with a partner in work, have high housing costs or more than one child, it is not hard for them to find themselves living in poverty despite their employment. Many other groups of workers are affected even more seriously.

Table 1 shows the proportion of children said to be living in poverty in 2019–21 by the UN measure. The percentage in the UK has been rising higher than any other country. It is also worth noting that this is an international measure. The local measure we use within the UK is higher still: nearly one child in three, with many children living only just above that level. Slightly more than one in three children in the UK no longer have any summer holiday at all (or any holiday all year).

Of course, it is not just children who suffer from poverty caused mainly by such high inequality, but all ages. For example, by 2021, according to official figures, some 2.1 million (18%) of pensioners in the UK lived in poverty. The poverty rate among pensioners rose after 2013–14, when 1.6 million (14%) lived in poverty. And as Age UK explained when it reported these figures:

> Some groups are at particular risk – 38 per cent of private tenants and 36 per cent of social rented sector tenants, live in poverty compared to 14 per cent of older people who own their home outright. 33 per cent of Asian or Asian British pensioners and 30 per cent of Black or Black British pensioners, are in poverty compared to 16 per cent of White pensioners.[14]

In the UK, the harmful effects of very high inequality and widespread poverty are felt even by the well-off, who tend to live lives surrounded by much more paranoia than the well-off do in more equal parts of Europe. In the rest of Europe, there is nowhere else where the rich try so hard to segregate and separate their children from others. Private schooling is one example: nowhere else in Europe is so much spent on private schools to ensure children do not mix with other children (the key word is 'private'). There is nowhere else where neighbours are so segregated from one another, nowhere where geographical segregation by income is so high, where regional inequalities are so great, where class differences are so extreme. No wonder so many of the very well-off in the UK are so scared of giving even a little away of their wealth. We do have the contrast of the 'patriotic millionaires' initiative, but they are just a couple of dozen millionaires and multimillionaires. The many thousands of other multimillionaires that have chose not to endorse these beliefs show just how great their fear of sharing has become.

Table 1 Child poverty rates

Rank	Country	% of children in poverty
1	Denmark	9.9
2	Slovenia	10.0
3	Finland	10.1
4	Czechia	11.6
5	Norway	12.0
6	Iceland	12.4
7	The Netherlands	13.5
8	Poland	14.1
9	Ireland	14.8
10	Japan	14.8
11	Estonia	14.8
12	Belgium	14.9
13	Germany	15.5
14	Cyprus	15.6
15	Republic of Korea	15.7
16	Latvia	16.3
17	Croatia	16.6
18	Australia	17.1
19	Canada	17.2
20	Sweden	18.0
21	Switzerland	18.0
22	Lithuania	18.3
23	Slovakia	18.9
24	Austria	19.2
25	Portugal	19.3
26	Malta	19.8
27	France	19.9
28	**United Kingdom**	20.7
29	New Zealand	21.1
30	Chile	21.6
31	Greece	22.3
32	Luxembourg	24.5
33	Italy	25.5
34	Bulgaria	26.1
35	United States	26.2
36	Spain	28.0
37	Romania	29.0
38	Türkiye	33.8
39	Colombia	35.8

Source: *Child Poverty in the Midst of Wealth* New York, UNICEF December 2023

WILL THIS LABOUR GOVERNMENT
SPARK SUFFICIENT CHANGE?

The short answer is 'no', because the longer we choose to tolerate living with very high income inequality and high child poverty, the worse the long-term effects are. Keir Starmer and Rachel Reeves have promised change coupled with stability, which will simply serve to perpetuate instability and continued pain.

In the summer of 2024, *Guardian* columnist Polly Toynbee wrote: 'I will eat my hat – or several – if Keir Starmer and Rachel Reeves don't get rid of the two-child cap soon.'[15] On the *Guardian* letters page, one reply to Toynbee read: 'As a grandad with less hair than he used to have, I have a number of tasteful hats. I'll be keeping the tastiest one for her.'[16] By the autumn, Toynbee was becoming worried that she might have to eat her hat, writing: 'Time is ticking for Labour to scrap the two-child limit – and then make Britain a welcoming place for children again.'[17] The stark fact is that nothing of any substance is being offered that will actually lift a single child or pensioner or working-age adult out of poverty, and nothing is being proposed that will reduce the gross inequality that underlies such high rates of poverty.

STABILITY OR RUPTURE?

During the General Election Keir Starmer made the oxymoronic promise of 'change and stability'.[18] However, it is impossible to have sufficient of the former while still maintaining an abundance of the latter. Any change to effect a transformation of an unequal Britain requires at least some destabilising of the vested interests of the rich and the greedy that caused, and preserve, the terrible state we are in. These vested interests in Britain have historic underlying anteced-ents, subsequently supercharged and expanded by a neoliberal globalisation. However, neither factor entirely explains why the UK is such a very unequal society. The callousness of successive govern-ments matters, governments made of up all major political parties: Conservative, Labour and Liberal Democrat. Successive British governments have tolerated inequality. One reason is the revolving door through which our top politicians almost invariably enter jobs in the finance industry, big tech or something even more lucrative upon leaving office. A Labour government entirely committed to transforming an unequal Britain would make a big difference. But it would not feather the future personal nests of the families of the leading Labour politicians.

This government can act if it chooses to do so, has the will to face down those who resist, and can cast aside the personal ambitions of so many minsters to have lucrative future jobs. There are simple measures that could be rapidly introduced to mitigate resistance. The policy solutions currently being used in Scotland by the Scottish National Party (SNP) are a model. These include measures which have reduced child poverty to the lowest levels across the UK. These are affordable, and could be reproduced across the rest of the UK. The rent controls introduced in Scotland by the SNP can be implemented just as effectively in England and Wales. The SNP has been a party that combines its civic nationalism with moderate social democracy. Labour in Scotland has mostly supported it in these polices – if not loudly. It must be more than a little embarrassing to be in the Labour Party in Scotland and watch another party do what Labour was originally set up to do.

As the Joseph Rowntree Foundation reported in January 2025:

SCOTTISH PROGRESS ON CHILD POVERTY 'TO OUTSTRIP REST OF UK'

Scotland's child poverty rate could fall to 21.8% by January 2029 from the current rate – believed to be 23.7%, according to forecasting data.[19]

By contrast, the Joseph Rowntree Foundation expects that, given current policies, England's child poverty rate, as measured by UK official measures, will rise from 30.8% to 31.5%.

IN THE ABSENCE OF CHANGE FOR THE BETTER

By 2029, one extra child in every ten will be poor in England compared to Scotland if Keir Starmer does not do for all of the UK what the SNP has done in Scotland. It is as simple as that.

And if most people in Britain do not see their living standards rise, they will not reward Labour in 2029. However, if leading politicians in the Labour Party cosy up to right-wing newspaper bosses and the Americans who control so much of our social media, some of them may wonder whether it could be possible for the media to help them stay in power, or at least exit gracefully. If you ever wonder why Labour ministers appear to be complicit in the continued dismantling of the welfare state, the cutting apart of the NHS, the evisceration of benefits for disabled people, be aware that they have other masters to serve. Masters who might in future offer them jobs when they are out of office. To be a career politician today is to look forward to a lucrative career in the private sector if you acted as a 'grown-up' while in office.

There is an obvious alternative to toadying to the rich. Currently, the rich pay too little in tax and the poor too high a share of their income in tax. Why would rebalancing this raise living standards? Or to put it differently, what should the extra be spent on: to benefit whom, and how? Just consider every single other country in Western Europe and look at their education systems, health services and public housing provision to imagine what is eminently possible.

A SPECTRE HAUNTING LABOUR

The greatest change between 2019 and 2024 was that 3 million fewer people chose to vote in 2024 than in 2019. There was a huge growth in apathy. In every single age group, apart from people aged 65+, more adults chose *not to vote* than to vote for *any* political party.[20] In part, this is a product of inequality. In general, turnout is lower in more unequal countries and when the voting population has lived with inequality for a very long time. At that point, it is easy to begin to think: 'Why bother?' In this regard, the UK has more in common with the USA than its European neighbours. Half the electorate in the USA does not vote, and the USA is even more economically unequal than the UK.

If a Labour government tackles inequality on the scale required, and that has a lived impact, it will galvanise a large proportion of the currently apathetic electorate to vote. It is the single best way to see off Reform UK. The risk is that Starmer's government doesn't have this scale of ambition. Instead, its leading members have personal financial ambitions, because even MPs' pensions may appear a little low to them in uncertain future times. Labour policy threatens to retreat into the worst sort of Treasury-brained thinking, performative declarations about growth in the South East, and desperately trying to be Donald Trump's new best friend. So far, to many, there appears to be a lack of any actual aspirational vision.

Perhaps instead, Starmer and Reeves, or whoever may replace them in office should there be a coup within the parliamentary party, should dust down the foundational document of the post-war welfare state, the 1942 Beveridge Report. The author, William Beveridge, was a Liberal, yet he knew precisely the urgent necessity to transform an unequal Britain. He wrote: 'A revolutionary moment in the world's history is a time for revolutions, not for patching.'[21] It was true then; it is even truer now.

In February 2025, Anneliese Dodds resigned from Starmer's cabinet.[22] She had been minister of state for development and minister of state for women and equalities since the July 2024 general election victory, and prior to that chair of the Labour Party from 2021 to 2024, shadow chancellor of the exchequer from April 2020 to May 2021, and shadow financial secretary to the Treasury from 2017 to 2020 (under the then shadow chancellor, John McDonnell). She was also a member of the Privy Council. Some of her fellow Labour MPs explained that the government's 'direction of travel' might have influenced her decision to resign.[23] She will not be the first to resign on a matter of principle. If that becomes the case, if more resign in future because there are more with such views in the current Parliamentary Labour Party, the Labour Party in the country, Labour voters and the broader public, then it is not impossible that this current government might become the change that is enough to begin to transform an unequal Britain – because the makeup of who runs the government might itself change.

ENDNOTES

1. Oscar Bentley and Chas Geiger 'Six Takeaways from Keir Starmer's "Plan for Change"' *BBC News* 5 December 2024 www.bbc.co.uk.

2. Abby Wallace 'Nigel Farage's Next Act: Hammer Labour on Energy Costs' *Politico* 30 January 2025 www.politico.eu.

3. Nicholas Timmins 'Why Has the UK's Social Security System Become So Means-Tested?' *Oxford Open Economics* 3/S1 (2024) pp. i1274–i1282.

4. Gordon Brown in his Labour Conference speech 2009.

5. Gordon Brown, Mohammad El-Erian, Michael Spence with Reid Lidow *Permacrisis: A Plan to Fix a Fractured World* Simon & Schuster, London 2023 p. 12.

6. Danny Dorling 'Permacrisis: A Plan to Fix a Fractured World – Review' LSE Review of Books 28 November 2023 www.blogs.lse.ac.uk.

7. 'Living Standards, Poverty and Inequality in the UK' Institute for Fiscal Studies 11 January 2024 www.ifs.org.uk.

8. Richard Wilkinson and Kate Pickett 'The Spirit Level at 15' The Equality Trust 22 July 2024 www.equalitytrust.org.uk.

9. OECD income inequality statistics: 'Danny Dorling, A Letter from Helsinki', *Public Sector Focus* (July/August 2022) pp. 12–15 www.dannydorling.org.

10. Oya Celasun, Dora Iakova and Ian Parry 'How Europe Can Protect the Poor from Surging Energy Prices' International Monetary Fund 3 August 2022 www.imf.org.

11. John Burn-Murdoch 'Britain and the US Are Poor Societies with Some Very Rich People' *Financial Times* 16 September 2022 www.ft.com.

12. Stephanie Flanders, quoted by Christiane Amanpour on X 2 February 2023 www.x.com/amanpour.

13. *Innocenti Report Card 18: Child Poverty in the Midst of Wealth* UNICEF Innocenti – Global Office of Research and Foresight, Florence December 2023 www.unicef.org.

14. 'Poverty in Later Life' Age UK January 2022 www.ageuk.org.uk.

15. Polly Toynbee 'Starmer Will Bin the Two-Child Benefit Cap and Outdo New Labour on Tackling Poverty – I'll Bet on It' *The Guardian* 19 July 2024 www.theguardian.com.

16. Paul Goatzee 'Why I'm Saving My Hat for Polly Toynbee' *The Guardian* 24 July 2024 www.theguardian.com.

17. Polly Toynbee, 'Time Is Ticking for Labour to Scrap the Two-Child Limit – and Then Make Britain a Welcoming Place for Children Again' *The Guardian* 3 October 2024 www.theguardian.com.

18. Keir Starmer 'My First Steps for Change' Labour Party 28 June 2024 www.labour.org.uk.

19. 'Scottish Progress on Child Poverty "to Outstrip Rest of UK"' *STV News* 29 January 2025 www.news.stv.tv.

20. Danny Dorling 'Elections – Theatres of Fears or Circuses of Hope?' *Public Sector Focus* (May/June 2024) pp.12–15 www.flickread.com.

21. Frontispiece of the Beveridge Report *Social Insurance and Allied Services* Cmd. 6404 (1942) www.nationalarchives.gov.uk.

22. See Pippa Crerar 'Anneliese Dodds Resigns over Keir Starmer's Decision to Cut Aid Budget' *The Guardian* 28 February 2025 www.theguardian.com.

23. Daniel Green 'Anneliese Dodds Resigns from Government over Foreign Aid Budget Cuts' Labour List 28 February 2025 www.labourlist.org.

There is Always an Alternative

James Meadway

If there is a political epitaph to Keir Starmer's time as prime minister, it will most likely be the grubby domestic failures, and the worst of these would be, by quite some distance, failure on the economy. If current pessimistic forecasts[1] of continuing economic stagnation matched by rising inflation prove to be broadly correct, they will reveal the inability or unwillingness of Starmer, his advisors and his key cabinet allies to understand the severity of Britain's multiple, deep-rooted economic failures in a world that no longer operates on the old rules, and finish them politically. Without a significant change of economic direction, the sort requiring a change of key personnel, including the chancellor and, most likely the Prime Minister himself, the chances of Labour winning the next election would become slender indeed. International plaudits for Starmer's adventures in diplomacy and migrant-baiting at home, and his ruthless control of dissent in his own party, will not ease the cost of living crisis or deliver meaningful investment across the country. Severe cuts to social security payments for those with disabilities only reinforce the case.

What Starmerism presents is a tragic edition of reversion to the mean. Elected as Labour leader in 2020 on the promise of Corbynism with the rougher edges smoothed off, Starmer's time as opposition leader was marked by a series of political panics that saw frantic, repeated relaunches dragging him ever rightwards, reducing whatever social democratic promises he once offered a misshapen sheen. His first shadow chancellor, Anneliese Dodds, was removed after Labour's disappointing results in the May 2021 local elections,[2] replaced by a figure from Labour's right, Rachel Reeves. Reeves, working against type but with the grain of Labour's support, started off by floating the idea of wealth taxes, and at the 2021 Labour Conference, proposed a £28 billion-a-year investment in the energy transition[3] – a colossal sum, certainly by the standards of Britain's low investment past, and larger even than the annual sum Jeremy Corbyn pitched in the elections of 2017 and 2019. Both Starmer and Reeves stuck, with surprising doggedness, to the amount and this pledge throughout the next two years – happily avoiding the kind of relentless, if frequently economically illiterate and occasionally unhinged, scrutiny Corbyn's pledges had been subjected to.

A closer inspection would have raised concerns about how, precisely, this substantial sum was to be funded while Reeves also planned to meet her own 'fiscal rules'. In brief, what these amounted to were: mandating that the current budget (government spending on day-to-day items like salaries and electricity bills) should match taxes over time, while also insisting that total government debt should fall at the end of parliament. This, in principle, would allow a very substantial amount of capital investment (spending on long-lasting infrastructure projects such as new schools and hospitals) to take place, assuming interest rates remained low and growth moderate. For the rest, judicious increases in taxes could cover the extra spending on recruiting more nurses, teachers, police and other key workers.

Precious few commentators pointed out just how closely these rules resembled those of her Corbynite predecessor, John McDonnell.[4] Of course, the fundamental difference between Reeves and McDonnell was their respective willingness to either exploit, or be constrained by, these rules. For McDonnell, the rules were there to provide the stable foundations for economic expansion. McDonnell set out his position well before the 2017 general election, promising to expand borrowing for investment to the maximum those rules would allow, given the official forecasts, and continued to press the case after Labour had done so much better than critics expected:

By focusing on the cost of government borrowing (currently close to an all-time low, thanks to tiny interest rates) rather than the enormous social and financial returns on investing that money, the right creates a narrative that investment costs society rather than benefits it.'[5]

What this amounted to for McDonnell was £250 billion over a ten-year period, and announced well before the election, too.[6]

This was a dramatic – though entirely credible and popular – move. In making it, Labour broke with two decades of political practice, having laid the basis for this break in that 2017 election by pledging to increase taxes only on the top 5% – an election which saw an extraordinary swing of 9.6% to Labour since 1945, the first election since 1997 where the party actually gained seats, and a vote share of 40%. In 2024, the Starmer 'landslide' swing was a paltry +1.6% and the vote share of 33.7% – the lowest ever for a party to form a government. Such are the vagaries of our electoral system and mainstream political commentary: one Labour campaign is treated as a disaster, the other a triumph. It's the economy which will judge such a treatment.

CORBYNISM'S SECRET

There was, admittedly, a secret ingredient for Labour to successfully exploit in both 2017[7] and (less happily) 2019. Since the 2008 crash, interest rates around the world had plummeted to the lowest values in recorded human history. A paper from the Bank of England surveying eight centuries of global real interest rates from 1311 2018[8] showed the secular decline of rates from just before the Black Death to the World Cup finals of 2018; meanwhile, records from ancient Mesopotamia point to very much higher rates prior to that, of around 20%. In real terms, after allowing for inflation, interest rates were even negative. Low interest rates are a potential positive, since they mean the cost of financing longer-term investments by government can be very low indeed: the repayments it has to make to its creditors when interest rates are low are relatively small. Better yet, if the investment makes some contribution to future economic growth, then meeting future repayments will become easier – simply put, the government will most likely get more tax revenue coming in.

Following that 2008 crash, Gordon Brown reached straight for the 'Keynesian' playbook: if a recession had started because people were not spending enough – and this was the mechanism driving recession in 2009, as financial panic translated into worried households and businesses spending less – then it was up to the government to step in. By borrowing a lot more and spending more, including a surge in government investment spending, the Labour government was able to rapidly stabilise the economy so that by the time of the 2010 election, real wages had begun to recover.

But following that election, the new Cameron-Clegg coalition rapidly curtailed Brown's brief rush of spending. And the same curtailment occurred internationally, in Europe via the tender mercies of the European Commission-International Monetary Fund-European Central Bank troika, egged on by Germany in particular, and in the US under Obama. The result everywhere was weak growth overall, and weak growth of wages and salaries in particular – even as low interest rates by central banks encouraged speculative booms in property prices. 'Quantitative easing' further exacerbated this situation. The programme was introduced in Britain in early 2009, in the midst of the financial crisis, and allowed the Bank of England to use its powers to issue more money, which it then distributed to major financial institutions. The original intention was to try to stoke up lending and spending; the reality was that asset prices, like London property prices, were inflated by newly cash-rich financial institutions and wealthy individuals chasing returns, while the rest of the economy was largely untouched.

General inflation in developed world economies reached dramatic lows by the mid-2010s, aside from property and asset prices. It is true that food prices initially surged, creating the conditions for political upheaval, in 2011 most dramatically across the Middle East during the 'Arab Spring' in Bahrain, Egypt, Libya, Syria, Tunisia and Yemen.[9] By the mid-2010s, oil prices had briefly threatened a sustained rise.[10] But by 2014, the low-inflation environment established in the 1990s appeared to have returned and held. Central bankers continued to congratulate themselves for this, even though the very policies they previously claimed were responsible for low inflation now barely seemed to operate. Cutting interest rates (in some cases, like the Swiss National Bank, to weird, new negative levels) seemed to make no real difference to economies. The flood of cheap manufactured goods that was the secret to sustained low inflation continued to travel from east to west in increasing numbers and varieties as smartphones became ubiquitous and the online world took its modern shape.

Low interest rates *and* low inflation should have been treated as the biggest possible signal for governments to spend, spend, spend. Instead, governments in the developed world cut, cut, cut. Nowhere was this pattern more marked than in Britain, where the 2010 Cameron-Clegg government pursued an internally coherent if socially abominable strategy of domestic austerity, intended to support international financial expansion. The mechanism is simple and horrible: by clearing the public finances *today*, the 'fiscal space' is made available to deal with financial upsets *tomorrow*. To maintain an extremely large, debt-laden, strongly internationalised financial system, it is also necessary to keep spending and borrowing on everything else to a minimum. Or as Maurice Obstfeld, when director of the International Monetary Fund Research Department, put it in 2018: 'Basically, you kind of want to build up your buffers when times are good. You want to keep your powder dry for when you really need it.'[11] Big finance means big cuts.

What this meant in Britain was spelt out by George Osborne in his first 'emergency' budget in June 2010: capital spending slashed, by £17 billion and rising[12] – an act of socio-economic vandalism against the future. Welfare spending was reduced, causing endless misery for millions, while essential services were stripped to the bone, and often beyond. Deprived of the spending, a sickly economy sickened further.

All of this pre-dated Brexit, although the slump in business investment (never high) after the 2016 vote is pronounced; what Brexit challenged, more fundamentally, was the primacy of Britain's financial system and its happy half-in, half-out arrangement with the EU's capital markets; and the ability of any government to pursue austerity. The twin elite nightmares of a disorderly exit from the EU and the spectre of anti-austerity Corbynism eventually produced their political reaction in the form of Boris Johnson's version of Conservativism, forged in the chaotic period between Theresa May's exit as prime minister and December 2019's general election. Johnsonism embraced both a barebones exit deal with the EU, while promising austerity would finally be halted, with the 2019 manifesto promise of 'levelling up' and even more bounty to come.[13] Johnson paid little or no heed to fiscal rules, ramping up borrowing even before Covid, and then, during the pandemic itself, allowing spending to soar to unimaginable levels[14] – spending tacitly financed by the Bank of England itself via a precisely matched expansion of quantitative easing.[15] Cuts afterwards were not forthcoming: even Johnson's exit never brought a return to Osbornism. Kwasi Kwarteng, somewhat unconvincingly, pledged both dramatic tax cuts and no spending cuts, allowing the projected course of borrowing to soar; Jeremy Hunt, his successor, recognising the political writing on the wall, pledged cuts only *after* the next general election.[16]

By the time that election came in 2024, Britain's economic performance lagged behind even the weak standards of its peers in Europe, having already fallen seriously behind US growth rates too.[17]

END OF THE LINE FOR SOCIAL DEMOCRACY

Even as Reeves and Starmer made their £28 billion annual spend pledge in 2021 to promote 'green prosperity', the world was changing around them. Covid had broken the back of the low-inflation economy: prices surged at the end of lockdown, and despite the firm belief of the economics establishment that this was merely 'temporary', surged again with Russia's 2022 invasion of Ukraine, and then – perhaps most ominously – have continued to rise ever since across critical, essential goods, notably including food. The price of what we eat has, in particular, become subject to the pressures of climate change in a manner unprecedented in previous history. Droughts have wiped out Mediterranean olive harvests; unprecedented levels of rainfall then severe droughts have knocked out cocoa production in West Africa, where 60% of the world's crop is grown. The prices of orange juice, coffee, butter and eggs have all been subjected to variants of these environmental pressures.[18] Interest rates are a useless tool to restrain inflation arising from geopolitical turbulence and environmental crisis on this, and rising, scale. The Bank of England base rate cannot stop Vladimir Putin invading Ukraine nor end a drought in Ghana. In this situation, the old methods no longer work. The entire fiscal and monetary setup of recent decades, the combination of central bank 'independence' and a minimal role for government spending and economic intervention, stands exposed.

IN LIZ WE TRUSST?

Liz Truss' brief tenure as prime minister, in this regard, was less of an upset than is commonly supposed. On one level, her diagnosis of Britain as a failing economy, requiring a new course, was correct; her prescription was, of course, deeply flawed, and in any case never likely to pass a market smell test – the financial panic her government was subjected to, although aided and abetted by the Bank of England itself at a crucial moment immediately prior to her downfall, reflected very real conditions. One symptom of Britain's historically low investment is its continued very significant current account deficit: we import 50% of our food, we import 50% of our gas, we rely on imports for an incredible range of manufactured goods no longer produced here, and as a result we depend heavily on what former Bank of England governor Mark Carney called the 'kindness of strangers'[19] in continuing to lend us, or at least our various financial institutions, money to cover the gap. We are, as a result, singularly and collectively exposed to turns of market opinion – our economic setup is such that what happens on the bond market can translate pretty rapidly into what happens to people's wallets.

It was Truss' response to one of the post-Covid price shocks, the surge in energy prices of summer 2022, that really sealed her fate. Pledging £150 billion in borrowing to cap domestic energy prices via the Energy Price Guarantee may have been a price worth paying to head off an alarming surge in popular anger. The Don't Pay non-payment campaign was judged by the electricity industry itself to be an 'existential' threat to their business models.[20] But it knocked all projections for future borrowing out of line.

Removing Truss did not, however, somehow restore pre-Truss 'normality'. Interest rates remained high, as they did across the developed world, reflecting our new, high-inflation environment. And it was these elevated interest rates that removed Starmer's last gasp of redistributive radicalism. At higher interest rates, the £28 billion green investment pledge no longer complied with Reeves' rules. It was ditched in spring 2023, never to be seen again. However, Reeves has not returned to the neoliberal norms of the past. Across the world, these norms are being abandoned as a combination of competitive pressures, primarily from China, geopolitical turmoil and environmental crises place more and more demands on governments. Reeves herself has identified much of this, committing herself to 'securonomics'[21] and, as she laid out in her Mais Lecture[22] proposing a decisively more interventionist role for government than any government from Thatcher's onwards, including support for industrial strategy, a publicly owned energy generator, and a national wealth fund. External pressures, from water company failures to Trump tariffs, would provoke any government of any political stripe to become more interventionist than in the past (as the Tories since 2019 had demonstrated). But this willingness to intervene for capital was not matched by a willingness to intervene for labour, or wider society. Spending pledges were kept to an absolute bare minimum for the 2024 Labour manifesto.

This bodes ill. Life in the new high-interest, high-inflation world is harder and more serious than Labour's leadership had ever considered. Even after their arrival in office, followed by the obligatory denunciations of the previous government's fiscal incontinence, there is little sign that they truly understand what they are up against. Whatever the question, Reeves has only one answer: growth. Which in terms of substance has more often than not meant simply grabbing the Treasury's off-the-shelf big projects and presenting them as if new and decisive: Heathrow and other airports' expansion on one side,[23] a new 'Silicon Valley' between Oxford and Cambridge on the other. These are stale in the extreme as proposals, and do nothing whatsoever for Labour's supposed heartlands – where, one presumes, a diet of migrant-bashing and occasional culture war jabs are supposed to keep the locals at least reasonably content – and are unlikely even to do much for growth. The same goes for Labour's extraordinary enthusiasm for the resource-guzzling monsters of the data economy, the vast new data centres it is pledging support for. These capital-intensive projects produce few jobs per spend (Blackstone's proposed hyperscale datacentre in Teesside will produce 1,600 jobs for £10 billion investment, or about £6.25 million a job), but their exceptional demands for water and electricity – a hyperscale data centre typically uses the same energy as around 30,000 homes – are already provoking local protests.[24] But from the government's point of view, such pledges may perhaps help charm their way to a small-scale deal with the Trump administration – pledging full support for US big tech in helping itself to public data and public resources, the better to sustain the flow of private profits back across the Atlantic.

CLINGING TO THE CENTRE

At every step, the reaction of Starmer's Labour to any problem is to cleave closer and closer to the presumed safety of Britain's centre ground on the economy. It has no appreciation of the extent to which Britain's economic failures are the fault of that centre ground. It has no understanding that the challenges Britain faces cannot be met from that centre ground: an insistence that finance must retain its primacy, and that the economy might, at a pinch, be merely rebalanced around its elevated status will no longer function. Reeves' clinging to the fiscal rules is an institutional expression of that primacy – a hard-wiring of the demand, inherent to an economy with an over-extended financial system, that government borrowing, and therefore government spending, be shrunk.

It's pretty clear Starmer himself has little to no interest in, or understanding of, economic issues, placidly handing the brief over for Reeves' complete control. Starmer's vision of economic management, such as it is, appears to live in those seemingly halcyon days before the 2016 referendum, and perhaps even before the 2008 financial crisis. David Cameron handed over the economic reins to George Osborne and his junior partners in the Lib Dems, preferring himself to indulge in diplomatic flights of fancy – his own Munich speech, pints with Xi Jinping. Tony Blair had a similar arrangement with his chancellor, Gordon Brown, who was also granted a wide brief over economic policy. Both models suited the Treasury as an institution: somewhat increasing public spending during the boom years pre-crisis, cutting heavily post-crisis.

The result is a catastrophic reversion to the mean of Treasury control, increasingly reinforced by growing demands for re-militarisation. A much-unappreciated bounty of recent years has been the post-1989 peace dividend of declining military expenditure, allowing for significant increases in social spending – on education, health and pensions – that will be much missed once it's gone.

Starmer and Reeves' economic strategy is in stark contrast to Germany's, the biggest villain and primary architect of Europe's austerity madness of the 2010s, but which in the 2020s has rediscovered the apparent virtues of government spending and debt funding. In Britain, meanwhile, political economy is now tightly locked into attempting to maintain the primacy of finance and a growing military commitment. The losers in all this, whatever Starmer's half-baked claims about jobs and investment via defence – research has consistently shown that military spending is extraordinarily inefficient in creating jobs[25] – will be wider society.

Corbynism has long since shuffled away. As Reeves pledges spending cuts to come, and as Labour ministers berate those rising numbers of the sick and unable to work, the last vestiges of social democracy have been finished off. The result for Starmerism is a strange new construction: more interventionist than New Labour, but also more miserly. Self-consciously taking an axe to the aid budget in order to fund the increased military budget is a carefully calculated move.

Increasingly, Starmer's government resembles nothing so much as Labour's old right of mid- to late 1970s-vintage James Callaghan's ill-fated premiership, egged on by the likes of the Electrical, Electronic, Telecommunications and Plumbing Union's leader Frank Chapple. They are the current victors of Labour's factional permawar of the last four decades – suddenly and dramatically elevated to high office. It is a faction living in a past long gone, for which the culture war entreaties of Blue Labour[26] are no doubt a good fit. It has little to say in a world of repeated economic shocks, of surging prices and environmental turmoil, to an ageing society where more and more of us are falling ill. Starmer's government is setting itself up for failure, but a failure driven by its own poor choices. It could choose differently – as Spain has chosen, for example, to intervene to protect consumers from rising prices, and to insist that climate financing is kept out of Europe's debt rules; or Mexico, where a hugely popular, left-wing president is seen as standing up to Washington. There are always alternatives. Starmer's failure will be in rejecting them.

ENDNOTES

1. See, for example, Richard Partington and Heather Stewart '"Stagflation" Fears as Bank of England Cuts Growth Forecast and Warns of Price Rises' *The Guardian* 6 February 2025 www.theguardian.com.

2. See Sally Hickey 'Labour Replaces Shadow Chancellor after Elections Disappointment' *FT Adviser* 10 May 2021 www.ftadviser.com.

3. See Jessica Elgot 'Labour Promises to Spend £28bn a Year on Tackling Climate Crisis' *The Guardian* 2 September 2021 www.theguardian.com.

4. See Conor Pope 'McDonnell Promises to Balance the Books with Fiscal Credibility Rules' Labour List 11 March 2016 www.labourlist.org.

5. John McDonnell interview: 'Labour Will Win Argument on Borrowing to Invest Says John McDonnell' *The Guardian* 26 November 2017 www.theguardian.com.

6. Ibid.

7. See my chapter 'Out of the Ruins' in Mark Perryman (ed.) *Corbynism from Below* Lawrence and Wishart, London 2019 pp. 242–249.

8. Paul Schmelzing 'Eight Centuries of Global Real Interest Rates, R-G, and the Surprasecular Decline, 1311–2018' Staff Working Paper No. 845 Bank of England, London 2020.

9. See Michael Safi et al. 'How the Arab Spring Engulfed the Middle East – and Changed the World' *The Guardian* 25 January 2021 www.theguardian.com.

10. For background to oil price rises and falls, see Paul Bolton 'Oil Prices' House of Commons Library, London 7 November 2022 www.commonslibrary.parliament.uk.

11. 'Transcript of the Press Conference on the Release of the July 2018 World Economic Outlook Update', International Monetary Fund, Washington, DC 16 July 2018 www.imf.org.

12. See 'Budget Key Points: At a Glance' *BBC News* 22 June 2010 www.bbc.co.uk.

13. For the end result, see Alex Nurse 'Levelling Up Has Been a Total Failure – Here's the Evidence' The Conversation 10 June 2024 www.theconversation.com.

14. See Philip Brien and Matthew Keep 'Public Spending during the Covid-19 Pandemic' House of Commons Library, London 12 September 2023 www.commonslibrary.parliament.uk.

15. See 'What Is Quantitative Easing?' Bank of England, London www.bankofengland.co.uk.

16. See Steve Schifferes 'Jeremy Hunt's Autumn Statement Is a Poisoned Chalice for Whoever Wins the Next Election' City St George's University of London 18 November 2022 www.citystgeorges.ac.uk.

17. See 'UK Economy Saw Zero Growth at the End of 2019' *BBC News* 11 February 2020 www.bbc.co.uk.

18. See Orla Dwyer 'Five Charts: How Climate Change Is Driving up Food Prices around the World' Carbon Brief 23 August 2024 www.carbonbrief.org.

19. Quoted in Jill Treanor and Nicholas Watt 'Mark Carney Fears Brexit Would Leave UK Relying on Kindness of Strangers' *The Guardian* 26 January 2016 www.theguardian.com.

20. See Keir Milburn 'Don't Pay Took Down Kwasi Kwarteng' Novara Media 18 October 2022 www.novaramedia.com.

21. See Sarah Ogilvie 'What Rachel Reeves Means When She Talks Securonomics' *Prospect* 15 August 2024 www.prospectmagazine.co.uk.

22. Rachel Reeves 'Mais Lecture' Labour Party 2024 www.labour.org.uk.

23. For a critical response, see George Monbiot 'Look at Labour's Acts of Environmental Vandalism and Ask: Did I Vote for This?' *The Guardian* 30 January 2025 www.theguardian.com.

24. See Tamlin Magee 'Not Just Nimbys – Why Data Centre Protests Are on the Rise' Raconteur 30 July 2024 www.raconteur.net.

25. See, for example, Khem Rogaly 'Military Spending Is Touted as a Remedy for Britain's Ailing Economy. Here's Why It Won't Work' *The Guardian* 7 March 2025 www.theguardian.com.

26. See the latest version of Sienna Rogers and Tim Scotson 'Blue Labour v Reform: The Pro-Worker, Anti-Woke Plan to Beat Farage' Politics Home 1 February 2025 www.politicshome.com, and for the ideological underpinning, see Maurice Glasman *Blue Labour: The Politics of the Common Good* Polity Press, Cambridge 2024.

No Democratic Reform, No Change

Jess Garland

On a range of measures, the electoral legacy inherited by Keir Starmer's government is an unfavourable one. A decade and more of political turmoil has fractured and fragmented the electoral landscape, leaving few political certainties intact. It has left in its wake a frustrated and disappointed electorate which is in no mood to give anyone a second chance.

This mood is being felt across Western democracies. Incumbent governments elected before or during the pandemic are being ousted. In the UK general election, not only did many incumbent MPs lose their seats, but those who retained them had their majorities severely trimmed. An anti-Tory sentiment was indisputably the dominant mood of the 2024 general election, but it came with an undercurrent of 'a plague on all your houses', which reflects another, more important, development: across this landscape, there is a chill wind of rising populism and democratic backsliding.

Turning the tide of public disillusionment and distrust enough to secure a second term is a massive challenge for Starmer's party, but it is also one being undertaken within a political system that works against achieving those ends. Both for voters and for those working within political parties, the system itself can be the problem, actively working against achieving a better, more engaging democracy. Meeting the populist right's challenges to democracy cannot mean propping up a redundant system that doesn't serve, but finding a way to renew the system to better serve the values and principles that we are trying to defend.

DISAPPOINTMENT, DISILLUSIONMENT ... DELIVERY?

Checking the vital signs of our democracy reveals a worrying prognosis. The general election in 2024 had the lowest turnout since 2001

– when turnout dropped just below 60% for the first time since universal suffrage; 40% of the registered electorate chose not to vote. That figure is higher than the vote share of any of the parties, but it is only half of the picture. There is, on top of this, another missing, invisible electorate – those who are eligible to vote, but not registered to do so. The Electoral Commission suggests up to 8 million potential voters could be missing.[1] Adding this silent constituency to those who were registered but didn't turn out means that, of the eligible electorate, nearly one in two potential voters did not cast a ballot in 2024.

There are many factors that drive turnout. Some are contextual, such as how close the contest is and how much is perceived to be at stake. On this measure, many blamed the polls, which gave Labour such a clear lead in the run-up to polling day, for dissuading voters. Other factors are practical – how easy it is to vote, and whether there are barriers (such as new voter ID laws which appeared to have a deterrent effect on turnout[2]). There is, however, one factor that goes beyond the practicalities of voting: the feeling that party politics, whatever the party, whoever the leader, just isn't connecting.

While support for democracy in general remains high,[3] there is growing cynicism about how it works in practice. Trust, both in politicians and our political institutions, has reached record lows. In the year prior to the election, the percentage of people saying they 'almost never' trust the government to put the needs of the nation above the interests of their party was at 45%; 58% said they 'almost never' trust politicians to tell the truth in a tight corner.[4] To put that in context, in 2009, in the wake of the expenses scandal, the number of people who said they almost never trust politicians was only 2 percentage points higher. The UK currently sits second from bottom of 30 surveyed OECD countries for trust in government.[5]

This disillusionment and lack of trust undoubtedly had an impact on turnout at the general election. One-third (34%) of those who didn't vote said it was because they don't trust politicians; another 21% said it was because voting doesn't change anything.[6]

It is true, of course, that people tend to have higher levels of trust in government when the party they support is in power. Likewise, there is a connection between how well-off people feel under the system and how much they trust it. There is therefore a sound logic to the Starmer government's approach of focusing on delivery as an answer to the problem of declining trust. Tackling the sense that the political system isn't delivering as it should and that government has lost the power to make people's lives better is crucial. Similarly, moving away from the empty promises of boosterism seen under the previous Tory government is an important step in addressing the sense that politics continually disappoints. But while delivery is a necessary condition, it is not a sufficient one.

What 'deliverism' can't provide is a sense of individual empowerment, and it is often those who feel like they don't have a voice in the political system who do not trust it. There is a growing pessimism and anger in our politics, and this, combined with low trust, can easily create a toxic environment. Those most alienated from the political system and least likely to engage are also most likely to support populist alternatives. Hope not Hate research just after the general election in 2024 found that 37% of people believed that voting is not a credible mechanism for change – rising to 51% of those feeling financially desperate.[7]

The combination of disengagement, low trust and pessimism is a warning sign. These are the fertile fields for the seeds of right-wing populism, but barren ground for those promoting democratic life.

There isn't an easy answer to these problems, but often the way to grow trust is to be more trusting, so the solutions must surely start with trying to encourage greater participation and ensuring that people's participation matters. People need to feel empowered to make their own lives better and create positive outcomes for their families and communities. There are material issues as well, of course, but it is important, too, that people feel their voice is heard. And there is a relationship between this sense of intention and trust – if the system is responsive to you, you tend to trust it, and to engage with it.

This is where looking to the structures of our democracy and how they can be reinvigorated to improve connections can provide answers. Trust is a difficult relationship to construct in a political system that is set up in a way that makes politics feel like something that is done to you not with you, and it is hard, if not impossible, to foster mutual trust and respect from a system that is remote and unresponsive.

A good place to start would be to ensure that our elections and parliament reflect voters' views fairly and that people feel their vote is valued through a proportional representation system. Elections for most people are the only point at which they engage in the democratic process, but even at this very basic level, there are unnecessary barriers and complications, and too many people go to the polling station knowing their vote won't count. To begin to turn the tide on the political disconnect, it is essential that this fundamental voting experience is a meaningful one. There is broad and growing support for changing the electoral system at Westminster to a more proportional system.[8] This fundamental change would be a huge step toward forging a better connection with voters. Not only would proportional representation help ensure that all votes are meaningful, but it would reshape the political dynamic at Westminster, opening the door to a different political culture.

But it doesn't need to end there. There are ways to deepen democracy by considering how both local government and national government could foster spaces for people to come together and engage with issues in deliberative forums, whether that's through citizens assemblies on national issues or local citizen forums helping shape decisions affecting a town or city. Engaging citizens more deeply is another way to start to rebuild connections and trust.

PERILS OF THE MING VASE STRATEGY

When a system isn't working, it impacts on those within it; it's bad for voters, but it can also be bad for politicians and parties. These dynamics can affect how parties campaign and how they shape their policies, both in elections and in office. In an increasingly complex electoral environment, the system can narrow the options and create a straitjacket for those within it.

The increasing fragmentation of our politics means that general elections under our electoral system are, for parties, especially Labour, now a complex game of piecing together an optimally located voter coalition. This is partly because geography takes centre-stage in first-past-the-post (FPTP) elections. Labour has learned that it is more important to attract votes in the right places than to increase vote share overall, which inevitably means that the political offer is steered toward those voters who hold the keys to unlocking the election – from 'White Van Man' to 'Waitrose Woman', the (ideally located) target voter has an outsized influence on what matters. This also means that there are many who don't matter as much – traditionally anyone in a 'safe seat', but certain demographics, too; typically younger voters and those in more densely populated urban areas are overlooked, and of course, those who are unlikely to vote (an increasing number). But as the previous decade of political turmoil has exposed, ignoring any group of voters has the potential to backfire.

The necessary and limiting focus on the target voter encourages an electoral cognitive dissonance whereby the electoral offer (or at least the offer that takes centre-stage in the debate) is detached from the values or broader aims of the party. This dissonance shapes the direction of politics beyond the election, dictating policy choices once in office and affecting how well government policy matches up to public preferences. Comparative studies have shown that under Westminster-style systems, given the inbuilt need to persuade key voters in key seats, a narrow set of interests exerts the greater pull on policy choices. This means greater spending on targeted benefits such as key infrastructure in certain constituencies, over generalised public goods such as welfare spending. It means that policy choices shift toward certain interests. Far from creating a pull toward a popular unity, this converging on the median voter in the median district can actually skew policy away from the median because voters are themselves not evenly distributed.[9]

At the same time, parties are trying to please an electorate that is increasingly characterised by a mobility in its party loyalties.

Volatility, or voter switching, reached a new high in 2024, but this increased volatility has been in evidence since 2015. We have had a decade of electoral shocks and continued party dealignment, and as a result, our politics has seen voters switching party like never before. Cross-loyalty voters, those who find that they may feel closer to one party on economic issues and another on social issues, have helped shape this shift in the political environment. Many voters now struggle to know where their political home is or to find a party that represents them, and this adds to volatility, with voters making their minds up late in one campaign and more likely to switch party again before the next election.

This is an uncomfortable situation for parties and politicians. The oft-quoted 'Ming vase strategy' attributed to Starmer's election campaign, in which, like Blair, he exercised the caution of 'a man carrying a priceless Ming vase across a highly polished floor', is a reflection of this. The fear of a small last-minute shift in the polls affecting the election outcome is a genuine risk, particularly in a close race, and particularly facing a hostile media, but it is also a reflection of the fragility of FPTP results in an increasingly multi-party electoral system.

This fragility can be seen across the last decade of election results. The 2017 election resulted in a hung parliament, but it would have been a Conservative majority if just 533 voters in nine constituencies voted differently. In 2017, Labour received 3 million more votes than it did in 2024, but 149 fewer seats. Labour's landslide majority in 2024 was achieved on a 1.6 percentage point increase on its 2019 vote share. The Conservatives experienced the same switch in fortunes this decade. Their 2019 'landslide' was achieved on a 1.3% increase in vote share, while the previous election had seen the Prime minister lose her majority. Increasingly, under our system, a small shift in vote share can mean the difference between a huge win or crushing defeat.

This imbalance may not work as well for Labour at the next general election as it did in 2024. Labour's 2024 electoral coalition, pieced together to deliver a highly efficient vote spread, is not tightly bound ideologically. Mostly this is an electoral coalition based on a desire for change, and one which will be harder to hold together with a call for continuity. Even a modest Conservative recovery at the next election could see Labour out of power.

To date, Labour has not needed to listen as much to those voters it lost to the Green Party or Lib Dems; typically, these were younger voters in more urban areas where Labour's vote share stacks up without leading to more MPs. This may change. To secure a second term, Labour will need to expand its vote share, drawing votes from progressives, too. The electoral contest is no longer a case of the red wall or the blue wall, but rather a battle across many, sometimes contradictory, sites. The fragility of the electoral coalition carefully pieced together in 2024 will be hard to defend.

This is an electoral game that is increasingly difficult to play and win. It's not good for voters, but nor does it serve those trying to win elections. The reality of fighting FPTP elections in a multi-party and volatile electoral arena is one of high stakes and limited options. There is very little room to manoeuvre in campaigning, or in office, when so much can ride on so few and the margins are so narrow.

The structures of our politics dictate the possibilities within it. Voters are not the only ones limited by the choices they can make; those in power also find their options, the choices they can make, the changes they can bring about, are limited by the Westminster system. The Ming vase strategy is undoubtedly a sound one in these circumstances, but it is an unenviable position to hold.

A MAN WITH A PLAN

Our system may be failing voters and parties, but there is a view that if the system delivers, then how it arrives there is not important. Our democratic system draws heavily on the idea of outcome legitimacy. The problem is that it is often the system itself that prevents good outcomes, and worse, actively contributes to governing disasters.

Considering the role our democratic structures play in the outcomes they deliver is especially important when so much is resting on Starmer's government delivering on its core promises. On the face of it, our governance structures seem suited to a mission-driven approach. The guiding principle of the Westminster system, despite having been radically reshaped by devolution, is centralisation with power hoarded at the core.

British governments are rarely required to make compromises: they rarely need to negotiate with other parties, they are rarely challenged by the second chamber, which itself lacks legitimacy. Parliament is most often a passive player, responding to, but not initiating, change. This is, in theory, an asset for a government that wants to drive through a focused programme of repair and renewal. Many will forgive the system for locking them out of power for decades on the basis that they have an opportunity once in a while to take control of this powerful engine and steer it to their stated ends. But the absence of veto players and lack of friction in the system, far from being a strength, can actively contribute to preventing change, and even creating failures.

As Anthony King and Ivor Crewe famously argued in their book *The Blunders of Government*, 'the only trouble with a system in which it is easy to take decisions is that it is every bit as easy to take the wrong decisions as it is to take the right ones'.[10] They drew attention to how an absence of careful consideration, speedy decision-making and a lack of consultation or reaching out to others is a risk rather than a benefit, and has contributed to the major policy failures of past governments. It is within the very strength and decisiveness of this style of governing that the conditions for mistakes are created. Other academics have also noted how the speed of decisions, the lack of friction from veto players, and the scale of decisions (taken nationally, not locally) all contribute to making the Westminster system more mistake-prone.[11]

One of the other problems of a system with little friction is that it is highly volatile. Policies are made, only to be undone wholesale by the next administration. The nature of the system encourages governing parties to deliver on campaign promises regardless of how much analysis has gone into formulating them prior to taking office. The absence of input from other parties means that they are, in turn, pushed into opposing everything the government does, creating an imperative to undo those policies when they themselves are in office. This increased policy volatility in winner-takes-all systems combined with reduced constitutional and legislative checks and balances creates the conditions for significant policy flexibility. To date, this shift has been less visible as successive governments have secured several terms in office back-to-back. But an increase in voter volatility means we are likely to be entering an era when parties cannot rely on several terms in office. In these circumstances, shifts in policy at each election have the potential to be enormously destabilising.

Ironically, by centralising power, the system makes it harder to take decisive action. Prime ministers know that while they are not constrained by veto players in office, the electorate is the ultimate veto player, waiting for the next election to punish perceived failings.

The fear of taking necessary but unpopular decisions, with a media ready to jump on anything that may cause short-term pain, creates an environment in which dealing with major long-term political challenges, the 'wicked problems' such as climate change or social care, is an almost impossible undertaking.

If the problems stem from a lack of deliberation, then potentially the solution is to reach out and involve others. Some parliamentary committees have tried in recent years to crack difficult issues by involving citizens through deliberative assemblies. These were widely seen as helpful in the process, but more needs to be done to ensure that their outcomes contribute to real change. Finding a way through may also involve working cross-party to build pre-legislative consensus. Building consensus for policies and drawing from a wider range of views not only helps craft better policy, but also provides insurance against the proposals being ripped up at the next change of government. This would take a significant shift in Westminster culture (and a leap in trust), but is not entirely alien. Various cross-party and independent commissions have tackled major questions of policy over the years including the Scottish Constitutional Convention from 1989 onward, which paved the way for devolution in 1998.

There are, however, limits on what can be achieved within the system as it currently operates. The Westminster system is designed to centralise and concentrate power; it stands in opposition to consensus-based systems designed to facilitate power sharing and negotiation. Structural change is needed to shift toward a more effective model of government.

Starmer has already made clear that 'sticking plaster' politics is a symptom of this failing Westminster system.[12] This is absolutely right, and there are few current policy challenges that will be solved by short-term fixes. But breaking out of the addiction to the quick fix might need more than good intentions when the system itself is encouraging the dependency. In 2013, King and Crewe pointed to government blunders, including the poll tax, mis-selling of pensions and the Millennium Dome project.[13] It is not hard to find more contemporary examples: HS2, Covid procurement, the Truss 'mini-budget' all share the hallmarks of the same system failures. By encouraging strong and decisive government, the system is also contributing to creating fickle and fragile ones, highly prone to getting things wrong.

A RENEWED DEMOCRATIC OFFER

Our political system is failing to accommodate this shifting, multi-party new world. It is alienating voters and creating problems for those sustaining democracy in our elected political institutions. The game is rigged and even those playing it are struggling to find a way out.

Democratic principles are supported by the vast majority of the British public despite significant disappointment in their practical application. But it would be unwise to take too much comfort in that fact. Around the world, the threat to democracy comes not from an alternative, but from the subversion of democracy from within its structures, often framed within its own terms. With strongman politics and authoritarian leaders taking office across the globe, threats to democratic integrity coming from outside national borders, and the increasing power of tech over democratic discourse, we need not only to protect democratic principles, but to articulate a vision of what we are trying to defend. Public faith in democracy is a strong foundation to build on, but it desperately needs a new, more engaging practice in reality.

The changes made under previous Labour governments to our political system beyond Westminster have been amongst the most important – and long-lasting – shifts of the last thirty years. Devolution and the Human Rights Act have survived where other major policy shifts have been undone. The 2024 manifesto promised some positive democratic change, including steps to modernise the House of Lords, completing the project started in 1999 with the removal of the remaining hereditary peers, changes to voter registration and lowering the age of the franchise, further devolution, as well as important changes to political finance rules. But the scale of change is clearly much smaller – important, but more timid, steps reflecting the precariousness and fragility of the electoral inheritance.

Yet the scale of the challenge to democracy demands a more significant answer. A bolder democratic offer that re-models our democratic system to build better connections would not only improve the situation for voters, but would make things better for those within it too. There are many who say that this is a 'second term' project, but that is a gift the voters may not bestow.

ENDNOTES

1. '2023 Report: Electoral Registers in the UK' Electoral Commission, London 18 September 2023 www.electoralcommission.org.uk.
2. 'Voter ID at the 2024 UK General Election' Electoral Commission, London 29 July 2024 www.electoralcommission.org.uk.
3. Richard Wike, Janell Fetterolf, Maria Smerkovich, Sarah Austin, Sneha Gubbala and Jordan Lippert 'Attitudes toward Different Types of Government Systems' Pew Research, London 28 February 2024 www.pewresearch.org.
4. *Damaged Politics?* British Social Attitudes 41 National Centre for Social Research, London 2024.
5. 'Trust in Government' OECD, Paris 2023 www.oecd.org.
6. More in Common *Change Pending: The Path to the 2024 General Election and Beyond* More in Common and University College London Policy Lab, London 2024.
7. Anki Deo and Misbah Malik *Fear and Hate 2024: The Case for Community Resilience* Hope not Hate, London 2024 p. 41.
8. See the biannual tracker 'Should We Change Our Current British Voting System?' YouGov, London 29 January 2024 www.yougov.co.uk.
9. See, for example: Jonathan Rodden 'The Geographic Distribution of Political Preferences' *Annual Review of Political Science* 13 (2010) pp. 321–340 and Gian Maria Milesi-Ferretti, Roberto Perotti and Massimo Ristagno *Electoral Systems and Public Spending* IMF Working Paper WP/01/22 International Monetary Fund Washington, DC February 2001.
10. Anthony King and Ivor Crewe *The Blunders of Our Governments* Oneworld Publications, London 2013 p. 385.
11. See, for example: Patrick Dunleavy 'Policy Disasters: Explaining the UK's Record' *Public Policy and Administration* 10 (1995) pp. 52–70 and Sven Steinmo 'Political Institutions and Tax Policy in the United States, Sweden, and Britain' *World Politics* 41/4 (1989) pp. 500–535.
12. Kiran Stacey and Pippa Crerar 'Starmer Vows to Let Communities "Take Back Control" in Labour's First Term' *The Guardian* 5 January 2023 www.theguardian.com.
13. King and Crewe *The Blunders of Our Governments* pp. 41, 65 and 111.

From Climate Emergency
to National Renewal

Andrew Simms

A traveller pauses at a junction. Turn one way, and at first the journey is mostly comfortable, the road familiar, with just a few challenging stretches to navigate. Further along, however, just far enough to delay serious consideration, a lethal head-on collision awaits. Take the other turn, and the landscape is less familiar, more challenging. The traveller has to adapt, to leave their comfort zone, be confident, find courage and take risks. The difference is that in this direction, survival lies. The route needs more thought, but avoids the fatal crash. Surprisingly, on this other path the traveller also feels better. Which turn to take to go from climate emergency to national renewal?

This was the choice facing Keir Starmer's Labour government – and Labour has taken the first turn. The question is, can it change to a course that, for the UK and its role in the world, swerves around catastrophe and heads in a direction where people and the rest of nature can survive and thrive? Doing so will mean at least three key shifts: a culture shift, a shift in economic investment, and a shift in preparedness to handle predictable disasters.

TIED TO A SINKING ECONOMIC POLICY SHIP

In a much quoted speech from his 1968 Presidential campaign Robert F. Kennedy said that the calculation for economic growth measured everything 'except that which makes life worthwhile',[1] More than half a century later Labour in power has made the pursuit of growth its compass, mantra and lash. It is not difficult to see why. Despite the Conservatives' catastrophic economic mismanagement, from the national self-harm of Brexit to Liz Truss' short-lived attempt to actually use the playbook of right-wing market extremists as a method to govern, Labour feels the need to prove its economic credentials.

It does this by sending the usual signals to finance and economic commentators – that it can be relied on to take the side of business and the City of London, for example by reneging on a pledge to reinstate a cap on bankers' bonuses[2] (even after having presided over the City's light-touch regulation that was instrumental in the great financial crisis of 2007–2008), and relaxing rules on bank lending (ditto)[3] – and that it will pursue a conventional strategy of maximising growth.

But having the highest level of sustained growth among the Group of Seven nations, is not just a routine objective for Labour, it is its number one, all-eclipsing priority in government.[4] The discipline it applies to sending this signal means that if a potential clash arises between, for example, the protection of nature, which we are indivisibly part of, and the pursuit of growth, it is nature that must be publicly sacrificed.

When rolling out a growth-oriented change to planning rules that would allow more house-building on Britain's green belt land, it was spun clearly that this would take priority over nature.[5] And who could argue with the urgent need to provide more affordable housing (if indeed such planning changes would have that effect)? But such political semaphore distracts from a reluctance to take other more effective steps to increase affordable housing supply. Labour eschews policies that have been proven to do so and are common in other countries, such as rent controls and market measures to prevent speculation on house prices.[6] These approaches do not meet the optics test for a 'pro-growth' policy. Other landmark choices over, for example, the expansion of polluting airports and how to transition away from North Sea oil and gas, are set to test the government.

The discipline of Labour's signalling on putting growth before all else can be seen in decisions like the chancellor, Rachel Reeves, choosing to continue the freeze on fuel duty (a subsidy for pollution), in place since 2011. Yet, according to the Office for Budget Responsibility, by the end of the 2025 financial year the freeze will have landed the Treasury a massive £100 billion cumulative bill in lost public income, which has the effect of further tightening

Labour's self-imposed restrictions on spending.[7] At the same time, the costs of cleaner alternatives such as public transport are allowed to rise. It is a counter-productive, political choice that pushes people toward more polluting, less healthy transport choices – bad for human health (and hence more work for the NHS), bad for efficient infrastructure and bad for the climate.

Labour's actions clearly accord with a story it has told itself about how to get and hold power. It is probably true that many in government see this as a tactical and rhetorical necessity. But politics can be captured by its own signalling, and rhetoric often hardens into ideology. Whether something is deeply believed or not is less relevant if coherence with a chosen message becomes an acid test for actual policy.

Haunted by ghosts of the right-wing press depicting the party as anti-business, it's easy to see why Labour is doing this. Given the party's large majority, it is less easy to see why it is so fervent in its signalling. But it is also not difficult to see why this means it took that first turn at the junction toward inevitable collision.

HEAD-ON COLLISION

In 2024, six of the biosphere's nine systems and processes that underpin life on Earth – the so-called 'planetary boundaries' – had been transgressed, the result predominantly of human activity. A seventh – the acidification of oceans – was approaching a critical threshold.[8] Another red alert came from finding that the decade 2015–24 was the hottest on record,[9] and globally in 2024 emissions of carbon dioxide, the main gas responsible, continued to rise.[10] The point of ringing this doleful bell is not to alarm, but merely to note that something depressingly predictable will happen if we continue on a path of unconstrained growth and overconsumption.

The *Limits to Growth* report produced by scientists from the Massachusetts Institute of Technology (MIT) in 1972[11] that set out to model Earth's survival capacity was derided by many for alarmism. Yet 35 years later, a study by one of the world's leading scientific research institutes found that its original projections of resource depletion, with its environmental and human consequences, had been proved basically correct.[12] When the global model based on the work of the MIT scientists was run using multiple scenarios that allowed growth to continue, growth always overwhelmed technological cures. Irrespective of whatever techno-fix was applied to deal with how nature was being exhausted, Earth's ecological life support systems, and hence our civilisation, ended in fairly sudden collapse.

In a less often-quoted line from that 1968 speech, Kennedy said, 'Too much and for too long, we seemed to have surrendered personal excellence and community values in the mere accumulation of material things.'[13]

A vast review of scientific literature on the subject of collapse by academic Danilo Brozović in 2023,[14] surveying 361 studies and 73 books, came to much the same conclusion as the 2018 special report on 1.5°C global heating by the Intergovernmental Panel on Climate Change (IPCC).[15] Namely, the need for a rapid, radical transformation of society and the economy. Brozović's study found, however, that one of the major obstacles to taking action commensurate with the scale of the problem is 'convincing people of the necessity of such measures'.[16] This is the point at which a lack of political leadership (something Kennedy called the 'great task') guarantees catastrophic failure.

CULTURE SHIFT – HOW TO STOP PROMOTING OUR OWN SELF-DESTRUCTION

Despite all this, when making his first major intervention as prime minister on the impending environmental catastrophe, at COP29, the international climate conference, Keir Starmer made a calculated choice. While defending the UK's emissions reduction target, he pointedly added, 'What we are not going to do is start telling people how to live their lives .... We are not going to start dictating to people what they do.'[17] It was a comment coming from the same signalling playbook as Labour's comments on growth, and the priority growth is given over nature: the priority of an abstract measure over that which is essential to life. It was odd, for two big reasons.

First, it is a basic duty of government to keep its citizens safe. Regulating dangerous products and policing abusive behaviour, providing positive advice and guidelines is the very stuff of government. It happens all the time and is a basic civic function – think smoking, drunk driving etc. So why not do it when it comes to the biggest collective threat yet, the loss of a habitable climate?

Second, while rejecting a more active role for government and using the political framing of the right to escape that responsibility – not 'telling people what to do' – the government appears quite happy that a vastly larger, private information machine should be allowed to do just that. And the problem is that this machine, commercial advertising, is telling people to pollute as if tomorrow didn't matter, and to live high-waste, high-carbon lifestyles.[18] Almost everywhere, people are assailed with adverts promoting polluting flights, giant SUVs, greenwash propaganda from fossil fuel companies, and other heavily polluting products and services.

If the government won't let itself encourage people to do the right thing, why are heavily polluting industries allowed to encourage people to do the wrong thing? This is the logic behind the 'Badvertising' campaign[19] for a tobacco-style ban on adverts that fuel the climate crisis. It is the reason increasingly at town and city level, where action often prefigures national policy, places ranging from Edinburgh[20] to Amsterdam, Stockholm,[21] Sheffield[22] and Gothenburg are adding adverts for heavily climate-polluting products to the list of prohibited advertising, to reinforce public health and climate goals.

Labour's caution is not only cowardly, it is potentially disastrous. In its 2022 report looking at necessary emissions cuts, the scientists of the IPCC looked for the first time at the question of 'demand' – what, including social factors, increases consumption and carbon emissions.[23] It concluded that keeping to the maximum temperature increase target of 1.5°C is unachievable without managing demand. The UK's Climate Change Committee,[24] which has an official advisory role to the government, is clear that behavioural change has a central role to play in meeting climate targets. Even mainstream, economically conservative bodies such as the International Energy Agency[25] point out that behaviour change plays a key role in around two-thirds of all emissions reductions in scenarios to achieve net zero.

Labour's signalling that it will not engage in what the jargon calls 'demand management' rejects this expert consensus. With the government reneging on its responsibilities, civil society campaigning and advocacy have never been more urgent and important.

However, in case the argument falls into a false dichotomy between system and behaviour change, a very important clarification needs to be made. This is not about placing the burden on individuals and merely compelling them to make the right choices, in a world in which it can be inconvenient, difficult and expensive to do so.[26] It is about making less-polluting options cheaper and worse ones more expensive. It is about changing the layout of towns and the comfort and energy efficiency of homes. It is about questioning what for some have become almost default lifestyle choices whereby, for example, it is considered 'normal' to use a two-tonne SUV to drive to the supermarket for milk, or take multiple long-haul flights for holidays every year.

In other words, the government's role is to change the parameters within which we choose different products, services and lifestyles, the so-called 'choice architecture'.[27] System and behaviour change are self-reinforcing dynamics. Make it easier to walk and cycle in a town by changing road and pavement layouts, and more people will walk and cycle. As that happens, further policies for traffic reduction – less pollution, more and safer space for pedestrians and cyclists, greater use of public transport – become more politically popular. The embedded privilege, social norm and policy bias in favour of car-based travel starts to change. Health bills and accident rates reduce, the air gets cleaner and neighbourhoods more convivial.

The irony of Labour's timidity about showing leadership on behaviour change is that everything about the current system is already 'telling people what to do' in a different way. For example, it is telling them to 'drive a car' – from the car subsidy given through freezing fuel duty to the layout of roads and priority given to them, the design of towns, location of facilities, parking and disproportionate gifting of street space and, crucially, the cultural normalisation of cars, and demand induced for them, that results from the billions spent on their advertising.

From travel to just getting around, diet and overall consumption – the dice are loaded in favour of high-carbon choices. But these could be fixed with a range of low-cost measures and a focus on the worst excesses of the wealthy: the high-consuming polluter elite, frequent flyers and especially urban owners of large SUVs.

A private jet tax and frequent flyer levy would curb high emitters. Coupling those with an end to airport expansion and mandating the aviation industry to have a 'just transition' plan for its workforces would ease the shift to less damaging ways to get around. An end to the age of careless, disposable consumerism could be signalled with a combination of goods being redesigned to comply with a 'right to repair' and requiring products to be designed to last longer minimum times, and be part of a fully circular 'cradle-to-cradle' service economy, with manufacturers required to eliminate waste. Mass roll-out of accessible high street 'fixing factories' could help bring back a culture of repair that was second nature to earlier generations, and libraries of consumer goods for hire could make essentials more cheaply available when needed, without increasing waste.

Many of these initiatives are being piloted at local level through networks like the Transition Towns movement, Share Sheds, Tool Libraries and more, but they lack an enabling policy environment that would, for example, provide start-up funding and allow them to occupy empty high street retail space.

These issues have moved rapidly to centre-stage. In 2024, António Guterres, the UN secretary general, talked about the lethal collusion between fossil fuel companies and the advertising industry. He called it 'Mad Men fuelling the madness', and accused the oil and gas industry of spending billions of dollars on 'distorting the truth, deceiving the public and sowing doubt'. He added:

> I also call on countries to act. Many governments restrict or prohibit advertising for products that harm human health – like tobacco. Some are now doing the same with fossil fuels. I urge every country to ban advertising from fossil fuel companies.[28]

Does that sound like a big ask? In practice, it may prove as simple as making clear and implementing what is already implicit in current guidelines overseen by the Advertising Standards Authority, the UK industry-funded self-regulatory body. These state that: 'Advertising must not encourage behaviour grossly prejudicial to the protection of the environment.'[29]

The activities of fossil fuel companies, hard-to-abate sectors like aviation, and the heavily promoted shift to driving SUVs, whose high emissions have cancelled out pollution gains made elsewhere, all seem to fail the hurdle set of not encouraging behaviour grossly prejudicial to the environment. Following the precedent of ending tobacco advertising in order to promote public health, the UK House of Lords Environment Committee report into behaviour change in October 2022 recommended that: 'The Government should introduce measures to regulate advertising of high-carbon and environmentally damaging products.'[30]

In 2021, the Behavioural Insights Team, then a unit in Whitehall known more popularly as the 'nudge' unit, published the report *Net Zero: Principles for Successful Behaviour Change Initiatives* that concluded: 'We do not have time to nudge our way to net zero ...'. It went on to say:

> Looking at past government-led initiatives, significant societal behaviour changes related to, for instance, reductions in harm from smoking, increasing worker or motor vehicle safety or uptake of vaccinations have all involved taxes, bans, mandates and other regulatory measures beyond soft persuasion.[31]

In a 2023 report, *How to Build a Net Zero Society*, the same unit, now part of Nesta (the former non-departmental public body turned independent 'innovation agency') recommended the regulation of advertising and greenwash, saying that the UK should, 'in addition to cracking down on all forms of greenwashing, follow other countries' lead by restricting advertising of high-emitting sectors'.[32] This is one way to tackle the problem at source by reducing artificially stimulated, or 'induced', overconsumption. Given many would rather block adverts anyway, and the difficulty of changing infrastructure, ad controls could be an easy, even popular, political win.

A GREEN NEW DEAL

Infrastructural change is needed too, and here Labour's commitment to renewables and to create a new, publicly owned renewable energy company, Great British Energy, has been widely welcomed. It falls far short, though, of a sufficiently scaled and properly funded Green New Deal, whose popularity would come through nation-wide job creation, reskilling, home energy efficiency retrofits, lower energy bills and reduced national dependence on imported gas for heating.

The Green New Deal is a policy package designed to ensure a dynamic economy while delivering a rapid, socially fair, low-carbon transition to avoid climate breakdown.[33] It involves large-scale public investment that pays for itself through the creation of 'green-collar' jobs and clean economic activity across sectors ranging from housing to transport, energy and agriculture. The Green New Deal utilises readily available, mature technologies for household energy retrofit, energy generation, and electric, mass transit and active travel alternatives. Together, the approach harnesses a wide range of science and technology skills and incorporates training through mass apprenticeship programmes.

Widespread health and well-being benefits also come from its reduced pollution, healthier homes, active travel and lower energy costs. It is intended as a package for Labour's longed-for economic revival. At the same time, it delivers energy and climate security, and insulation from the geo-political shocks of global fossil fuel markets. It's an approach that would seem to tick all the boxes for Labour: a clean, cost-effective economic reboot for Britain, welcomed for its multiple positive effects by businesses, unions, and anti-poverty and environmental groups alike.

But Starmer's Labour, like the Conservatives before it, has restricted the scope for action by self-imposed and mostly arbitrary public spending limits. Research by the London School of Economics and Cambridge University in early 2024 said increased public green investment of 1% of GDP was needed, amounting to £26 billion annually, to make up for lost time, and that this would crowd in the equivalent of a further £51 billion from the private sector.[34]

Labour abandoned its initial pledge to invest £28 billion annually on green economic initiatives.[35] So many caveats now surround its plans that it is unclear what the pledge has been reduced to.[36] But the Green New Deal Group estimates that £150 billion of public money per year could be found,[37] relatively easily, to pay for the policy: just over £50 billion from changes to personal and corporate taxes, and closing loopholes to the oil and gas industries that work as hidden subsidies, and £100 billion from placing a green investment requirement on savings vehicles like ISAs and some pension contributions that enjoy tax breaks.

An even more important message to send, however, is about the false economy of failing to make the necessary investment. Failure to act will prove very, very expensive. Research published in May 2024 found that 'the macroeconomic damages from climate change are six times larger than previously thought',[38] and followed earlier work that found the costs of climate damage will be six times higher than the amount needed to invest to keep global heating below the 2°C level.[39] With the Liberal Democrats stronger in parliament and positioning themselves as bolder on the environment than Labour, plus the Green Party proposing a £40 billion annual public spending plan that would finance a Green New Deal programme, there is surely scope for cross-parliamentary work to align public investment with practical necessity.

In late 2024, energy secretary Ed Miliband won plaudits for a series of planning, funding and grid reforms that removed numerous obstacles to the roll-out of renewable energy.[40] Some doubts were expressed about potential funding going to ineffective and expensive carbon capture and storage, seen as an encouragement and subsidy to fossil fuel companies. But the larger issue remains that achieving climate targets is not just about increasing the supply of renewables, vital as it is, but about reducing demand for energy overall to speed the transition, and cutting back on high-carbon energy activities like flying and driving in particular. It means breaking the link that associates the idea of prosperity with increased consumption. It has long been known that growth, per se, can be 'jobless, voiceless, ruthless, rootless and futureless, and thus detrimental to human development'.[41]

SHIFT PREPAREDNESS – GIVE AGENCY AND RESOURCES TO FIRST-RESPONDER LOCAL COMMUNITIES

Perhaps nowhere is the gap between necessary action and urgent reality clearer than in how populations, the UK included, are being left to sink or burn due to a lack of climate preparedness.

In 2021, London was hit by flash floods that caused damage to homes and businesses across the city. In 2022 there was a heatwave, with temperatures hitting 40°C. The following year was the hottest on record globally, and the second hottest in the UK. In 2024, the interim report from the London Climate Resilience Review,[42] commissioned by the mayor of London, found London and the UK more widely to be under-prepared for the current frequency of extreme weather events and severity of climate change. It identified a lethal risk to the population, with certain communities, including low-income households, the elderly, minority groups, children and vulnerable health groups, being most susceptible. It called for a 'step change' in adaptation planning and investment to withstand more intense and frequent heatwaves, rainfall, flash flooding and sea level rise. Labour's challenge, for a party seemingly more comfortable with centralised political control, is that effective climate and disaster preparedness is founded on giving resources and decision-making powers to local communities. Delay in shifting how the UK prepares for disasters will cause avoidable deaths.

Early in 2025, a record number and scale of wildfires burned across Los Angeles, one of the world's richest cities. In the UK, widespread flooding devastated multiple communities in the North of England and elsewhere. Global heating was leading to weather 'whiplash', with temperature rises driving rapid swings in extreme weather.[43]

The London Review called for a multi-agency exercise to test the city's preparedness for extreme heat and requested Whitehall provide more funding and powers to councils. It said improvements in housing standards were needed to ensure resilience, action to prevent major flooding damage and collaborative efforts for a clear strategic vision for climate adaptation.

In 2024, the Climate Change Committee (CCC) analysed the government's national adaptation plan. Reviewing progress to date, the CCC commented that after the Climate Change Act was passed in 2008, 'the country is still strikingly unprepared'. As well as a lack of vision, the plan was failing in terms of governance, investment and monitoring, and needed strengthening to 'avoid locking in additional climate impacts'. It concluded that adaptation policy needs to be reorganised to become a 'fundamental aspect of policy making across all departments'.[44]

How could things possibly be this bad?

For one thing, this Labour government seems to share the previous Conservative government's hostility to climate protest, which makes sounding the alarm, and getting that alarm heard, difficult.

Professor Paul Rogers says that 'This overall elite response can be characterised as "keeping the lid on things" – or "liddism".' He says the strategy is pervasive, accumulates, and involves intense efforts to 'avert problems and suppress them should they arise'.[45]

But global warming is already proving that it can burn through or wash away any lid that elites might try to place on it. So how can communities, as first responders in any disaster, best prepare?

The answer can be found not only in the deep knowledge and experience of the humanitarian relief community, but in the UK's own not so distant past. It is about building resilience into infrastructure, but also having the network of local human relationships and assets in place before disaster strikes, and having people know and rehearse what to do.[46]

On the night of Saturday 31 January 1953, coastal communities of eastern England experienced an unprecedented spring tidal surge 18 feet above sea level, accompanied by hurricane force winds, reaching 126 m.p.h. Flooding killed hundreds in the English counties of Lincolnshire, Norfolk, Suffolk and Essex, 40,000 were left homeless and 160,000 acres of farmland were ruined by sea water.

But what prevented things from being much worse, argues Ken Worpole, writer on landscape and public policy, was the 'extraordinary way that so many individuals and local organisations swung into action in the middle of the night to rescue neighbours and near neighbours.'[47] Almost everyone, it seems, back then was a member of some local club or society, and people were in networks and in the habit of looking out for each other.

Things are different now, but one overriding characteristic of that terrible night in 1953 can be seen still today in disasters ranging from the Grenfell Tower atrocity to the Covid pandemic and the impacts of worsening weather extremes. In the face of failure of officially guided measures for pre-disaster preparedness, disaster response and post-disaster recovery, it is the communities affected themselves who are typically the first responders to disaster and the foundation for recovery. But invariably, these are communities that have not been resourced, equipped, given sufficient agency and control, or worse, been actively undermined, to best perform that role.

Labour should recognise and act on this reality. The remote, often authoritarian response of top-down, official 'civil contingency' planning could be re-engineered to create a genuinely civil society, locally organised, and a properly resourced approach to adaptation, disaster preparedness and response. Not only will this be more effective, it will save countless lives. Experience with citizens' juries, assemblies and commissions shows that when engaged, informed and given agency, the public go further than central government, choosing and supporting more ambitious policies likely to match the true scale of the problem being faced.[48]

The current local vacuum –with some existing bodies not meeting for years – has led to an independent initiative to establish 'climate emergency centres' across the UK, using empty buildings as community hubs to build resilience to climate and social crises.[49] Such networks can fill gaps at national and local government level, but despite being highly willing, are poorly resourced and barely recognised by government.

THREE KEYS TO SURVIVE AND THRIVE

It's hot, and getting hotter. Both in and beyond party politics, there is growing support for action. This is both necessary and possible.

We need (1) a culture shift around overconsumption and the behaviour of the polluter elite, and (2) an infrastructural shift away from an economy over-dependent on fossil fuels; (3) communities also need strengthening to look after themselves better when inevitable climate extremes strike.

These three elements are not a comprehensive or exclusive plan, but they are key to giving us any chance of holding on to a liveable climate and society. In other words, 'three shifts, or we're out'.

ENDNOTES

1.   Robert F. Kennedy 'Remarks at the University of Kansas' John F. Kennedy Presidential Library and Museum, Boston 18 March 1968 www.jfklibrary. org.

2.   Ethan Shone and Ruby Lott-Lavigna 'Finance Firms Gave Labour £2m in Two Years before Banker Bonuses U-Turn' Open Democracy 1 February 2024 www.opendemocracy.net.

3.   'Banks Could Offer More Large Mortgages as Labour Urges Regulators to Relax Rules' This is Money 17 January 2025 www.thisismoney.co.uk.

4.   'Mission-Driven Government' Labour Party www.labour.org.uk.

5.   'Housing Must Take Priority over Nature, Says Starmer in Green Belt Reform Plan' *The Guardian* 12 December 2024 www.theguardian.com.

6.   Hannah Gray and James W. Kelly 'Tenants Call for Rent Controls in Demonstration' *BBC News* 14 December 2024 www.bbc.co.uk.

7.   'Budget 2024: Green Campaigners Describe Chancellor's Fuel Duty Freeze as "Utterly Nonsensical"' *Sky News* 30 October 2024 news.sky.com.

8.   *Planetary Health Check Report 2024* Potsdam Institute for Climate Impact Research, Postdam www.planetaryhealthcheck.org.

9.   '2024 Is on Track to Be Hottest Year on Record as Warming Temporarily Hits 1.5°C' World Meteorological Organization 11 November 2024 www. wmo.int.

10. 'Global Carbon Budget 2024' Global Carbon Budget www.globalcarbon budget.org.

11. Donatella Meadows et al. *The Limits to Growth: A Report for the Club of Rome's Project on the Predicament of Mankind* Universe, New York 1972.

12. Graham Turner 'A Comparison of "The Limits to Growth" with 30 Years of Reality' *Global Environmental Change* 18 (August 2008) pp. 397–411.

13. Kennedy 'Remarks at the University of Kansas'.

14. Danilo Brozović 'Societal Collapse: A Literature Review' *Futures* 145 (January 2023).

15. 'Special Report: Global Warming of 1.5°C' Intergovernmental Panel on Climate Change, Geneva 2018.

16. Damian Carrington '"We Need Dramatic Social and Technological Changes": Is Societal Collapse Inevitable?' *The Guardian* 28 December 2024 www.theguardian.com.

17. Helen Corbett 'Starmer Not Telling People How to Live to Reach New Emissions Goal' *The Independent* 12 November 2024 www.independent. co.uk.

18. See Andrew Simms and Leo Murray *Badvertising: Polluting Our Minds and Fuelling Climate Chaos* Pluto Press, London 2024.

19. See Badvertising www.badverts.org.

20. See 'Edinburgh Introduces Landmark Ban on Advertisements for Fossil Fuels and Arms Manufacturers' Badvertising 29 May 2024 www.badverts. org.

21. See 'Stockholm Region Bans Fossil Fuel Advertising' Badvertising 23 January 2024 www.badverts.org.

22. See 'Sheffield Kicks out Polluting Ads in Groundbreaking New Policy' Badvertising 19 March 2024 www.badverts.org.

23. 'Sixth Assessment Report 2022: Working Group III Mitigation of Climate Change – Summary for Policymakers' Intergovernmental Panel on Climate Change, Geneva www.ipcc.ch.

24. *2021 Progress Report to Parliament* Climate Change Committee, London www.theccc.org.uk.

25. *Net Zero by 2050: A Roadmap for the Global Energy Sector* International Energy Agency, Paris 2021.

26. Noel Cass 'Why Leaving Climate Policy to Behaviour Change Will Never Be Fair' Centre for Research into Energy Demand Solutions, Oxford 30 March 2022 www.creds.ac.uk.

27. Peter Newell, Freddie Daley and Michelle Twena *Changing Our Ways: Behaviour Change and the Climate Crisis* Cambridge Sustainability Commission on Scaling Behaviour Change, Cambridge 2021.

28. António Guterres *Secretary-General's Special Address on Climate Action 'A Moment of Truth'* United Nations, New York 5 June 2024 www.un.org.

29. See 'The Environment: Misleading Claims and Social Responsibility in Advertising' Advertising Standards Authority 10 February 2023 www.asa.org.uk.

30. '*In Our Hands: Behaviour Change for Climate and Environmental Goals* 1st Report of Session 2022–23 Environment and Climate Change Committee, London www.parliament.uk.

31. Behavioural Insights Team, *Net Zero: Principles for Successful Behaviour Change Initiatives* Department for Business, Energy and Industrial Strategy, London 2021.

32. Behavioural Insights Team *How to Build a Net Zero Society* National Endowment for Science, Technology and the Arts, London 2023.

33. See The Green New Deal Group www.greennewdealgroup.org and Ann Pettifor *The Case for the Green New Deal* Verso, London 2020.

34. Dimitri Zenghelis et al. *Boosting Growth and Productivity in the United Kingdom through Investments in the Sustainable Economy* Grantham Research Institute on Climate Change and the Environment, London School of Economics, London 2024.

35. Kiran Stacey and Fiona Harvey 'Labour Cuts £28bn Green Investment Pledge by Half' *The Guardian* 8 February 2024 www.theguardian.com.

36. 'What Happened to Labour's £28bn for Green Projects?' *BBC News* 8 February 2024 www.bbc.co.uk.

37. 'How to Pay for a Green New Deal' The Green New Deal Group 4 March 2024 www.greennewdealgroup.org.

38. Adrien Bilal and Diego R. Känzig *The Macroeconomic Impact of Climate Change: Global vs. Local Temperature* Working Paper 32450 National Bureau of Economic Research Cambridge, MA May 2024.

39. Maximilian Kotz, Anders Levermann and Leonie Wenz 'The Economic Commitment of Climate Change' *Nature* 628 (2024) pp. 551–557.

40. 'Government Unveils New Powers to Approve Onshore Wind Farms' *BBC News* 13 December 2024 www.bbc.co.uk.

41. *Human Development Report 1996* United Nations Development Programme, New York 1996.

42. Emma Howard Boyd, George Leigh and Johanna Sutton *London Climate Resilience Review Interim Report* Greater London Authority, London 2024.

43. *2024 Summary Report* Global Water Monitor www.globalwater.online.

44. *2023 Progress Report to Parliament* Climate Change Committee, London www.theccc.org.uk.

45. Paul Rogers 'A Tale of Two Paradigms' Open Democracy 28 June 2009 www.opendemocracy.net; Paul Rogers 'Beyond "Liddism": Towards Real Global Security' Open Democracy 1 April 2010 www.opendemocracy.net.

46. Andrew Simms, David Boyle and Lindsay Mackie *Unprepared: The Case for Community Control of Civil Contingency Plans* New Weather Institute 2024 www.newweather.org.

47. Ken Worpole *The Great Tide of 31 January 1953* Open Democracy 25 January 2013 www.opendemocracy.net.

48. Rebecca Willis *Building the Political Mandate for Climate Action* Green Alliance, Lancaster 2018 https://green-alliance.org.uk.

49. See Climate Emergency Centre https://climateemergencycentre.co.uk.

THE OUTCOMES

Labour According to Morgan McSweeney

Emma Burnell

> There's no such thing as Starmerism and there never will be.
>
> Keir Starmer

These words are quoted in *Get In: The Inside Story of Labour under Starmer* by Patrick Maguire and Gabriel Pogrund.[1] They were said, somewhat testily, by Keir Starmer to Len McCluskey and Jon Trickett as they tried to calm the storm over the suspension of Jeremy Corbyn from the Labour Party. The book builds a narrative of the leadership of – well – Morgan McSweeney.

Ostensibly, the book is about Keir Starmer. But in reality, it's about McSweeney's plan to change the Labour Party in order to get it elected in service of the kinds of voters it once took for granted. For this, McSweeney needed an electable party leader. According to the book, it is McSweeney who chose his candidate – not the candidate who chose his strategist.

MCSWEENEYISM IS DEFINED BY WHAT IT IS NOT

McSweeney's view is that many on the left are far too willing to subjugate everything – including morality – to ideology. He has a convincing diagnosis of the dangerous tunnel vision of a certain way of doing leftism. For example, he was disgusted at the way vulnerable people were failed in Lambeth in the 1970s, 1980s and 1990s 'by an ideological cult'[2] who allowed child abuse to run rampant in the borough's children's homes and who saw any criticism of what was happening as politically – rather than morally – motivated.

The Labour Party needed to change out of this self-defeating, voter-repelling, aggressively defensive posture. It needed to change a lot. And it needed to change to win. And winning is an essential driver for political change. All the flowery speeches in the world won't change a single life for the better if you do not achieve power.

And a bit of ruthlessness doesn't go amiss in any pursuit of victory. In particular, a ruthless focus on the voters over party membership. Many Labour members would also agree with McSweeney that it is the voters who matter. In a democracy, parties have to meet the voters at least halfway. To be virtuous and powerless is not the role of a political party.

Throughout *Get In*, there are many good reasons why McSweeney has been repelled by the behaviour of the left. The example of Lambeth's children's homes is a particularly egregious one of an inability to self-reflect causing actual real-world harm. So was the antisemitism crisis in the party. Corbyn's inability to accept blame, back down and apologise – something it seemed that the Starmer leadership were pretty desperate for him to do – showed an inability to work for the good of the politics of the whole party and country rather than for the sake of a faction. The things that turned McSweeney's stomach turned plenty of others', too.

In many ways, what McSweeney did was necessary to bring the Labour Party back into the service of the British people. But one thing that jumps out when reading *Get In* is that McSweeney is just as fanatically obsessed with the hard left as the hard left are with Blairites (a broad term generally thrown at anyone not 100% behind the Corbyn project). He has his own brittle tunnel vision which often causes at least as much damage to the party as those he is seeking to expunge. It is not the ideology that is dangerous with any fanatic – it's the fanaticism. Discipline within a party is important. But it has to be even-handed to truly be discipline. Otherwise, it's just power – unevenly wielded and unjustly applied. And power that ignores poor behaviour because it is done by 'one of us' is power badly wielded on behalf of the powerful – not in aid of the powerless – no matter how radical or moderate the cause.

FACTIONALISM IS SELF-HARM

On election day in 2017 in the marginal constituency of Ilford North, you could see hundreds of people in Momentum and Corbyn T-shirts working to get Wes Streeting elected. Streeting is about as far from a Corbynite as it's possible to be. But these activists knew that getting Labour candidates elected was important for their politics, whoever they were. They poured into their nearest marginal (identified through a Momentum-run app) despite misgivings they may have had about the candidate. This is the better side of factionalism: the organisation of internal groups of people to campaign for the party.

An obvious example of the dark and self-harming side of factionalism boiled over at a crunch moment during the 2024 election campaign. The party's political grid had designated this 'NHS Week', but all anyone was talking about was the deselection of a number of candidates and sitting MPs. There was a public and media focus on the deselection of Corbynite economist Faiza Shaheen standing in Chingford and Woodford Green (CAWG) and on Diane Abbott – the first black female MP and stalwart of the Labour left long before Corbynism was a thing.

CAWG activists were divided over the treatment of Shaheen, but a significant number were upset at her treatment – upset enough to resign their party positions.[3] Shaheen ended up running as an independent, and the vote split, with her receiving almost exactly the same number of votes as the official Labour candidate. The incumbent, Iain Duncan Smith, was returned in a seat whose demographics had been trending toward him losing it for years.

But the treatment of Shaheen was not nearly as contentious as the treatment of Diane Abbott.

Abbott had been unwell, and rumours had been swirling that she was minded to step down as an MP. In the Corbyn leadership, she had been shadow home secretary, a peak she was unlikely to return to.

She had also been suspended from the party for a terribly worded letter[4] to the *Observer* that sought to diminish the impact of antisemitism and anti-traveller racism, likening them to the treatment of those with red hair.

What is now known is that the investigation had been concluded in December 2023 and Abbott had accepted a formal warning and undergone mandatory training. She had quietly done what was needed to have the whip restored and – it was widely assumed – to then finish her career as a Labour MP in 2024. However, someone jumped the gun, briefing *The Times*[5] that Abbott was to be blocked as a candidate.

Briefing about just how clever and politically 'hard' they are has become something of a perennial problem for Starmer's team. The desperate desire for them not just to act tough, but to be seen to do so by favoured journalists backfired spectacularly. The outrage over the treatment of Abbott – whom Starmer had been lauding after disgusting comments by Tory donor Frank Hester just days before this briefing – was too much even for Starmer's shock troops to counter, and after a bruising week of distraction, Abbott was accepted as a candidate. This suggests that those doing the briefing were significantly less clever than they were trying to portray themselves.

The campaign continued, but these incidents left a bad taste in the mouths of many activists at the contempt with which they felt they were treated by a small cabal around the leadership.

The public had been shown a party that – despite a much stronger public-facing appearance – still had significant divisions.

However, Labour activists were far from the most demoralised. At the 2024 election campaign, morale among Tory activists was already low following scandal after scandal, including 'partygate' and the Dominic Cummings' trip to Barnard Castle, as well as the disastrous and short-lived leadership of Liz Truss. It was not helped by an inept campaign that included astonishingly stupid mistakes such as Sunak leaving the D-Day commemoration early and a number of Tory MPs and staffers 'betting' on the election date.

The Tories behaved so badly that the factional behaviour from McSweeney and his team (that reached something of an apogee during the 2024 candidate selections) had less impact on the immediate morale of activists during a short campaign Labour activists thought they could win, although the success of independent and Green candidates positioning themselves to Labour's left (not least Jeremy Corbyn himself in Islington North) was a warning shot that Labour was clipping its own wings.

There will, however, be an impact on the morale of Labour activists in the longer term – not just those who belong to the faction that has been on the sharp end of deselections, but on those who don't, but who do feel that having a better internal process is important.

For example, John McTernan is a former political secretary to Tony Blair, a renowned political bruiser and factional fighter. If anyone in the world beyond Blair himself has earned the moniker 'Blairite', it is McTernan, and yet he wrote an article for the *Spectator* titled 'Diane Abbott Has Been Treated Abysmally'.[6] This feeling was widespread across the party, with Starmer's (sometimes uncomfortable and separately elected) deputy, Angela Rayner, also speaking out, and saying that Diane Abbott should be allowed to stand for Labour.

The leadership didn't just pick an unnecessary fight; they lost it too. But this was about far more than one selection, one woman, one fight. It was about the culture of the Labour Party.

PARTY CULTURE MATTERS

Human beings are tribal. Political people especially so. But this tribalism also creates a protectionism of one's own that, at best, tunes out and, at worst, turns against any criticism of a leader.

This is not a left/right divide in Labour. Those who criticised Corbyn supporters for being blind to his faults get angry with those who criticise Starmer, and vice versa. It's a natural human instinct that is heightened by the emotional needs politics can fulfil for people.

It is worth remembering that whoever is in charge of the Labour Party, they and their team have frequently bent and broken the rules in ways that benefit whichever factions back them. This is not a defect of the right or left of the party, but of the way the party is set up and has long learned to behave. It is a defect of power and how it changes us. It is a defect the party should recognise and embed processes to deal with, but never does.

In the same way that parties elected under first-past-the-post have little reason to change the voting system, those who get their hands on the levers of power inside the party have little incentive to change the process that got them there. They might be wrong, short-termist and short-sighted, but it is important to understand that compulsion in the moment. Trying to make sure that our politics outlast ourselves is a strong motivational driver. If one has a tool to make that happen, however ugly, the temptation is to use it. But it also leaves that tool available to those who will inevitably beat you as the wheel turns.

There is a sense among many Labour members that the rules are unclear, both in their written form and their interpretation. And all factions have, at times, felt the rulebook was used not as a tool for sensible, effective party management, but of factional oppression. This was felt by the centrists under Corbyn, and is felt by the left now.

It's not new for a faction who were once down to enact their own extreme interpretations of the rules when they come to the top. The left will almost certainly be back in charge of the party one day. And since Starmer's premiership has had a wobbly start, it may well be that the wheel will turn faster than anticipated by McSweeney and his team. They may find themselves at the sharp end of rules they used ruthlessly against others.

All of which should make the conversation about defactionalising the implementation of the rules and bureaucracy of the party more – not less – urgent.

The Labour Party is – or, at least, should be – a broad church. It has always been a party that spans the left side of the political spectrum from the centre to the hard left. It contains Catholic socialists who oppose abortion and libertarian socialists who oppose any restrictions on bodily autonomy. There are unilateralists and multilateralists, gender-critical feminists and trans rights activists, Blue Labour social conservatives and ultra-liberals, people who want to abolish private schools and people who send their children there. Many members have very strong views on all of these topics and will fight to get their views adopted as party policy. But in doing so, no one should argue that those who oppose them within the party have no right to do so or no space on the broad left.

However, the rules do not seem to be enforced equally and fairly. Women have been complaining for many years about the inadequacy of the system around complaints of sexual harassment and abuse. There are complaints from many members around political differences tipping over into abusive behaviour, and the 2023 Forde Report[7] highlighted areas of problematic behaviour in the party that went beyond the headlines around the antisemitism crisis and which still need to be dealt with.

So what do party members need from each other when it comes to the pact they make on joining up and the rules they agree to abide by?

They need to know that these rules and their application are sensible. That their application is fair and balanced and that punishments are not arbitrary or unjust. The Labour Party should be run as members would like to see it run the country – not by fiat or dictatorship, but not 'anything goes' either. There needs to be agreement from those leading and those led what it means to be a party member, both in terms of rights and responsibilities.

The way the Labour Party is organised, with endless internal elections at branch, Constituency Labour Party (CLP) and regional level, as well as onto national bodies such as the National Executive Committee (NEC), National Constitutional Committee, Conference Arrangements Committee and the National Policy Forum (and probably many more forgotten here), means that a great deal of the political energy of Labour Party members is spent in opposing each other rather than fighting for the party against the parties it needs to defeat to win elections. It shouldn't be that way.

When people are volunteering their time and effort without an expectation of favour or reward (which is true for the vast majority of members of all parties), there is an obvious need to defend our own reasons for doing so. This can easily become blind faith or slide into a kind of defensiveness that means that the right questions aren't being asked.

But this not only misses that those with the greatest skills may come from a different faction, but also denies the wider application of the skills of the membership.

Take the NEC, for example. This is the body that acts as the governing board of the Labour Party. Its members are supposed to act much as charity trustees do to oversee the governance of the organisation. But how they are chosen affects how the NEC behaves. It is a body made up of some people appointed by the trade unions and socialist societies, some chosen by the Parliamentary Labour Party (PLP, appointed by the leadership, and so loyal to them), and others directly elected by the membership. Elections to the NEC inevitably become a factional bunfight.

Charities often advertise for trustees with accounting skills. The Labour Party is not a charity, but has many similarities. It is run on the goodwill of passionate volunteers who come from a huge range of backgrounds with a joint cause. Sadly, though, it is probable that no one has ever stood up in a Labour meeting to say, 'I am a forensic accountant and wish to utilise these skills to properly interrogate the finances of the party.' But these are precisely the kind of skills that would be most useful on the NEC. Instead, members are deluged with messages of support for one faction or another, or policy positions that have absolutely nothing to do with the governance of the party. Members may deeply agree with a candidate's views on Gaza, but fail to ask how this will help them interrogate the party's accounts and governance procedures. They are never encouraged to do so.

Political parties are made up of people who are statistical outliers. Fewer than 2% choose to pay dues to a political party.[8] But these are also people who are civic-minded by their nature – seeking to give something to national and local political life through activism. And while electoral campaigning is and always will be an important part of that activity, the jealous guarding of roles within the party and the barriers to members offering those skills to be put to good use mean that all too often members are simply treated as leafletting fodder. They not only find themselves unable to give the best of their skills to the party, but often feel they are resented for trying.

But there are signs that Labour can get this right. In the run-up to, during and immediately after the 2024 general election, the Labour Party's training unit found innovative and clever ways to engage with members and make them feel a valued part of the team. That they released a (very funny) video[9] which leaned into the fact that during the campaign they had managed to make 'Gail from Labour' a meme showed a sense of personality and willingness to humanise Labour staff that tight discipline doesn't always allow for. It wasn't factional – it wasn't even political – it just let Labour members feel valued and in on the action and the joke. It showed a section of the party that was comfortable with its relationship with the members. It felt like the staff had looked at what Momentum had achieved in its heyday, and instead of dismissing it, had incorporated the best of that digital relationship-building.

After the 2024 landslide, there is a sense from some that nothing needs to change, but, as Labour are already finding, it isn't as simple as that. If Labour wants to continue to be a successful party, then it will need reform to modernise, professionalise and de-factionalise. This isn't instead of putting the country first. This should not be the choice. Labour must have the skills to govern both the country and itself. And only by doing the latter well is it likely to succeed in running the country well in the longer term.

This is why being in government makes this more – not less – urgent. Look at what brought down the Tories. The chaos of that party during 2015–24 didn't come from nowhere. It came from excessive factionalism leading to the rise of deeply unsuitable people to high office, culminating in the rule-breaking of Boris Johnson and the economic trust-breaking of Liz Truss. This didn't happen because they were the best the Tories have to offer – Labour isn't that lucky. It happened because the internal politics of the Tory Party was allowed to fester. That allowed the rot to set in, and that rot destroyed it. Labour must do what is needed to avoid that fate.

MCSWEENEY CAN SUCCEED, AND WE SHOULD HOPE HE DOES

It is not enough to only seek power without an end. Power is a tool, not a goal. So while 'protest or power' is a question Keir Starmer rightly answers by choosing the latter, it is actually a choice between methods – not ends.

It is a fair critique of Labour – particularly under Corbyn – that it has too often forgotten that seeking power is the better tool for social change than protest.

But Labour must have both power and a purpose.

If Labour is to succeed with a mission-led approach to government, it has to have a mission, and that mission must be understood and adopted by its membership. The policies that help it achieve that are secondary. Too many in the Labour Party become wedded to concepts rather than outcomes. Good politics avoids that. For example, nationalisation isn't an end in itself. It's one way of ensuring the national wealth is more fairly shared between citizens.

If Labour can find another way to do that – fine. It is the goal that matters. One can be pathway-neutral if the destination is clear.

But in all the discussion of the Starmer project, in all the talk of missions, in all the sense that the party is being led by serious people with a serious project for the country in mind, we do not see a sense of the real purpose of government. Nowhere is there an explanation of what it's all for beyond winning elections. Even in politics, winning elections is not everything. Power with a purpose is great. OK – tell us the purpose.

Because if Labour cannot articulate a goal, there are others out there who can and who will. And if it turns out that McSweeney's clarity of vision began and ended with his changing the Labour Party, it may well be that his usefulness to Starmer and the party will run out.

For now, credit where credit is due. McSweeney is – by all accounts – a superlative campaigner. To effect lasting change, Labour needs to win again in 2029, and his sense of permanent campaigning is not a bad one for a party that needs to stay in constant contact with voters and their needs.

But there is a difference between campaigning from opposition and doing so while in government. If Labour cannot get beyond the pure campaigning mindset of opposition, if it cannot articulate a vision of the journey it wants to take this country on, if it cannot deliver and show itself to be delivering, then all the internal strong-garming in the world won't help it.

All too often, the people behind Starmer – and McSweeney in particular – seem not to see that changing the way politics is done – to and with each other – matters, that poor culture and poor behaviour are poor in and of themselves – and not excusable when it's 'one of us' exhibiting it. And the large number of people who have been poorly treated or cast aside should worry McSweeney. Not least because somewhere out there will be someone on the other side who will be doing just as he did during the Corbyn years; sitting on the sidelines and plotting what comes next. And if it is as bloody and as brutal as he has been – well, that's politics.

As Labour's membership falls, the less the party will hear from a variety of voices in communities across the country. And however attractive it might sound to live free of challenge, doing so will fundamentally blunt its ability to make an argument. That's no good to anyone. Because if Labour's leadership think the challenge they get inside the party is tough, wait until they have to face the voting public at the next election.

There has been a clunkiness in the way Starmer's team have dealt with internal dissent that has made this an inward-looking storyline when it didn't need to be. To pivot to leading the country, Starmer and McSweeney need to loosen their own focus on their power games with the membership – from the PLP to the grassroots. Let go a little. Not completely – every party needs discipline – but they should recognise that the vice-like grip has gone from necessary control to a chokehold. People who are a long way off from wanting there to be no rules are starting to feel uncomfortable about quite how much control is being exerted.

These weren't things that were going to lose Labour the election in 2024. There wasn't much that would. But as they persist, they might well be things that stop the party being an effective internal alliance. And that will have a long-term impact on its ability to govern well and remain in office.

Forget factional infighting. Forget which side you're on. Forget the noise. Look again at the cover of Labour's 2024 manifesto, and think about that single word emblazoned across it: CHANGE.

It's never too late to think about all the possibilities that word allows for.

ENDNOTES

1. Patrick Maguire and Gabriel Pogrund *Get In: The Inside Story of Labour under Starmer* Bodley Head, London 2025.
2. Keir Starmer, quoted in ibid p. 32.
3. The author's father was one of them. He stepped down as a branch secretary, and ended up volunteering his time for the party in a different constituency.
4. Letter from Diane Abbott to *The Observer* 23 April 2023 www.theguardian.com.
5. Patrick Maguire and Steven Swinford 'Diane Abbott to Be Banned from Standing for Labour' *The Times* 28 May 2024 www.thetimes.com.
6. John McTernan 'Diane Abbott Has Been Treated Abysmally' *The Spectator* 29 May 2024 www.spectator.co.uk.

7. Martin Forde *The Forde Report* Labour Party National Executive Committee, London 19 July 2022 www.labour.org.uk.

8. See 'Research Briefing: Membership of Political Parties' 31 August 2022 House of Commons Library, London www.commonslibrary.parliament.uk.

9. See 4 July 2024 tweets at www.x.com/Labour training.

The Unions Make Us Strong

Gregor Gall

For as long as I can remember, as a socialist activist and industrial relations academic, all shades of left-wing critics of Labour have always reminded us that the trade unions founded Labour in the form of the Labour Representation Committee in 1900. Their point is that Labour as a political party is no longer – and has not been for a long time – the party of the unions. And, by implication, neither is Labour the party of the organised working class or even of the working class itself. For many, there's a fundamental truth to these facts. For others, they are factoids. But what flows from this leftist critique is less laudable, namely the suggestion that Labour should and can become this party again – *a*, if not *the*, party of unions and workers.

This puts unions on a pedestal, which is problematic for several reasons. First, unions represent a specific form of political agency seeking labourism rather than socialism itself. They are organisations which are long-standing largely because of their conservative, centralised and bureaucratic tendencies. Labourism is a specific form of social democracy emanating from the unions, seeking state intervention in the processes of the market in order to ameliorate their outcomes. Second, unions represent all sections of the labour movement, including those that are often disparagingly referred to as its 'backward sections' – that is, those that do not hold progressive and egalitarian views in terms of race, gender, manufacture of armaments, and the environment.

Such points seem somewhat facile when contemplating the much-reduced influence of affiliated unions in Labour today. Harking back to what was, what might have been and what should be in these terms are not pressing agenda items for Labour's 13 affiliated unions.[1] What they seek is the implementation of mild reforms to undo the worst excesses of the neoliberalism of both Labour and Tory governments since 1979. There are few voices at the top of the union movement that call for radical reforms – other than repealing all the anti-unions laws. And they are not able to do much about that.

Radical social democracy and reformism, let alone socialism and revolution, barely get a mention from union leaders. Former National Union of Rail, Maritime and Transport Workers (RMT) general secretary (2021–25) Mick Lynch became one of the few union leaders to openly articulate a coherent social democratic perspective,[2] but the RMT has not been affiliated to Labour for 20 years, and despite Lynch's prominent public profile, it is a small union. Lynch naively called upon Starmer to reveal his 'true self'. Starmer has done this: he is a social liberal, and not a social democrat. Social liberalism is 'neoliberalism with a heart', a form of neoliberalism with a touch more social conscience than 'normal' neoliberalism.[3] By enabling neoliberalism, it seeks to generate the tax receipts to provide for a minimal level of welfare state. Matt Wrack, former Fire Brigades Union (FBU) general secretary (2005–25), was another of the very few union leaders to espouse a genuinely radical worldview within and outside his union. But the FBU is an even smaller union than the RMT, and it is a specific occupational one. Other leaders of much larger left-wing affiliated unions, like the Communication Workers Union (CWU), general secretary Dave Ward, and Unite, general secretary Sharon Graham, have not set out any such complete and coherent social democratic worldview. They have responded to events inside Labour which affect their members in a piecemeal way. Graham's predecessor, Len McCluskey, only did so when he left office, in the form of his autobiography.[4]

Some may argue that the unions will be bolder in better times, but this is not the time. Such is the current context that must be recognised in order to understand the relationship between the unions, especially the affiliated ones, and Starmer's Labour Party. The union with Labour may not make the unions much stronger, but paradoxically, without it they may be much weaker still.

STATE OF THE UNIONS

It would be easy to think 'the unions are back' and on the 'up' following the 2022–23 fightback against the cost-of-living crisis which saw the highest level of strike action for 40 years. Indeed, it would be easy to think 'the working class is back', as Lynch proclaimed in the autumn of 2022. Of course, the working class never went away, but what is more significant is that the primary organisations of the working class, the unions, have not received any boost from their resistance to the cost-of-living crisis. Union membership fell by 200,000 in 2022, with only a 90,000 increase in 2023. Union density – the proportion of workers in unions – was just 22.4% in 2023, compared to 32.4% in 1995 and 55% in 1980.[5] One reason for the lack of growth since 2022 is that very few strikes won pay rises of much more than the rate of inflation.[6] Wages were sacrificed during industrial action (the use of strike pay is not widespread), and clawback of falls in the value of real wages since 2010 was not achieved. Although the poor might have said they refused to be poor any more, to quote Mick Lynch from that autumn of 2022, that is what continued to happen. Even the RMT experienced membership loss – 81,197 in 2021, 81,543 in 2022 and 78,889 in 2023 – it still claims on its website to be 'Britain's fastest growing union'. Membership participation, judged by turnouts in internal union elections for general secretaries and national executives, remains low at around 10%.

Ironically, this profound weakness has not necessarily made all in the leadership of the union movement more moderate. Some, like Unite's Sharon Graham, have become more militant so that they have become trenchant critics of Starmer. They recognise that even while pursuing a strike strategy to protect and advance members' pay and conditions,[7] there is a need for state intervention to help equalise the relationship between capital and labour.

During the 2022–23 fightback, it was no surprise that Starmer gave no significant support to unions. He only wished for disputes to be resolved, rather than arguing the unions' case. This is because he believes rising wages cause inflation, and not vice versa. Consequently, and under instruction from Starmer not to, only a handful of Labour MPs were ever seen on picket lines in these disputes. One, Sam Tarry, was sacked from the shadow cabinet and then deselected from standing in the 2024 general election.[8]

One recent attempt, initiated by the RMT and CWU, to provide unions with an effective left-wing political voice, called 'Enough is

Enough', quickly ended up being a damp squib. Initially, it showed greater promise than similar previous attempts such as the Coalition of Resistance and People's Assembly, but despite packed-out and enthusiastic rallies across the country, it was wound up by the unions almost before it had begun.

CONSIDERATIONS ABOUT
THE CONTEMPORARY CONTEXT

To understand the context of the unions' position under a Starmer-led Labour Party and Labour government, it is necessary to take a few steps back in time. More than 50 years ago, sociologist Tony Lane in the *Union Makes Us Strong*[9] argued that labour throughout its whole history – via the unions – innately seeks accommodation with capital, and that Labour cannot and will not be a socialist party. In a controversial piece in *Marxism Today* in 1982, Lane further argued that unions, riven by sectionalism, have never resolved what they are for: short-term sectional economic gain for members, or creating social democracy for all.[10] A decade later, historian Lewis Minkin merely termed the relationship between unions and the Labour Party a 'contentious alliance'.[11] Nevertheless, Lane and Minkin could agree that Labour and the unions were not one and the same, and neither was Labour merely and happily the political arm of the unions.

Although Minkin concerned himself with the 1980s, he could also be taken to be referring to the late 1970s, when conflict between the two different wings of the labour movement was particularly sharp. This was a result of the formal 'Social Contract' between the Trades Union Congress (TUC) and the Labour government. In return for moderating wage demands to control inflation in a situation of economic decline called 'stagflation', the unions would gain certain reforms to employment law and the social wage. This contract ran aground on the rocks of the 'Winter of Discontent' of 1978–79 which helped usher in Thatcher to victory in the May 1979 general election.

Although a long period of being out of office from 1979 did much to rekindle the flames of the romance of the relationship between Labour and the unions, it remained contentious. More importantly, major internal party battles were often eased out of existence by the party leadership's use of the union block vote to outmanoeuvre the more left-wing Constituency Labour Parties. The clamour from the unions was the need to provide an electable Labour to roll back the Tories' attacks. Compromises with – and concessions to – the Labour leadership abounded. This 'new realism', first advanced after Labour's defeat in the 1983 general election, was reinforced within the unions by the defeats of the miners, printers, seafarers and dockers in the mid- to late 1980s.

Come Labour's return to office as 'New' Labour under Blair in 1997, the union–party relationship was, for the Labour leadership, pretty much child's play. Affiliated unions moaned in the run-up to and after the 1997 general election about being only wanted for their donations to the party so that they felt, in the words of then TUC general secretary John Monks, like embarrassing elderly relatives at a family gathering. But they pretty much kept criticism to themselves.

BLAIRISM AND 'NEW' LABOUR

Several left-led unions were wary of Blair, especially after he abolished their sacred Clause Four of the party constitution on public ownership in 1995 and then initiated the creation of the 'third way' social liberal variant of neoliberalism. They naively equated public ownership with socialism, a term itself never mentioned in Labour's founding and enduring constitution of 1918–95. The 1918 Clause Four, often printed on membership cards, and drafted by the famous Fabian social democrats Beatrice and Sidney Webb, read:

> To secure for the workers by hand or by brain the full fruits of their industry and the most equitable distribution thereof that may be possible upon the basis of the common ownership of the means of production, distribution and exchange, and the best obtainable system of popular administration and control of each industry or service.

Blair's new Clause Four read:

> The Labour Party is a democratic socialist party. It believes that by the strength of our common endeavour we achieve more than

we achieve alone, so as to create for each of us the means to realise our true potential and for all of us a community in which power, wealth and opportunity are in the hands of the many, not the few, where the rights we enjoy reflect the duties we owe, and where we live together, freely, in a spirit of solidarity, tolerance and respect.

These left-led unions sought to orientate more toward the likes of Gordon Brown and John Prescott to provide a counterbalance to Blair and his allies, especially Peter Mandelson. But a number of factors meant disagreements were very much kept behind closed doors, if expressed at all. These included the size of the Labour majority in 1997, most of the new intake of Labour MPs being Blairites, the strength of the 'good riddance to the Tories' feeling, not wishing to be blamed for creating difficulties that would give succour to the Tories, and an expanding economy, which allowed for significant increases in public expenditure on welfare.

Significant and overt union opposition did not surface until after the 2005 general election. Despite the introduction of the minimum wage, most unions were disappointed and somewhat angered by Blair on two particular counts. The first was that not only were the Tory anti-union laws kept in place, but Blair boasted in the Foreword to the 1998 'Fairness at Work' White Paper that even after his limited reforms, Britain would still have 'the most lightly regulated labour market of any leading economy in the world'. The second was that to make good on his notion of 'social partnership' between capital and labour, Blair allowed business, through the Confederation of British Industry, to co-determine critical aspects of the statutory procedure for gaining union recognition under the Employment Relations Act 1999 (derived from 'Fairness at Work'). This watered down the 1997 manifesto pledge that 'where a majority of the relevant workforce vote in a ballot for the union to represent them, the union should be recognised'.

Blair believed the Employment Relations Act 1999 was the settled will on industrial relations reform, but the angered affiliated unions worked hard through the National Policy Forum to gain the Warwick Agreement in 2004. It formed the basis of the party's manifesto for the 2005 general election. On paper, some relatively minor gains were made, but not of all of these were implemented, highlighting that the so-called 'union paymasters' of Labour did not control the party or its leadership.

Union opposition was principally led by new leaders of affiliated and unaffiliated unions. They were quickly dubbed the 'awkward squad'.[12] The appellation hid significant differences between them. Though all critical of 'new' Labour, they were split over whether Labour could be won back for the left, or whether a new party of labour needed to be created. RMT general secretary Bob Crow was firmly of the latter view, and was the only significant figure to put effort into doing so.[13]

STARMERISM PRE- AND POST-ELECTION

Some of Blair's ability to control Labour derived from his charisma; some of it derived from his willingness to include people from the soft left, such as Brown and Prescott, in his ruling circle. He promised a 'new Britain' through a 'fair' meritocratic form of neo-liberalism. He was for a considerable time a 'vote-winner' with widespread support within the party and the country. Starmer has no such appealing personality, and is a technocrat. He has administratively expunged the left of all shades from the party, rather than try to work with the more palatable – to him – parts of it. Reeves is no counterbalance as Brown was to Blair. Rayner may yet fulfil her belief that she is 'John Prescott in a skirt' by giving Starmer left-wing cover. Although he has embraced British nationalism to a degree that Blair did not and did not need to, Starmer has promised much less. With the economy in a poor shape compared to the mid- to late 1990s, Starmer has had to promise 'fiscal responsibility' to the markets to suggest that economic growth, not tax rises, is needed to generate more tax revenues.

Compared to 1997, Labour's 2024 victory was loveless and shallow. Prior to the election, Starmer made clear that 'the taps [of public spending] won't be turned on' if Labour won. He effectively dampened down expectations; hence the loveless nature of the landslide. He was supported by the likes of Lynch, who told voters to 'grow up'[14] and make sure a Starmer-led Labour won. Despite Starmer's attempts, there were still some lingering hopes among unions and their members, whether affiliated or not, that Labour would put an end to austerity and begin to take the first steps to rebalancing the economy toward more equitable outcomes.

But for the unions, the 'New Deal for Working People' was the clincher. In their view, it was the one thing that made Labour worth voting for. They had worked long and hard to move it in its entirety from the National Policy Forum to a Green Paper and then to the election manifesto commitment. They largely succeeded. But the consequent Employment Rights Act 2025 saw a further watering down still. It made Starmer's social partnership pledge to be simultaneously both pro-worker and pro-business – as Blair had, but without Blair's panache – seem ever hollower. The settling of long-running pay disputes with doctors and railway workers was not an indication of beneficence, but just removing, for then, inherited problems.

All this places the unions, especially the affiliated ones, in a strange place. The shallowness of the landslide means Starmer is in a weak position, potentially providing the unions with more leverage. That Labour's first budget could be termed 'tax and spend' indicated this. Yet the unions will not want to push Labour too far for fear of not allowing Labour to settle into government after a long spell in opposition, and in the process undoing a Labour government. For the most part, and in Lynch's words, their thinking is that the most right-wing Labour government will always be better than the most left-wing Tory one. This means that the desire of union leaders like Graham, Lynch, Ward and Wrack to hold, in their words, 'Labour's feet to the fire' is difficult to deliver. The old ways of using sponsored MPs, parliamentary groups and motions passed at party conferences are not sufficient anymore (if they ever were).

Unite is, after UNISON, the second largest union and the second largest affiliate. It is the most left-wing of the major affiliated unions. Its position is instructive. Although there were significant strategic differences between Graham and her predecessor, close Corbyn ally Len McCluskey, under Graham, Unite has emerged as the most trenchant critic of Starmer. Graham won the leadership of Unite on a 'back to the workplace' pledge because many members believed McCluskey spent too much of Unite's time and money on Corbyn's Labour with little to show for it in their pay packets. After her election in August 2021, Graham consciously chose not to attend that year's Labour Conference. However, as the general election neared, Graham positioned Unite as the major union critic of Starmer and Reeves, covering an array of issues from public spending, public investment and employment law to welfare benefits. And while Unite under Graham has taken part in Labour's National Policy Forum, it has acted on its own and outside Labour in pursuit of its political objectives with the likes of its 'Unite for a Workers' Economy' and 'Take Back the Power' campaigns. Both targeted, among other issues, fuel poverty. Forcing and winning a vote on a motion to repeal the winter fuel payment cut at the first party conference after the election was notable. No one could now accuse Graham of making Unite abstentionist, or even syndicalist. While some other leaders of affiliated unions may have privately demurred and doubted Starmer's leadership, they have not made this public. Graham has, repeatedly. But for all that, Unite has had no discernible influence on Starmer and Labour.

DISUNITED BROTHERS AND SISTERS

Divisions among the unions, especially the affiliated ones, emanate primarily from which political faction has dominated the union for decades. For example, UNISON and the General and Municipal Workers' Union (GMB) continue to be on the right of the union movement despite changes in full-time leaderships. Through its full-time general secretary, UNISON especially has provided political support to Starmer, even though the left dominates its national executive.[15] However, some divisions do emerge from the composition of union memberships. UNITE and the GMB are argued by many to take stances which are not environmentally progressive, and both support armament manufacture because of the desire to protect their members' jobs in these particular industries. Sexism and misogyny continue to be issues, especially in the GMB and Transport Salaried Staffs Association (TSSA), prompting some other unions, like the Associated Society of Locomotive Engineers and Firemen (ASLEF) and the FBU, to survey their own members to ascertain whether this was a problem in their own unions.

THE BACKWARD MARCH OF LABOUR

Under Starmer, to bastardise Eric Hobsbawm's famous phrase,[16] the backward march of (organised) labour continues. In the late 1970s, Hobsbawm detected a historic inability of unions from the 1950s onwards to maintain their previous dynamism, primarily resulting from changes in intra- and inter-class composition. He termed it the 'forward march of labour halted'. In 50 years, the Labour Party has not helped to put unions into a forward gear. Indeed, recalling Minkin's motto, the union–Labour relationship remains contentious on both sides. With the Labour leadership, Parliamentary Labour Party and Labour Party all having their own independent resources and powerbases, unions have still yet to work out how to mobilise their members to impose their social democratic will on the party in and out office. This is as much a problem for affiliated unions as it is for non-affiliated ones. Some left-led unions make better attempts than others, but there are also some unions which are more or less enthusiastic cheerleaders for Starmer. How long this balance will last will depend on future public sector pay settlements, expenditure on public services, and the fate of the implementation of the measures in the Employment Rights Act 2025. Yet pressure to fall in line to the party leadership's tune once again will undoubtedly happen in good time for the forthcoming 2029 general election.

ENDNOTES

1. Associated Society of Locomotive Engineers and Firemen (ASLEF) for train drivers; Community for all industries/sectors from steel, education and justice to the self-employed; Communication Workers Union (CWU) for post and telecommunications; Fire Brigades Union (FBU) for firefighters and other workers within fire and rescue services; General and Municipal Workers' Union (GMB) for general workers in the public and private sectors; Musicians Union (MU) for performers, writers and teachers; National Union of Mineworkers (NUM); Transport Salaried Staffs Association (TSSA) for road, sea, rail and travel white-collar staff; UNISON for those employed in the public, private or voluntary sectors providing public services; Unite for general workers in the public and private sectors; and the Union of Shop, Distributive and Allied Workers (USDAW) for retail and distributive workers. The RMT disaffiliated in 2004, and the Bakers, Food and Allied Workers Union did so in 2021. The

FBU disaffiliated in 2004, re-affiliating in 2015. The Broadcasting, Entertainment, Communications and Theatre Union disaffiliated in 2017 as a condition of its merger with the larger union Prospect. The largest unaffiliated unions are drawn from the public sector among civil servants, doctors, nurses and teachers.

2. Gregor Gall *Mick Lynch: The Making of a Working-Class Hero* Manchester University Press, Manchester 2024.

3. Gregor Gall 'SNP: Neo-Liberalism with a Heart?' *Scottish Left Review* 87 (June 2015).

4. Len McCluskey *Always Red* OR Books, London 2021.

5. See 'Trade Union Statistics' www.gov.uk. The number of workers covered by collective bargaining has fallen even more precipitously.

6. These were mostly to be found among Unite members in transport (buses, lorry drivers, airport workers) because of a combination of strategic leverage and giving strike pay.

7. After Graham was elected general secretary in August 2021, some 215,000 Unite members had taken strike action in 1,551 disputes by December 2024, where the win rate was 84%. See Suzanne Muna, 'Unite executive discusses challenges under a Labour government' 8 January 2025 www.socialistparty.org.uk.

8. Gall *Mick Lynch.*

9. Tony Lane *The Union Makes Us Strong: The British Working Class, Its Trade Unionism and Politics* Arrow Books, London 1974.

10. Tony Lane 'The Unions: Caught on the Ebb Tide' *Marxism Today* (September 1982) p. 38 www.banmarchive.org.uk.

11. Lewis Minkin *The Contentious Alliance: Trade Unions and the Labour Party* Edinburgh University Press, Edinburgh 1991.

12. Andrew Murray *A New Labour Nightmare: The Return of the Awkward Squad* Verso, London 2003. Among the initial union leaders were Bob Crow (RMT), Jeremy Dear (National Union of Journalists), Andy Gilchrist (FBU), Billy Hayes (CWU), Mick Rix (ASLEF), Mark Serwotka (Public and Commercial Services Union), Derek Simpson (Amicus) and Tony Woodley (Transport and General Workers Union). These were replaced by Dave Ward (CWU), Matt Wrack (FBU) and Len McCluskey (Unite).

13. Gregor Gall *Bob Crow: Socialist, Leader, Fighter* Manchester University Press, Manchester 2017.

14. 'Mick Lynch Says Voters Must "Grow Up" and See Starmer Is Only Alternative' *The Guardian* 24 February 2024 www.theguardian.com.

15. Once in Number Ten, Starmer appointed Claire Stewart, former aide to UNISON general secretary Christina McAnea, as director of trade union relations.

16. Eric Hobsbawm 'The Forward March of Labour Halted?' *Marxism Today* (September 1978) pp. 279–286 www.banmarchive.org.uk.

Biting the Hand That Doesn't Feed Us

Yasmin Alibhai-Brown

I came to Great Britain in 1972, from Uganda, where I was born and raised. Freedom was exhilarating; the new nation was full of optimism and anticipation. In August 1972, Amin ordered Asians to leave Uganda. Within three months, my birthland was ethnically cleansed. And the economy dived. Under British rule, Ugandans had no democratic rights. A decade after independence, a military megalomaniac took charge. Democracy had lasted only a few years.

COMING TO THE COLD MOTHERLAND

At the age of 23, I began a new life in the old Motherland, a place at once familiar and indecipherable. Like other incomers, those early days and years were daunting and also comforting. The country was secure and stable. For me, after Uganda's descent into tyranny, the chance to vote without fear of persecution was precious. Between the 1950s and early 1980s, most immigrants supported Labour, even though, when in power, it had repeatedly maligned them to pacify anti-immigrant forces, which can never be pacified.

The 1960s are much mythologised as a time of cultural liberation from old Blighty's greyness and oppressive values. Those who came to stay never saw it that way. How could we? While the flower power chicks and chaps were lost in drugs and dreams, migrant labour was being exploited, racism stalked swarthy and dusky incomers, and politicians pandered to the voters who demanded an end to immigration from the Caribbean, South East Asia, Africa and other 'coloured' colonies.

In the 1964 general election, Peter Griffiths, the Conservative candidate, stood in Smethwick, a Labour stronghold.[1] Among the Tories' campaign slogans was 'If you want a nigger for your neighbour, vote Labour.' Griffiths denied using the slogan himself, but never denounced those who did. Griffiths won.

But it was a Labour government that was elected, and it was the Labour majority that passed the 1968 Immigration Act. This created a two-tier citizenship structure for overseas British subjects. Those with ancestral connections to the UK – that is, white people – had full entry rights, while non-white British passport holders were subjected to severe restrictions. *The Times* thundered:

The Labour Party has a new ideology. It does not any longer profess to believe in the equality of man. It does not even believe in the equality of British citizens. It believes in the equality of white British citizens.[2]

Just a month after the act was passed, Enoch Powell, the nativist folk hero, made a racist speech in Wolverhampton denouncing 'coloured' immigration and immigrants. The opposition leader Ted Heath expelled him from his shadow cabinet. Two years on, the Conservatives won the 1970 election, ironically, because many of Powell's fanbase believed the party was tougher on immigration than Labour ever would be.[3] Harold Wilson won in 1974. He led a minority government. In spite of labour's discriminatory immigration laws, black and Asian voters stayed loyal. Jena, my mum, and I both rejoiced. Our joy didn't last long.

This long-established democracy could, we learnt, unleash disorderly, xenophobic forces.

Between 1974 and 1979, with a Labour government in power, immigrants went through very hard times.

I remember the fear every time we stepped into a public space. Our neighbours called us cockroaches and threw rubbish at my mum. Eventually, she won them over with humble smiles and offerings of home-made curries.

On 30 January 1978, my son was born in Radcliffe Hospital, Oxford. On that day, Margaret Thatcher moaned on TV about the country being 'swamped' by people of other cultures. I hated her from that moment onward.

Andi Oliver, the musician and celebrated TV chef, recalled her own tormented childhood in Bury St Edmunds in the 1970s:

It was awful ... constant racism and bullying. [At school] every day I would be called all sorts of disgusting names .... A teacher referred to me as 'you people'. I was the only Black girl for 20 miles. So I learned to fight, physically and verbally.[4]

Most ethnic minority families who lived through the late 1960s and 1970s have their own stories of suffering and survival.

LABOUR AND THE BLIGHT OF FAR-RIGHT MOVEMENTS

Since the end of World War Two, liberal Britons have internalised the belief that the UK will never surrender to the far right. Churchill and patriotic citizens beat Hitler; their descendants would see off new-generation Nazis. It's a long-standing national delusion. Throughout modern history, neo-fascist and racist parties have garnered strong support across the UK. And their biggest moments do seem to come when Labour is running the country. The left needs to explore why this happens. And why the party's responses are so often weak, abject and dishonourable.

When Wilson and then Callaghan ran the country, the National Front became bigger, louder and more vehement than ever before. I went on the anti-NF demo in Southall on the eve of the 1979 general election, where Blair Peach was killed by the Special Patrol Group. I became a fierce, unbounded activist after that march.[5] I still am. Few politicians stood up for us then.

Under Labour during 2005–10, the British National Party, originally a small operation, gained saliency and presence. In 2009, the BBC invited the BNP leader Nick Griffith onto a *Question Time* panel, which gave him respectability.[6] During the 2000s, the BNP won more than 50 seats in local government, one seat on the London Assembly, and had two members elected to the European Parliament.[7]

And today, cynical forces are extending the appeal of racial nativism across the four nations. Their brazen project began with Brexit and the heroisation of Nigel Farage. The mainstream parties and most of the media, panicked by the growing support for Reform, are choosing to flatter and court its supporters and leaders.[8]

Many of us feel that old, cold dread again. Increasing numbers of second and third generations of black and Asian Britons are feeling the same, but for the first time. Are we going to be safe with Starmer as prime minister? Or at least safer than we were before?

We so, so want Labour to succeed and bring together a diverse country in which all lives can hope and thrive. The early signs are not promising.

JULY 2024: THEIR TIME COMES

The first serious test for the new government came soon after the 4 July election. In August, more than 30 anti-immigrant, racially motivated riots broke out in towns and cities in the UK, mostly in the North.

On 29 July, a man had carried out a savage knife attack on a dance class in Southport. Three young girls were killed; eight others and two teachers were injured. Collective grief and fury spread fast through the land. All too soon, fake news and rumours online captured the narrative. The killer was described as an illegal asylum seeker, a Muslim who was being watched by MI6. White rioters – mostly angry men – took to the streets, tried to torch a hotel housing asylum seekers, attacked mosques, black and brown people and police officers, set fire to police cars. The insurrections were led by the far right and fired by anti-immigrant hate.[9]

Hate against strangers, outsiders and diverse others can easily be activated by social media. And sometimes by previously reliable sources of information in our society. In some of the post-riot analysis, the entirely unjustifiable racism and violence was justified.[10] Once again, the focus shifted to the 'forgotten' white people who languished at the bottom of society. We were urged to understand their woes.[11]

In a robust rebuttal, the historian David Olusoga discredited the excusers:

To put the violence directed at British Muslims, Black Britons and asylum seeking down to 'legitimate grievances' is to fall for one of the most toxic and intentionally divisive falsehoods in the populist handbook; the myth that class and race are diametrically opposed and that, the assertion that non-white people have no class identity.[12]

This was the moment for the new prime minister to say exactly that. Instead, Starmer, the former lawyer, framed the disturbances as lawlessness, and called for tough punishments for those found guilty. Ever mindful of 'red wall' voters, he didn't engage with the issues of racism and migration. And seemed unbothered about those non-white Labour voters and members who argued he should. The *Guardian* columnist Andy Beckett observed:

> Only when people involved with or influenced by the far right have broken the law, as in the summer's race riots, has the government been assertive. And even then, rather than accompany the arrests with a proper, sustained condemnation of right-wing extremism and the myths it propagates, Starmer offered only a few terse, formulaic-sounding words, attacking 'far-right thuggery'. The much broader problem of anti-immigrant prejudice went unaddressed.[13]

It gets worse. In September 2024, Starmer took advice from, and happily posed with, Georgia Meloni, Italy's prime minister, whom the journalist Alexander Stille has outed as:

> the shapeshifter [who] presents different sides to different audiences ... scrupulously moderate when addressing the EU and international audiences, but a populist firebrand on the campaign trail. When addressing a rally of the Spanish right-wing party Vox, she denounced the threat from 'the secularism of the left and Islamic radicalisation', and called for a defence of 'our civilisation' against 'those who want to destroy it'.[14]

In January 2025, Meloni cheerfully announced she was in 'fine tune' with Starmer on immigration.[15] Welcome to their world.

IMMIGRATION, IMMIGRATION, IMMIGRATION AND REFORM

In one of the most thought-provoking pieces on Starmer's political choices Aditya Chakrabortty asked his readers to guess who had made the following assertions:

1. Rishi Sunak was the most liberal prime minister we have ever had on immigration.
2. Mass immigration happened by design, not accident.
3. The UK is a one-nation experiment in open borders.[16]

No, not Nigel Farage, but Keir Starmer. Yet he expects migrants, their children and grandchildren to trust and believe in him. Are we fools?

Starmer has not accorded any time or energy to making the irrefutable case for immigration, past and present. He could – indeed, should – acknowledge that from the post-war period to today, immigrants and their descendants have kept the country moving and afloat. He could – indeed, should – defend demonised immigrants, including asylum seekers.

His leadership is messy and inconsistent. He lacks authority and authenticity. More and more of us who voted Labour are getting restive and speaking out. It seems clear to me that Starmer sees anti-racist, left-wing, pro-human rights and pro-Palestine Labour supporters as pesky, out-of-touch saddos he can well do without. The approach is mad, bad and dangerous. But Labour's movers and shakers are immovably and unshakeably committed to this strategy.

As Rachel Cunliffe astutely observed in the *New Statesman*: 'Put bluntly, there are people high up in Starmer's Labour team who believe a big high-profile altercation with the left wing of the party is good for the campaign.'[17]

According to Ipsos, Labour in the 2024 general election lost more than a third of its share of the ethnic minority vote.[18] Jabeer Butt, chief executive of the Race Equality Foundation, points out the grave implications of this collapsing support:

[How] Labour addresses the concerns of these communities, such as a disproportionate experience of poverty, excess deaths during the pandemic and now Palestine, is likely to be crucial in whether this is a blip or becomes a trend.[19]

WITH US OR AGAINST US?

After 14 years under the Tories, the pressure is on Labour supporters to be grateful, obsequious and uncritical of Starmer's government.

But the most reasonable – helpful even – position, surely, is to be both: with the Labour government on matters when it is right, and against it on those when it is wrong.

In the 2024 general election, Labour majorities were slashed in many multi-racial constituencies. In Leicester South, Jonathan Ashworth, who was expecting to become paymaster general, lost to Shockat Adam, an optician who ran as an independent pro-Palestinian candidate. Three others – all British Muslims whose campaigns focused on Gaza – won seats from Labour. In Ilford North, Wes Streeting won by just 528 votes. His opponent was Leanne Mohammed, a young British-Palestinian woman.[20]

The pro-Israel columnist Stephen Pollard ominously branded the results 'sectarian voting'.[21] Writing in the *Telegraph*, Jake Wallis Simons, editor of the *Jewish Chronicle*, warned that the election of the Muslim MPs gave us a 'glimpse into the horrifying future'.[22]

Funny how there was little 'horror' when for decades Muslims were used as election fodder by Labour. And how those who called for Muslims to integrate into British society are frantic when they do precisely that. These four Muslim, pro-Gaza candidates actively and intelligently participated in our democratic system. And up against the Labour machine, they won.

Labour's response has been a mix of arrogance and ignorance. Ashworth's allies clearly believed he, and only he, could represent Leicester South, because, you know, it's a Labour colony. For a while, Shockat Adam was hounded and smeared. Ashworth, in an unwise tweet, linked him to a terrorist. Then, when threatened with legal action, he deleted it. The political establishment is behind the curve. It needs to catch up fast.

So how are the new Indies faring? The Commons and Lords are clubs where some are consciously or unconsciously seen as interlopers. They know they have made history, and many of us hope that, in time, they will transform national politics.

Interviewed soon after they entered parliament, Adam was upbeat and excited:

We have no party whip. We have issues that impact our constituents, and we vote and will support any amendment, any policy that benefits our constituents. ... Politicians, when they have healthy majorities, become complacent.... This election has demonstrated that people are disillusioned with party politics and if they see hypocrisy, they are not frightened to support independence.[23]

LABOUR AND ETHNIC MINORITIES:
AN UNSTABLE, UNEQUAL DEAL

Between 1767 and 1922, more than a dozen MPs of Indian origin or mixed heritage, and one Armenian, had been elected by various parties.[24] After that, the House of Commons had turned white again, and almost wholly male.

History was made in 1987 when Diane Abbott, Paul Boateng, Bernie Grant and Keith Vaz entered parliament. This current parliament now has 90 black and Asian MPs; 60 are Labour, 15 Conservative, five Liberal Democrats and four Independents. Labour deserves huge credit for changing the colour of parliament.

However, that first big breakthrough in 1987 owes as much, if not more, to a broader, more assertive black politics in the 1980s. This emerged out of the ashes of the 1981 riots across Britain, fury about Thatcherism and its economic and social marginalisation of millions. This fed, and was sustained by, the campaign for Labour Party Black Sections. Labour's Black Sections, a caucus of Asian, Caribbean and African labour party members, were formed to push back against internal racism and for proper political representation. They knew seats could be lost without the ethnic vote. Until then, their votes were taken for granted.

Lessons have not been learnt. Bad judgements are being repeated.

FROM BAD TO WORSE

To show he was a man of action on becoming party leader in 2019, Starmer appointed Martin Forde KC to look into the party's structures and culture. Forde's brief was to investigate:

the extent of racist, sexist and other discriminatory culture within Labour party workplaces, the attitudes and conduct of the senior staff of the Labour party, and their relationships with the elected leadership of the Labour party.

Forde's conclusion was stark: Labour was, 'in effect operating a hierarchy of racism or of discrimination'.[25]

Forde had told truths that Starmer and his allies did not want to hear. Following the report's publication, Forde wasn't shy in describing what he'd uncovered: 'Anti-black racism and Islamophobia is not taken as seriously as antisemitism within the Labour party, that's the perception that has come through.'[26]

In May 2024, the Tory MP Natalie Elphicke's defection to Labour was acclaimed by Starmer. He smiled a lot, and seemed in good cheer as he welcomed Elphicke to the Labour benches. Prior to defecting, Elphicke was best known for denouncing Marcus Radford's free school lunch campaigns and for relentlessly demonising migrants and asylum-seekers.[27] Welcome to Starmer's Labour Party, Natalie.

This was a moment that crystallised Starmer's dependence on poor advice and gesture politics, and his final metamorphosis into an uncertain and unreliable politician so entirely different to his positioning when he stood for and won the Labour leadership. It was during his campaign to win that leadership that Starmer described Jeremy Corbyn as 'a colleague and a friend', and then, almost as soon as it was over, made Corbynism a political swearword.

My views on Corbyn have not changed over the years. He is a decent man who has often been on the right side of history. But he is too stubborn, tribal and myopic to be a leader. So, it turns out, is Starmer.

Faiza Shaheen was deselected as a Labour Parliamentary candidate – a young, female, globally respected Muslim academic and writer on equality who, as Labour's candidate in the midst of the disastrous 2019 campaign, had reduced Iain Duncan-Smith's majority in his Chingford and Wood Green constituency to just 1,262 votes.

I met her soon after the 2024 election, and she was still asking, 'How can they treat people this way?' They can. They do. And Rachel Cunliffe believes there is method in their actions: 'for all the vocal left-wingers outraged by the treatment of Shaheen (and, similarly, Abbott) there are voters in the centre who are reassured by it'.[28]

Diane Abbott's decapitation came next. In April 2023, she sent a letter to the *Observer* in response to a column penned by the

British-Nigerian journalist Tomiwa Owolade on a newly published report in which more white than black and Asian people claimed to have experienced racism.[29]

Her letter was emotive, and uninhibited:

It is true that many types of white people with points of difference, such as redheads, can experience this prejudice. But they are not all their lives subject to racism. In pre-civil rights America, Irish people, Jewish people and Travellers were not required to sit at the back of the bus. In apartheid South Africa, these groups were allowed to vote. And at the height of slavery, there were no white-seeming people manacled on the slave ships.[30]

I know Diane. She fights against all forms of inequality and injustice. And she does it her way, often eschewing the niceties of political manners. When Nigel Farage or Lee Anderson do that, they are described as 'real' and 'authentic'. But Diane, speaking her mind, is typecast as an uncontrolled, angry black woman.

To many journalists, commentators and politicians, she is too black, too left wing, too close to Corbyn, too bolshie. They relished her discomfiture, debasement and suspension as a Labour MP, all of which were aimed at preventing her from standing for Labour in the forthcoming general election. Her apologies were swept away in the media storm. Then, just before the July election, while still suspended, Abbott was caught up in a race scandal involving Frank Hester, a millionaire Tory funder.

During a meeting in 2019 at his company HQ in Leeds, Hester had allegedly said:

It's like trying not to be racist but you see Diane Abbott on the TV, and you're just like I hate, you just want to hate all black women because she's there, and I don't hate all black women at all, but I think she should be shot.

The remarks were leaked to the media.[31]

Starmer stood up in parliament to attack Hester and the Tories, and to back the MP he had himself exiled. It was posturing, opportunism and a display of amoral white, male power. During the debate, Abbott herself stood up 45 times, yet was not called once by the Speaker. She was spoken about, but wasn't allowed to speak for herself. That second, very public dishonour revived her spirit. She fought for the right to stand again for Labour in her Hackney North and Stoke Newington constituency.[32] She stood, and she won. But her vote was down; it was the Greens who enjoyed the biggest increase in their vote, overtaking the Tories to come second.

GAZA, THE UNSTOPPABLE BLEED

The depletion of support caused by the Labour's obdurate and unlawful backing – verbal as well as practical – for Israel's punitive actions in Gaza, the Occupied Territories and the Lebanon continues. It's a depletion too often dismissed by Starmer's allies as the product of antisemitism. I have been on the pro-Palestinian marches, a rainbow coalition of protesters, including a sizeable Jewish bloc. Labour's leadership are trying to alter reality. It's not working.

The support is politically broad, too. Layla Moran, a Liberal Democrat MP of Palestinian lineage, and the peer and former co-chair of the Conservative Party, Sayeed Warsi, are among the most outspoken critics of what Israel is doing to Gaza. Kit Malthouse, once a Tory cabinet minister, has long campaigned for Palestinian rights. He denounced the Starmer government's policy on Gaza and Israel as 'inherently racist'.[33] Which it is.

Starmer and his coterie, thus far, have been unconcerned. And unmoved. They don't seem to care. Meanwhile, we are expected to put up with what they are doing, supposedly in our name, and to shut up.

THE PRESENT AND THE FUTURE

I want Labour to get another term. I know the populist right are on the attack and determined to bring the government down.

In this environment, any appeasement of, or imitating, the Tories and Reform will mean Labour will lose more votes than it gains. Gaza and immigration are the two tests. He must do better on both, or else lose it all.

The *Guardian* columnist Nasreen Malik advises:

Starmer's weakest feature is his inability to paint a rousing vision of our modern country. One that isn't just about safe streets and working hard and paying the bills and getting on. ... We don't live in Gotham City, waiting for a mayor to clean the streets of villains. We are not just atomised individuals running our own public limited companies, but part of something bigger, part of a nation that has miraculously expanded, absorbed and assimilated people from all over the world, one that has manifested the best and most natural of human impulses – to get along and make a common home.[34]

Few have provided better advice. But is Starmer listening?

ENDNOTES

1. The most detailed and well-sourced accounts of this period were penned by Paul Foot in *Immigration and Race* Penguin, London 1965 and *The Rise of Enoch Powell* Penguin, London 1969.
2. Both sources cited by Kenan Malik in 'The Problem Is Not Immigration, It's the Obsession with It' Pandaemonium 20 April 2013 www.kenanmalik.com.
3. For a full account, see Zig Layton-Henry *The Politics of Immigration* Blackwell, Oxford 1992.
4. See Michael Segalov's interview 'Andi Oliver: "Life's Too Short to be Appalling"' *The Observer* 29 December 2024 www.theguardian.com.
5. See Yasmin Alibhai-Brown *The Settler's Cookbook: A Memoir of Love, Migration and Food* Portobello Books, Edinburgh 2008 pp. 328–329.
6. Thus began the accommodation and normalisation of far-right politics. Reform UK is the beneficiary of this betrayal of post-war values.
7. See Nigel Copsey *Contemporary British Fascism* Palgrave Macmillan, London 2008.
8. See Yasmin Alibhai-Brown 'Labour Must Expose Farage for What He Is' *The i Paper* 30 September 2024 www.inews.co.uk.
9. See 'Southport Stabbing: How the Knife Attack Unfolded' BBC Verify 7 August 2024 www.bbc.co.uk.
10. See, for example, 'Planet Normal: Toby Young Warns of Chilling Crackdown on Free Speech' *The Telegraph* 29 August 2024 www.telegraph.co.uk.
11. See Gaby Hinsliff 'The Grifters behind the Southport Riot Are Only Getting Started' *The Guardian* 2 August 2024 www.theguardian.com.
12. David Olusoga 'There Can Be No Excuses. The UK Riots Were Violent Racism Fomented by Populism' *The Guardian* 10 August 2024 www.theguardian.com.

13. Andy Beckett 'Bullies Can Sense Weakness – Which Is Why Labour Must Not Shy Away from Taking on the Global Far Right' *The Guardian* 9 December 2024 www.theguardian.com.

14. Alexander Stille 'The Shapeshifter: Who Is the Real Giorgia Meloni?' *The Guardian* 19 September 2024 www.theguardian.com.

15. Athena Stavrou 'Far-Right Italian PM and Musk Fan Giorgia Meloni Says She Is In Tune with Keir Starmer' *The Independent* 3 January 2025 www.independent.co.uk.

16. Aditya Chakrabortty 'All Starmer's Failings Play into the Hands of Farage – the Prime Minister Is the Gift That Keeps on Giving' *The Guardian* 19 December 2024 www.theguardian.com.

17. Rachel Cunliffe 'How the Faiza Shaheen Row Helps Keir Starmer' *New Statesman* 30 May 2024 www.newstatesman.com.

18. See Nadine White and Alicja Hagopian 'Labour Lost Almost a Third of Its Black and Asian Support at Election, Report Finds' *The Independent* 29 July, 2024 www.independent.co.uk.

19. Ibid.

20. See @LeanneMohamad www.x.com/leannemohamad and www.leannemohamad.co.uk.

21. Stephen Pollard 'Imagine If It Had Been the Jewish Vote Rather Than the Muslim Vote' *Jewish Chronicle* 19 July 2024 www.thejc.com.

22. Jake Wallis Simons 'Why the Muslim Vote Campaign Is a Glimpse into a Horrifying Future' *The Telegraph* 7 July 2024 www.telegraph.co.uk.

23. Interview quoted in Ruby Lott-Lavigna 'I Was an Optometrist. Now I'm an MP. I Had to Sink or Swim' Hyphen 10 October 2024 www.hyphenonline.com.

24. Rebecca Lees 'Who Were the First MPs from Ethnic Minority Backgrounds?' House of Commons Library, London 28 October 2020 www.commonslibrary.parliament.uk.

25. *The Forde Report* Labour Party www.labour.org.uk.

26. See Jon Stone 'Labour leader Keir Starmer Announces Urgent Investigation into Leaked Party Antisemitism Report' *The Independent* 13 April 2020 www.independent.co.uk and on YouTube, Al Jazeera English 'The Labour Files – Episode 1 – The Purge' 23 September 2022, 'The Labour Files – Episode 2 – The Crisis' 25 September 2022, 'The Labour Files – Episode 3 – The Hierarchy' 27 September 2022, 'The Labour Files – Episode 4 – The Spying Game' 30 September 2022, 'The Labour Files – The Forde Response' 16 March 2023 www.youtube.com.

27. See Jennifer McKiernan 'Natalie Elphicke: Who Is the Former Tory MP Who Defected to Labour?' *BBC News* 8 May 2024 www.bbc.co.uk.

28. Cunliffe 'How the Faiza Shaheen Row Helps Keir Starmer'.

29. Tomiwa Owolade 'Racism in Britain Is Not a Black and White Issue. It's Far More Complicated' *The Guardian* 15 April 2024 www.theguardian.com.

30. Diane Abbott 'Racism Is Black and White' *The Observer* 23 April 2023 www.theguardian.com.

31. See Rowena Mason 'Police Investigate Alleged Racist Remarks by Frank Hester' *The Guardian* 22 March 2024 www.theguardian.com.

32. See the detailed account of what happened and how she felt, in Diane Abbott *A Woman Like Me* Penguin, London 2024.

33. See Harry Taylor 'Government Should Be Ashamed of Policies on Gaza, Former Cabinet Minister Says' *The Independent* 7 January 2025 www.independent.co.uk.

34. Nesrine Malik 'After the Riots, Keir Starmer Should Tell Us The Truth about Our Country. This Is Why He Won't' *The Guardian* 19 August 2024 www.theguardian.com.

Pragmatic, Social Democratic, Radical

Eunice Goes

To the exasperation of pundits, Keir Starmer's typical answer to questions about his vision is vague and impatient. As his biographer noted, 'Starmer has always disliked the obsession with "vision" because he is neither given to grand abstractions nor easily located in a particular ideological framework.'[1] If pushed, Starmer admits he is 'a socialist', but a 'practical one.'[2]

This reaction suggests that the Labour leader is out of his comfort zone when asked about his political thinking. He prefers to be thought of as a leader trying to fix the problems that afflict Britain. He does not have time for self-indulgent discussions about political ideas. He is a doer and a fixer, not a thinker. As Starmer himself has put it, he came into politics 'to get things done, to strive, each and every day, to make a difference to the lives of working people'.[3] This has been Starmer's refrain since he was elected Labour leader in April of 2020. He has now taken it into government. From the doorstep of Downing Street on his first day as prime minister, he told the nation that he would lead a government 'unburdened by doctrine'.[4]

Starmer's lack of interest in ideas permeates his team of political strategists. From the early days of his leadership, Starmer was advised by them to avoid making references to values and ideas that are too closely associated with socialism or social democracy because they may potentially turn off floating voters. Deborah Mattinson, who was Starmer's head of strategy until 2024's general election, advised Starmer to adopt a language that reflects the socially authoritarian values of 'red wall' voters.[5] She advised the Labour leader to show voters 'his love of the country'.[6] Peter Hyman, who also left Starmer's team following the election, proposed 'missions' as the technocratic buzzword to disguise a potentially transformative political project.[7]

His speech-writer, Alan Lockley advised Starmer to resist appeals to explain 'his vision' and to focus instead on explaining the values of the voters Labour represents.[8] His reasoning was that British politics 'has typically been more rooted in competing class interests, than a philosophical contest of ideas'.[9]

The perception of those in and around Starmer's office was that it was Labour's shift to the left during Corbyn's era as leader that had made it unelectable. If Labour wanted – and needed – to widen its electoral coalition, the party had to address the concerns and priorities of a broad variety of voters, including of those who had voted Conservative at the 2019 election. Most voters are not very interested in politics, and for them, references to ideological traditions or to the party's history can become barriers to political engagement.

But the avoidance of social democratic language reflects a mindset in Starmer's team, one of contempt for allegedly self-indulgent intellectual debates.[10] This contempt was on show when one of Starmer's advisers told a *Times* journalist that the typical centre-left reply to the question of how it might repair trust in politics, was usually 'a Fabian festival of ideas that are all bad ideas'.[11] Previous Labour leaders have encouraged the development of a diverse ideational infrastructure composed of think tanks, including the Fabian Society, academics, leading columnists and public intellectuals, who contributed to the development of the party's programme and narrative. Starmer, by contrast, has been mainly associated with Labour Together, a think tank which was founded by his chief of staff and main political strategist Morgan McSweeney, and which is mostly known for conducting surveys and focus groups of key sections of the electorate.[12]

SOCIAL DEMOCRACY FOR THE 'PRACTICAL-MINDED'

Starmer's lack of interest in debates about ideas and visions may upset Labour observers and long-term supporters, but they are not entirely a novelty in the party's history. In reality, they are part of the Labour tradition of privileging pragmatism and realism over principles and ideas. Labour has always benefited from the contributions and support of committed socialist intellectuals, but their voices have rarely set the tone of the party's manifestos. Even for a self-declared proud socialist like Clement Attlee, moderation and pragmatism were important restraining forces of the socialist mission. As he put it, 'Socialism cannot come overnight, as the product of a weekend revolution. The members of the Labour Party, like the British people, are practical-minded men and women.'[13]

Like other socialist movements in Europe, there were many traditions of socialism, including Marxist ones, that jostled to influence the shape of what later became the Labour Party. The thinker and artist William Morris and the Social Democratic Federation of H.M. Hyndman tried to imbue the British socialist movement with Marxist ideas, but they lost their battle. As Ross McKibbin explained, the combination of 'pomp and fairness' encapsulated in Crown and Parliament, together with the patterns of socialisation of a highly fragmented working-class movement, helped produce an ideology of rights 'which was both permissive and restraining'. Labour being a party led by workers and not by an intelligentsia at least in part explains the weak influence of Marxism over the Labour Party.[14]

Instead of Marxist or other radical traditions, Fabianism and the labourism of the trade unions won over time the battle of ideas in the Labour Party. The party that emerged in the early 20th century rejected the key Marxist tenets of class struggle and revolution and proposed instead a parliamentary road to socialism which paid reverential homage to all the conventions of the Palace of Westminster.[15] This choice, as well as the path charted by successive Labour leaders, dictated that the type of socialism the party subscribed to was of a reformist kind. When the Labour Representation Committee was finally founded in 1900, what emerged was largely a reformist party which was 'not only non-Marxist but anti-Marxist'.[16]

But if Marxism, with its historical materialism and commitment to the class struggle and revolution, was seen by British socialists as a form of dogma, 'reformism' and 'parliamentarism' became Labour's own dogmatism. These, in turn, would lead to the emergence of the tradition of labourism, which Ralph Miliband dated back to the publication of the 1918 document *Labour and the New Social Order*.

As Miliband explained, this tradition committed the party to 'piece-meal collectivism within a predominantly capitalist society'.[17]

Alongside reformism and incrementalism, labourism was elitist in its approach to the socialist principle of common ownership of the means of production. Unlike Britain's own Guild Socialists or the Swedish Social Democrats, or the German SPD, or the Austro-Marxists, the Labour Party was far more insistent on the nationalisation of some parts of the economy than on the adoption of a more pluralist and democratic concept of common ownership of the means of production, which entailed developing economic democracy and building countervailing power to capital.

The social democratic thinker David Marquand concurred. He argued that in the 20th century, labourism was the dominant tradition in the party's thinking and practice. As he put it, Labour had 'deliberately chosen to identify itself as the instrument of the labour interest rather than as the vehicle for any ideology'.[18] As such, labourism was, in the words of Tony Wright, 'an untheoretical meliorism'.[19] In practice, this meant a commitment to guarantee the survival of capitalism and to the general improvement of workers' lives through full employment, better working conditions and an extensive and robust welfare state, rather than the wholesale transformation of society.

If labourism contributed to the landslide victory of 1945, it was also the cause of the party's demise, which, according to Marquand, promoted a:

> kind of woodenness, a lack of political imagination, a hardness of the intellectual arteries, which prevented Labour ministers from creating new opportunities and turning the flanks of their opponents in the way that Roosevelt and Lloyd George so often did.[20]

Wright agrees that labourism ended up having a stultifying effect in Labour's trajectory. The party's reluctance to engage in theoretical debates led to the sanctifying of certain symbols, namely Clause Four from Labour's constitution. As a result, argued Wright, 'Labour increasingly lived in a theoretical void, living off its past ... and content to settle for a pragmatic political practice.'[21]

LABOURISM AND SOCIAL DEMOCRACY

Of course, labourism has significantly improved the lives of the British working classes. It has strengthened workers' rights, expanded the welfare state, substantially reduced poverty, and contributed to greater social mobility and a stronger public realm. However, labourism should not be confused with social democracy. This is because social democracy is an ideology that, despite its diversity, has a clear conception of the good society shaped by an understanding of historical change and human nature.

Social democrats agreed that human beings, and in particular workers, could only be free to live the lives of their own choosing in a society shaped by the values of cooperation and equality. Because capitalism was seen as the great obstacle to the enactment of that vision, social democrats were committed to replace it with a socialist mode of economic production.

There were heated debates about how to turn this conception of the good society into a reality. Different varieties of social democracy emerged, but on the whole European social democrats came to a broad and shared understanding about the goals of their mission and over the steps (which involved adopting a critical approach to capitalism) that needed to be taken to turn that vision into a reality.

This being said, social democracy was and remains a contested term. Following the European revolutions of 1848, social democracy was seen as a moderate form of socialism, but by the 1860s, social democracy was associated with a radical politics committed to the socialist revolution and the overthrow of capitalism. Following the Russian Revolution of 1917, social democracy referred to the pursuit of socialism and the overthrow of capitalism via the parliamentary road. After World War Two, social democracy became a reformist ideology which merely sought to achieve socialist ends through a reformed form of capitalism. Even today, there is no settled meaning associated with social democracy. In countries like Britain and France, social democracy is normally associated with a very moderate form of democratic socialism. In Scandinavia, it means a more ambitious egalitarian project.[22]

The transformation of social democracy resulted from dealing with the real world. Their doctrines had to adapt to the electoral, political, economic and social realities they encountered. This transformation narrowed the gap between social democracy and labourism. In the process, social democracy lost its distinctive critical approach to capitalism and its commitment to the emancipation of workers and citizens in general.

The first doctrinal change social democracy underwent was about the 'means' to arrive at a socialist society. In the mid-19th century, male universal suffrage offered socialists a new way of overthrowing capitalism and developing a socialist society. Many socialists renounced violent revolution, endorsed the parliamentary road to socialism and became social democrats. But then they realised that the parliamentary road to socialism had many obstacles. To gain political power, social democratic parties needed to attract the support of a majority of voters, and to achieve that goal, those parties needed to tone down the most radical aspects of their programmes.[23]

As social democrats had their first taste of power, they realised they had never developed a distinct economic model which would become a substitute for capitalism. They had a rough idea of what needed to be done, but that rough idea did not amount to a detailed blueprint. Lacking a specific economic strategy, social democrats ended up improvising. They borrowed from other traditions and adjusted to the hard realities of governing at times of economic crises. Eventually, they accepted that a state-regulated form of capitalism could deliver social democratic goals.

This transformation of social democracy did not happen at the same speed and in the same way across Europe. Different political and economic circumstances and different intellectual traditions resulted in different varieties of social democracy. In the post-war period, most (though not all)[24] social democrats across Europe accepted that a tamed form of capitalism could be compatible with socialist goals. In the case of Labour, the revisionist thinker Anthony Crosland revisited the arguments made by the German Eduard Bernstein at the turn of the 20th century and by the Austro-Marxist Rudolf Hilferding in 1917–19 on how a transformed capitalism was compatible with a social democratic vision of society. Crosland noted that:

the [Marxist] belief that the 'inner contradictions' of capitalism would lead to a gradual pauperisation of the masses, and ultimately to the collapse of the whole system, has by now been rather obviously disproved.[25]

Instead, he argued, the 'business class had lost its commanding position' and in its place the state accepted responsibility 'for full employment, the rate of growth, balance of payments and the distribution of incomes'.[26]

Crosland and other revisionist thinkers were right in their assessment. By the 1950s, capitalism was very different in nature from the capitalism Marx and the early socialists experienced and theorised. In many European countries, governments had nationalised key industries, had introduced robust competition laws, had enacted active industrial policies, had strengthened the bargaining power of citizens in the workplace through co-determination mechanisms or workers' councils, had developed extensive welfare states which offered protection from cradle to grave, had promoted full employment, and had taxed heavily private profits and top incomes.

This type of capitalism generated high levels of economic growth across Europe and North America. Crucially, social democrats (but also conservatives and Christian Democrats) used the proceeds of economic growth to redistribute wealth, strengthen welfare states, promote solidarity and contribute to the emancipation of all workers by giving them power over economic life.

There was a key ingredient in this revisionist take on social democracy that was missing from the tradition of labourism. While labourism articulated an accommodation to capitalism,[27] revisionist social democrats claimed the state had a role in guaranteeing that capitalism served the common good. It was this critical approach to capitalism that ensured that the revisionism of the 1950s and 1960s had kept social democracy alive. It was also this critical approach to capitalism that led European social democrats such as Willy Brandt, Bruno Kreisky and Olof Palme to make the case for economic democracy in the 1970s.[28] As they witnessed the unravelling of the Bretton Woods economic order and the growth in power of multinational corporations, Brandt, Kreisky and Palme argued that workers needed to develop countervailing power to capital.[29] The solution was 'economic democracy', which would give workers the right to participate in economic decision-making.

This animated social democrats until the 1980s. But a new capitalist transformation forced a new social democratic revisionism, which this time changed not only the 'means' of social democracy, but also its 'ends'. The capitulation to neoliberal capitalism by social democratic parties had a profound impact on social democracy. This was no longer a transformative project committed to developing a socialist (and solidaristic) society of free and equal citizens. The accommodation to capitalism meant that social democrats were now merely committed to the gradual improvement of workers' living standards, though not necessarily to their emancipation. Rather than defending the reform of the capitalist economy to deliver the social democratic goal of human emancipation in a society based on co-operation and equality, social democratic parties believed that their role was to equip workers with the necessary skills to compete in the globalised and competitive economy. Social democrats accepted with reluctance the neoliberal settlement which depended on the weakening of trade unions and collective bargaining mechanisms, as well as on the promotion of insecure and flexible labour markets.

In the 1990s, this vision of society was presented as a 'third way' between socialism and neoliberalism, but it can also be seen as simply a new form of labourism adapted to the economic and political conditions of the time. Not all social democratic parties succumbed to this vision. For instance, the French Socialist Party led by Lionel Jospin argued that 'social democracy is a way of regulating society and of putting the market economy at the service of people'.[30] Several other European social democrats defended a social Europe which would act as a counterpoint to the neoliberal experiments of the single market and monetary union. But these were isolated laments. Most European social democrats capitulated to the forces of neoliberalism.

This capitulation to neoliberal capitalism came to bite social democrats. One by one, they started to lose elections. The opposition benches offered some time for reflection. Across Europe, social democratic parties started to realise their mistake and thought they could rediscover their transformative mission. In Britain, the

Labour leaderships of Ed Miliband and to a lesser extent Jeremy Corbyn were engaged in these debates, and even Starmer has attacked trickle-down economics and argued for transformative change.[31] But this process of rediscovery has been harder than they had imagined. Since the global financial crisis of 2008, a succession of crises has left social democrats disorientated. Rising inequalities, stagnating economies, a climate emergency and rising concerns with migration are complex problems that present social democrats with difficult decisions. This problem is compounded by a certain intellectual inflexibility. The new generation of social democratic leaders was intellectually shaped by the debates of the 'third way' and triumphant neoliberalism. On the one hand, they attack the shortcomings of neoliberalism and now believe that social democracy can offer solutions to today's multiple crises. On the other, they only know how to operate with the pre-crises remedial policy kit.

LOCATING STARMERISM

The trajectory of the Labour Party since 2010 reflects the disorientation of the European social democratic left. Labour shifted left under the leadership of Ed Miliband, then moved further to the left under the leadership of Jeremy Corbyn, but with Starmer as leader, it has returned to the centre.

Starmer's avoidance of ideological language, his ambiguous positioning on taxation and social affairs, and his notorious lack of interest in intellectual debates about the multiple crises that affect Western democracies[32] has created some confusion about the nature of his project. On the left, commentators like Oliver Eagleton have argued that Starmer's agenda represents 'a journey to the right' whose sole purpose is to 're-establish the Right's monopoly on power'.[33] However, this interpretation seems to ignore Starmer's positioning on key issues such as promoting the role of the state in industrial policy or expanding workers' rights. Starmer's positioning on political economy suggests, as Karl Pike has argued, 'some clear "moving on" from New Labour thinking'.[34] However, 'moving on' from New Labour does not necessarily mean that Starmer's agenda is social democratic. In truth, as Pike puts it, Labour seems to have returned to the 'recognisable yet amorphous political tradition' of labourism which 'does not set a clear direction towards the "good society"'.[35]

In a respectful nod to the labourist tradition and in a rejection of New Labour's approach to globalisation and free markets, the Labour Party led by Starmer claims to be at the service of working people. Labour's proposals for stronger workers' rights and trade union powers, as well as the national minimum wage rise and the commitment to deliver growth to all parts of the United Kingdom, reflect the labourist approach: a commitment to the general improvement of living standards for workers while at the same time adopting a less generous approach towards those who do not work. The two-child benefit cap, the capping of the winter fuel allowance to pensioners relying on pension credit, the promise to crack down on welfare fraud and make work pay are not only about kowtowing to the readers of the *Daily Mail*. These stances on welfare benefits have always been a familiar feature of Labour and labourist approaches to welfare spending.

Similarly, the party's 'securonomics' centred around a new industrial strategy designed to decarbonise the economy and create new jobs sits comfortably with a labourist conception of the role of the state in the economy. Starmer's promise of a partnership with the business sector, his willingness to subcontract to the private sector the running of public services, his reluctance to tax the wealthy in a substantial manner,[36] and his unwillingness to regulate multinational corporations and the financial services industry reflect the labourist reflex of accommodation to the capitalist economy. This positioning on capitalism suggests that Starmerism represents a new form of labourism. Even the revisionist tradition of the social democracy of the post-war period adopted a more critical approach to capitalist interests.

This Labour vision matches those of a labourist agenda. Starmerism in action articulates an active view of the state, a commitment to strengthen the power of workers in economic relations and in improving living standards, but leaves largely untouched the economic, social and political structures that contributed to high levels of inequality and to a depleted public realm. Even the welcome announcements of a rise to the minimum wage and of new spending on public services will not, as James Meadway has warned, be sufficient to avoid a new round of austerity.[37]

Perhaps more worryingly, Starmer does not tolerate dissent within the Labour benches. The withdrawal of the whip from the seven Labour MPs who rebelled over the two-child benefit cap and the way Starmer forced the resignation of the popular secretary of state for transport Louise Haigh suggests a degree of intellectual insecurity. This intolerance of dissent can condemn the party to what Marquand defined as an 'intellectual woodenness' which can prevent Labour from innovating and which contrasts with the intellectual self-confidence of the New Labour governments. Famously, Tony Blair welcomed members of the soft left like Robin Cook and Clare Short into New Labour's tent and was largely magnanimous towards the left-wing rebels of his PLP.

Nonetheless, there are hints of some social democratic possibilities. The Labour leader claims that Labour wants to do more than merely offer a red sticking plaster for Britain's problems. He seems to be personally disturbed by structural inequalities which prevent the less privileged pursuing the lives of their choice. Labour's articulation of a new role for the state in the economy, its critical approach to globalisation and its emphasis on class and workers' protection open the door to a more critical approach to capitalism and to a commitment to the social democratic goal of human emancipation.

But to repeat those apt words of Clement Attlee, these are not changes that can be implemented over a weekend. The key test for Labour's social democratic mission remains the goals the party sets out to fulfil. Labour needs to want to transform the capitalist economy in ways that serve the public good, and it needs to keep on trying to enact that transformative change. While Labour does so, the social democratic flame can remain alight.

ENDNOTES

1. Tom Baldwin *Keir Starmer: The Biography* London, William Collins 2024 p. 255.

2. Keir Starmer 'Our Radical Socialist Tradition Must Remain at the Heart of Labour' *The Independent* 22 February 2020 www.independent.co.uk.

3. 'Keir Starmer's New Year Speech' Labour Party 4 January 2024 www.labour.org.uk.

4. 'Keir Starmer's First Speech as Prime Minister: 5 July 2024' www.gov.uk.

5. Deborah Mattinson *Beyond the Red Wall: Why Labour Lost, How the Conservatives Won and What Will Happen Next?* London, Biteback 2020 p. 229.

6. Mattinson, quoted in Anushka Asthana *Taken as Red: How Labour Won Big and the Tories Crashed the Party* London, Harper North 2024 p. 14.

7. Peter Hyman 'Keir Starmer Must Remember His Mission' 30 November 2024 www.newstatesman.com'.

8. Alan Lockey 'What Should Keir Say?' Medium 9 September 2021 lockey-alan.medium.com.

9. Ibid.

10. Tom McTague 'The Kingmaker in Labour Who's Ensuring Keir Is No Heir to Blair' *The Times* 10 May 2024 www.thetimes.com.

11. Starmer adviser, quoted in Patrick Maguire 'Sir Keir Starmer's Modest Ambition: Don't Scare the Horses' *The Times* 27 June 2024 www.thetimes.com.

12. Think tanks like the Institute for Public Policy Research and the Resolution Foundation have influenced Labour's policy development, but Labour Together has been the most influential.

13. Clement Attlee, quoted in Ralph Miliband *Parliamentary Socialism: A Study in the Politics of Labour* London, Merlin Press 2009 p. 278.

14. Ross McKibbin 'Why Was There No Marxism in Great Britain?' *English Historical Review* 99/391 (1984) pp. 297–331, at p. 330.

15. George Bernard Shaw *Essays in Fabian Socialism* London, Constable 1961.

16. Tony Wright *Socialisms: Old and New* London, Routledge 1996 p. 10.

17. Miliband, *Parliamentary Socialism* p. 62.

18. David Marquand *The Progressive Dilemma: From Lloyd George to Kinnock* London, Heinemann 1992 p. 17.

19. Wright *Socialisms* p. 126.

20. Marquand *The Progressive Dilemma* p. 21.

21. Wright *Socialisms* pp. 126–127.

22. Eunice Goes, *Social Democracy* Newcastle upon Tyne, Agenda Publishing 2024 pp. 3–10.

23. Ibid. pp. 133–137.

24. The French and Italian socialist parties were slower in their revisionist journeys.

25. Anthony Crosland *The Future of Socialism* London, Constable 2006 [1956] p. 5.

26. Ibid. p. 9.

27. Eric Hobsbawm *The Forward March of Labour Halted?* London, Verso 1981 p. 17.

28. Willy Brandt, Bruno Kreisky and Olof Palme *La Social-Démocratie et l'Avenir* Paris, Gallimard 1976 p. 143.

29. Ibid. p. 36.

30. Lionel Jospin *Modern Socialism* Fabian Pamphlet 592 London, Fabian Society 1999 p. 1.

31. Eunice Goes 'The Labour Party Under Keir Starmer: Thanks, but No "Isms", Please!' *Political Quarterly* 92/2 (2021) pp. 176–183.

32. The lack of intellectual curiosity of Starmer and his team is discussed at length in Sally Davison, Sue Goss, Neal Lawson and Paul Thompson 'Putting the Critical into "Critical Friend"' *Renewal* 31/2 (2023) pp. 25–33.

33. Oliver Eagleton *The Starmer Project: A Journey to the Right* London, Verso 2022 p. 185.

34. Karl Pike *Getting Over New Labour* Newcastle upon Tyne, Agenda Publishing 2024 p. 124.

35. Ibid. pp. 93–94.

36. The first budget of the Starmer government announced rises to capital gains tax, to the tax on the profits of private equity and the scrapping of the status of non-domiciled resident, but the rises were modest, and it left out corporation tax, which remains low in comparison with other G7 economies and a wealth tax which, if well designed, can raise significant amounts of revenue.

37. James Meadway 'The Budget Is Socialism for the Rich, Austerity for the Poor' Novara Media 31 October 2024 www.novaramedia.com.

UNDERSTANDING KEIR STARMER'S LABOUR PARTY

A Guide to Labour
Battleground Seats at
the Next General Election

On 4 July 2024, Labour won a 174-seat majority. Ordinarily, this would virtually guarantee Labour to win the next general election and a second term.

But elected with the lowest vote share ever for a party to form a government, 33.7%, this was an entirely disproportionate result. This conclusion is reinforced by losing 500,000 votes since Jeremy Corbyn led Labour to a calamitous defeat in 2019, yet Starmer's Labour in 2024 won 211 more seats than Corbyn's Labour in 2019.

The switch is almost entirely explained by the right-wing vote in 2024 being split between the Conservatives and Reform UK, whereas in 2019 there was an electoral pact, a 'regressive alliance', between Boris Johnson's Tories and Nigel Farage's Brexit Party. At the same time, in 2024 Labour targeted all its efforts and resources at Tory seats with low majorities where it was clearly the main challenger. And where it wasn't, it withdrew all campaign resources in favour of the better-placed challenger, the Liberal Democrats. But a victory based on a divided vote – Tory/Reform – versus vote efficiency – Labour/Liberal Democrats – is highly vulnerable to voter volatility.

At the next general election, Labour's problem will be fivefold.

First, while a formal Tory-Reform pact is unlikely, the same practice, but this time by the right, of seeking vote efficiency could result in heavy Labour losses.

Second, if either the Tory or Reform vote implodes to establish one or other as the main challenger, Labour's chances of retaining sufficient seats to form a government would be much more seriously reduced.

Third, Labour's drift in government, particularly prioritising growth over a serious effort to reverse the climate emergency, could enable the Green Party to build further on its historic 2024 breakthrough.

Fourth, Labour recorded 36 gains in Scotland, the SNP losing 39 seats. Any kind of SNP recovery, even if not enough to topple Starmer, would nevertheless be a significant contribution to such an outcome.

Fifth, the election of Jeremy Corbyn and four other 'independents' was a mix of a left-of-Labour vote personified by Corbyn with a mainly communal Muslim vote agitated by Labour's non-position on Gaza. The Workers Party led by George Galloway also did creditably too, failing to win seats, but finishing a close second in a number of them. As much as adherents to these various versions of this 'outside left' might like to believe this can be sustained to 2029, it is almost impossible to predict the scale to expect.

So there are five fronts, and to win power again, Labour will have to fight and win on all of them.

Votes won't remain static between 2024 and the next general election, but as a starting point, these are the second-placed challengers from 2024 Labour will have to beat again:

Labour majority of under 1,000, under 1% swing to lose seat

Conservative Party	22 seats 2nd
Independent Left	2 seats 2nd
Workers Party	1 seat 2nd

Labour majority of 1,000–2,000, 1–2% swing to lose seat

Conservative Party	14 seats 2nd
Reform UK	1 seat 2nd
SNP	1 seat 2nd
Independent Left	1 seat 2nd
Workers Party	1 seat 2nd

Labour majority of 2,000–3,000, 2–3% swing to lose seat

Conservative Party	16 seats 2nd
Workers Party	1 seat 2nd

Labour majority of 3,000–4,000, 3–4% swing to lose seat

Conservative Party	14 seats 2nd
SNP	1 seat 2nd

Labour majority of 4,000–5,000, 4–5 % swing to lose seat

Conservative Party	19 seats 2nd
SNP	5 seats 2nd
Reform UK	2 seats 2nd
Independent Left	2 seats 2nd
Liberal Democrats	1 seat 2nd

Labour majority of 5,000–6,000, 5–6% swing to lose seat

Conservative Party	20 seats 2nd
SNP	5 seats 2nd
Green Party	1 seat 2nd
Plaid Cymru	1 seat 2nd

Labour majority of 6,000–7,000, 6–7% swing to lose seat

Conservative Party	16 seats 2nd
Reform UK	5 seats 2nd
SNP	2 seats 2nd
Independent Left	4 seats 2nd

Labour majority of 7,000–8,000, 7–8% swing to lose seat

Conservative Party	7 seats 2nd
Reform UK	4 seats 2nd
SNP	4 seats 2nd
Green Party	1 seat 2nd

If all these swings happen, Labour will lose its majority.

The following tables show each party's top ten Labour targets.

Labour's top ten defences from second-placed 2024 Tory candidates

Constituency	Labour MP	Labour majority	% swing for Tory win
Hendon	David Pinto-Duschinsky	15	0.02
Poole	Neil Duncan-Jordan	18	0.02
Cambs NW	Sam Carling	39	0.04
Peterborough	Andrew Pakes	118	0.14
Chelsea & Fulham	Ben Coleman	152	0.16
Middlesborough South	Luke Myer	214	0.28
Forest of Dean	Matt Bishop	278	0.29
Derbyshire Dales	John Whitby	350	0.34
Sittingbourne	Kevin McKenna	355	0.43
Somerset North	Sadik Al-Hassan	639	0.59

Labour's top ten defences from second-placed 2024 Reform UK candidates

Constituency	Labour MP	Labour majority	% swing for Reform gain
Llanelli	Nia Griffith	1504	1.85
Amber Valley	Linsey Farsnworth	3554	4.18
Montgomery	Steve Witherden	3815	4.41
Great Grimsby	Melanie Onn	4803	6.56
Hull East	Karl Turner	3920	6.57
Bradford South	Judith Cummins	4392	6.65
Makerfield	Josh Simons	5399	6.70
Barnsley South	Stephanie Peacock	4748	6.77
Durham North	Luke Akehurst	5873	7.06
Rotherham	Sarah Champion	5490	7.43

Labour's top ten defences from second-placed 2024 Green Party candidates

Constituency	Labour MP	Labour majority	% Swing for Green gain
Huddersfield	Harpreet Uppal	4533	5.64
Bristol East	Kerry McCarthy	6606	7.16
Bristol South	Karin Smith	7666	8.83
Sheffield Central	Abtisam Mohamed	8286	13.03
Bristol NE	Damien Egan	11167	13.30
Leeds Central	Alex Sobel	8420	13.33
Stratford and Bow	Uma Kumaran	11634	13.39
Manchester Rusholme	Afzal Khan	8235	14.18
Poplar	Apsana Begum	12560	14.59
Norwich South	Clive Lewis	13239	14.68

Labour's top ten defences from second-placed 2024 SNP candidates

Constituency	Labour MP	Labour majority	% Swing for SNP gain
Stirling	Chris Kane	1394	1.40
Edinburgh East	Chris Murray	3715	4.08
Glenrothes	Richard Baker	2954	4.09
Ayrshire North	Irene Campbell	3551	4.20
Glasgow SW	Zubir Ahmed	3285	4.60
Glasgow South	Gordon McKee	4154	4.90
Cumbernauld	Katrina Murray	4144	5.06
Ayr, Carrick & Cumnock	Elaine Stewart	4154	5.07
Glasgow North	Martin Rhodes	3539	5.09
Glasgow East	John Grady	3784	5.34

Labour's top ten defences from second-placed 2024 Independent Left/Workers Party candidates

Constituency	Labour MP	Labour majority	% Swing for Independent/ Workers Party gain
Ilford North	Wes Streeting	528	0.56
Bradford West	Naz Shah	707	0.95
Birmingham Yardley*	Jess Phillips	693	0.96
Bethnal Green	Rushanara Ali	1689	1.81
Rochdale*	Paul Waugh	1440	1.81
Birmingham Hodge Hill*	Liam Byrne	1566	2.29
Slough	Tanmanjeet Singh Dhesi	3647	4.21
Birmingham Ladywood	Shabana Mahmood	3421	4.68
Oldham West	Jim McMahon	4976	6.45
Walsall & Bloxwich	Valerie Vaz	4914	6.61

Note: * In these constituencies, second placed were Workers Party candidates

For those who fancy a spot of their own psephology, a weekly Friday-morning visit to www.x.com/electionmapsuk provides council by-election results from the day before. The corresponding website www.electionmaps.uk provides a huge range of the latest shifts in voting behaviour.

Visit www.electionpolling.co.uk for all parties' defences and targets, along with regular updates using polls to identify changes in which target seats are most likely to determine the result of the next general election.

Symptom of What? Further Reading and Other Resources

For readers who are interested in the framing of this collection by a quote from Gramsci and would like to know more of his work, the best book to begin with remains *Gramsci's Political Thought: An Introduction* by Roger Simon, with the added bonus of an introductory essay, 'Reading Gramsci', and a postscript, 'Gramsci and Us', both by Stuart Hall. Peak 'Gramscianism' was the late 1970s, following the English translation of his Prison Notebooks and other writings. A taster of his influence at the time is provided by Anne Showstack Sassoon's edited collection *Approaches to Gramsci*. Ernesto Laclau and Chantal Mouffe's *Hegemony and Socialist Strategy: Towards a Radical Democratic Politics* remains the most influential 'revisionist' interpretation and application of Gramsci's work. That influence is maintained by Mouffe's writings, most recently *Towards a Green Democratic Revolution: Left Populism and the Power of Affects*. To help readers understand the Gramscian concept of the 'conjuncture' as applied to current politics and culture, John Clarke's *The Battle for Britain: Crises, Conflicts and the Conjuncture* is absolutely excellent

The work of Stuart Hall is featured strongly in Mark Perryman's Keynote Essay in this volume. *Stuart Hall: Selected Political Writings*, edited by Sally Davison, David Featherstone, Michael Rustin and Bill Schwarz, features a wide range of Hall's work from the birth of the 1956 New Left to New Labour. *Understanding Stuart Hall* by Helen Davis places his work squarely in the context of debates he helped shape, and serves as a very good introduction to Hall's ideas.

For an overview of labourism, *A Century of Labour* by Jon Cruddas is a most original critical history of Labour in government.

For a comprehensive account of the enduring significance of Labour's 1945 'Now Win the Peace' general election victory and the establishing of the welfare state, read Jim Fyrth's two edited collections *Labour's High Noon: The Government and the Economy*

1945–51 and *Labour's Promised Land? Culture and Society in Labour Britain 1945–51*.

By 1979, 'Now Win the Peace' had turned into a 'Winter of Discontent', and to help understand why, *In and Against the State* was published that year, a book that pioneered an understanding of the welfare state as a site of contestation among users, producers and service providers rather than simply a cause to defend. The 2021 reissue of the book contains a new introduction and afterword which locate this contestation following the rise and fall of Corbynism and the continuing neoliberal hegemony.

Two accounts of Rock against Racism's 'joyful symptom' provide a well-deserved break from 'morbid symptoms'. Long out of print, *Beating Time: Riot 'n' Race 'n' Rock 'n' Roll* by David Widgery is far and away the best contemporary account – beg, steal or borrow a copy if you can. *Reminiscences of RAR: Rocking against Racism 1976–1982*, edited by Roger Huddle and Red Saunders, is a superb history of this most day-glo of social movements. David Widgery's richly varied case 'against miserabilism' is compiled in the collection *Against Miserabilism: Writings 1968–1992*, edited by Juliet Ash, Nigel Fountain and David Renton. The largely untold story of Red Wedge is included at length in Daniel Rachel's *Walls Come Tumbling Down*.

Edited by Martin Jacques and Stuart Hall, *The Politics of Thatcherism* contains all the key *Marxism Today* articles on the subject. Otherwise, see the *Marxism Today* online archive for the original articles, www.banmarchive.org.uk/marxism-today.

The ideas Tony Blair shaped into a programme for government are critiqued in *The Blair Agenda*, edited by Mark Perryman. An uncritical insider's account from the period is provided in Peter Mandelson and Roger Liddle's *The Blair Revolution: Can New Labour Deliver?* Revived for one special edition of *Marxism Today* to critically assess Tony Blair's Labour with the strapline 'Wrong', it can be read via the *Marxism Today* online archive.

The challenges Blair posed for a left response was the theme of *The Moderniser's Dilemma: Radical Politics in the Age of Blair*, co-edited by Mark Perryman with Anne Coddington, while Liz Davies recorded her and others' experiences of an oppositional Labour left during Blair's first term, 1997–2001, in *Through the Looking Glass:*

A Dissenter inside New Labour. From this period, too, read *Making Sense of New Labour* by Alan Finlayson, the best critical account of Blairism as a set of ideas. And accompany it with two books of retrospective analysis, *Futures of Socialism: 'Modernisation', the Labour Party and the British Left 1973–1997* by Colm Murphy, and Karl Pike's *Getting Over New Labour*.

Jeremy Corbyn's election as Labour leader was a huge shock to the system of 'labourism'. How big a shock is variously assessed by Alex Nunn's account of how and why Corbyn was elected leader, *The Candidate: Jeremy Corbyn's Improbable Path to Power*, and *The Corbyn Effect*, edited by Mark Perryman, which accounts for why, rather than leading Labour to a widely expected wipe-out at the 2017 general election, Corbyn's radical 'For the Many Not the Few' manifesto wiped out the Tories' overall majority. Why did Corbynism fail? Richard Seymour unpicks the project's weaknesses from its strengths in *Corbyn: The Strange Rebirth of Radical Politics*. Mark Perryman's *Corbynism from Below* brings together a wide range of approaches to help us understand the eventual unfulfilled promise.

To understand Labour's 2024 general election campaign, combine reading two very different reports for a rounded view: from Labour Together, *How Labour Won*, and from Compass, *Thin Ice: Why The UK's Progressive Majority Could Stop Labour's Landslide Melting Away* (both available free online). Keep up to date with what has happened to all the parties' votes since via Paula Surridge's Substack, *PS:Polling Snippets*, and Tim Bale's blog, www.timbale.com. For those who aspire to be an amateur psephologist, a weekly Friday visit to @electionmapsUK on X, where all the council by-election results from the day before are listed, will help to track the parties' ups and downs.

Edited by Gerry Hassan and Simon Barrow, and published in association with Compass, *Britain Needs Change: The Politics of Hope and Labour's Challenge* combines both analysis of the vote and a wide range of policy challenges facing the new government. Anushka Asthana's *Taken as Red: How Labour Won Big and the Tories Crashed the Party* is a journalistic account following the 2024 general election campaign. From Patrick Maguire and Gabriel Pogrund, *Get In: The Inside Story of Labour Under Starmer* is full of exclusive revelations to tell the story of Starmer, both as party leader and prime minister.

Two books that give an insight into Jeremy Gilbert's theorisation of Starmerism are Gilbert's *Twenty-First Century Socialism* and *Hegemony Now: How Big Tech and Wall Street Won the World (and How We Win It Back)*, co-authored with Alex Williams. Gilbert's website carries all his most recent writing and archived works: www. jeremygilbert.org. Gilbert's work can also be followed via the *Culture, Power and Politics* and *#AFCM* podcasts.

How to understand the ways racism constructs a 'racial capitalism'? Read *Empire's Endgame: Racism and the British State* by Gargi Bhattacharyya and others, accompanied by *Uncommon Wealth: Britain and the Aftermath of Empire* by Kojo Koram.

Joe Kennedy first articulated his theory of authentocracy in the book *Authentocrats: Culture, Politics and the New Seriousness*. To apply the theory yourself, start with a read of Tom Baldwin's *Keir Starmer: The Biography* (authorised version) and Oliver Eagleton's *The Starmer Project* (unauthorised version).

Compass is the home of a 'soft left' characterised by a plural politics of all parties and none: www.compassonline.org. The Labour version is best represented by, although it doesn't use the label, *Renewal: The Journal of Social Democracy* at www.renewal.org.uk. Straddling the Kinnock-Blair years, Robin Cook's autobiography *Point of Departure* provides an excellent insight into the hard choices a soft left, then and now, is forced to make. Before being bound by the rules and discipline (hard choice number one) of cabinet collective responsibility, Ed Miliband's book *Go Big: 20 Bold Ideas to Fix Our World* and Lisa Nandy's *All In: How We Build a Country That Works* could be pretty much read as manifestos for a new soft left. Sitting on the Labour back bench naughty step means not being bound by any such responsibility, and Clive Lewis (www.clivelewis.org) and Nadia Whittome (www.nadiawhittome.org) give a very good representation of what a 'soft left' might look like.

Reading up about the Conservative Party may not be at the top of the list of priorities for most readers of this book, but understanding why Sunak lost so heavily in 2024 is every bit as important as understanding why Starmer won by a landslide. *The Party's Over: The Rise and Fall of the Conservatives from Thatcher to Blair* by Phil Burton-Cartledge (blog www.averypublicsociologist.com) and Tim

Bale's *The Conservative Party after Brexit: Turmoil and Transformation* provide the very necessary analysis.

Jon Bloomfield and David Edgar's short book *The Populist Right* is a key text for understanding the ideas behind this most unwelcome of phenomena. *The Far Right Today* by Cas Mudde provides the best historical and theoretical framework to plot where the phenomenon might take us, if we let it. To prevent such a drift, the campaigning organisation Hope not Hate confronts the Reform UK threat via undercover investigations, in-depth polling and support for practical local initiatives that unite, not divide, communities. For updates, visit www.hopenothate.org.uk.

After the 2019 general election defeat, with *Our Bloc: How We Win* James Schneider provided one blueprint for an 'independent left'. Four decades earlier, in 1979, Sheila Rowbotham, Lynne Segal and Hilary Wainwright's *Beyond the Fragments: Feminism and the Making of Socialism* provided another. With *A New Politics from the Left*, Wainwright sought to connect this previous effort of the late 1970s to the present.

Danny Dorling's writings on inequality are an essential introduction to the subject. Read his collection *Peak Injustice: Solving Britain's Inequality Crisis* for an insight into the breadth and scale of the problem. Keep updated by visiting www.dannydorling.org. *The Only Way Is Up: How to Take Britain from Austerity to Prosperity* by Polly Toynbee and David Walker is both a powerful testament to the sheer scale of social division across post-landslide Britain and a brilliant indicator of the potential breadth of a coalition to reverse it should there be the political will to do so.

For non-economists, the weekly podcast *Macrodose* from James Meadway is the perfect entry point to a better understanding of the world of money and how to change it for the better. On *The Curve* podcast, Meadway is joined by fellow economist Grace Blakeley for a fortnightly conversation on all matters economic. The Common Wealth think tank www.common-wealth.org provides a constant stream of new, radical and accessible thinking on the economy. Founder of Common Wealth Mathew Lawrence and Adrienne Buller collaborated to write the short book *Owning the Future: Power and Property in an Age of Crisis*, the perfect antidote to Rachel Reeves.

Edited by Christine Berry, *The New Foundations: A Future Built on Democracy* includes chapters on the state, the economy, the environment and more, each dissected by how current failings could be reversed via democratisation, and is available as a free e-book from www.politicsforthemany.co.uk. To keep up to date with the pressure from inside the Labour Party for democratic reform, visit www.labourforanewdemocracy.org.uk.

Cancel the Apocalypse: The New Path to Prosperity by Andrew Simms provides a positive approach to how we can use this moment in human history to transform both the economy and society for the better, for all. The programme for a 'green government' in Mathew Lawrence and Laurie Laybourn-Langton's *Planet on Fire: A Manifesto for the Age of Environmental Breakdown* is the perfect tool to measure how far along, or far away, the Starmer government is in achieving that label. Combining Rachel Reeves' mantra of 'growth' with sustainability is key to that achievement. Raphael Kaplinsky's *Sustainable Futures: An Agenda for Growth* shows how.

Labour Together was where Morgan McSweeney first made his mark on the Labour Party. The Labour Together website is at www.labourtogether.uk. Labour to Win is the pro-Starmer faction organising to win internal Labour elections: www.labourtowin.org. First founded during the Corbyn era Momentum continues to represent the broad left in the party www.peoplesmomentum.com. A 430-page account of the twists and turns of Labour Party democracy might not sound like a riveting read, but in the hands of David Kogan his book *Protest and Power: The Battle for the Labour Party* is almost a thriller, such are the patterns, directions and consequences of change he meticulously plots. Most of all, Kogan maps the terrain the likes of McSweeney navigate to their own ends.

Follow Gregor Gall at @leftacademic on X for daily updates on industrial relations and the trade unions. Gall's book *Mick Lynch: The Making of a Working-Class Hero* is both an insightful account of the rapid rise of Lynch to become the best-known trade union leader of recent times and an invaluable insight into the varied models of trade union militancy. Two classic texts crucial to understanding the role of trade unionism in any renewal of labourism are Eric Hobsbawm's book *The Forward March of Labour Halted?* (the original *Marxism Today* article that gave rise to the book is available via the online *Marxism Today* archive) and Tony Lane's *The Union Makes Us Strong: The British Working Class, Its Politics and Trade Unionism* (much of Lane's ground-breaking critique was subsequently contained in his *Marxism Today* article 'The Unions: Caught on the Ebb Tide', also available via the online Marxism Today archive).

Yasmin Alibhai-Brown's exploration of race and racism can be traced via three of her many books: the autobiographical *The Settler's Cookbook: A Memoir of Love, Migration and Food*, a hugely original account of what a multicultural Englishness looks like, *Exotic England: The Making of a Curious Nation*, and *In Defence of Political Correctness*, a powerful rebuttal of voices on the right, sometimes on the left, too, who argue that taking a stand against racism and other versions of discrimination is an optional extra.

The varied potential of social democracy to overcome the apparently binary opposition of being both pragmatic and radical is interrogated by a number of historical accounts. *One Hundred Years of Socialism: The West European Left in the Twentieth Century* by Donald Sassoon takes the long view. *Social Democracy* from Eunice Goes combines the historic with the thematic, from parliamentary socialism to globalisation. The most significant internal alternative to Labour's particular version of social democracy has come from various versions of the Bennite left. At its peak in the 1980s, *Labour: A Tale of Two Parties* by Hilary Wainwright detailed how this alternative evolved, survived and thrived when the party leadership were so fulsomely against it. *The Searchers: Five Rebels, Their Dream of a Different Britain and Their Many Enemies* by Andy Beckett continues that account via the stories of Tony Benn, Ken Livingstone, Diane Abbott, John McDonnell and Jeremy Corbyn. Ralph Miliband's *Parliamentary Socialism: A Study in the Politics of Labour* remains a hugely influential critique of Labour's particular version of social democracy. Miliband's critique was developed and updated by Leo Panitch and Coin Leys in their book *Searching for Socialism: The Prospect of the Labour New Left from Benn to Corbyn*.

As a means toward transforming all this Gramscian pessimism of the intellect into Gramsci's own urging, optimism of the will, I suggest two admirably short but succinct reads. Both advocate the potential for social democracy as both a pragmatic and radical project. Combine Neal Lawson's *Beyond Monopoly Socialism*, available as a free download from www.compassonline.org.uk, with his *The Left Wing of the Possible: The Case for Radical Pragmatism*, available via www.renewal.org.uk. And add *Don't Stop Thinking About Tomorrow: The Labour Party after Jeremy Corbyn* by Mike Phipps to a regular session of Bryn Griffiths' *Labour Left* podcast for a rounded view of a left politics in the making, still.

If that little, or rather big, lot isn't sufficient treat yourself to the 21st volume of *The British General Election* series dating all the way back to 1945, now there's a Labour landslide that was anything but loveless. The latest, for the 2024 General Election, is written by Robert Ford, Tim Bale, Will Jennings and Paula Surridge. The perfect read for readers of *The Starmer Symptom* to come up with their own 'diagnosis'.

Notes on Contributors

Mark Perryman Prior to *The Starmer Symptom* Mark mapped the limits of labourism under two Labour leaders. Firstly in *The Blair Agenda* and *The Moderniser's Dilemma: Radical Politics in the Age of Blair* (co-edited with Anne Coddington). And secondly, with *The Corbyn Effect* and *Corbynism from Below*. Actively committed to a plural left culture of 'organic intellectuals', to this end he organises an annual Labour Party Festival of Ideas in Lewes for which the only entry requirement is an open mind.

Clive Lewis is the Labour MP for Norwich South. A member of the Socialist Campaign Group of Labour MPs, he also works closely with the think tank Compass and is a strong proponent of co-operation across the parties of the 'progressive bloc'. Follow Clive on X: @LabourLewis

Paula Surridge, with Tim Bale, Robert Ford and Will Jennings, co-authored the definitive analysis of Labour's 'landslide', *The British General Election of 2024*. Professor of Political Sociology at Bristol University, her research of the British electorate began with the 1992 Scottish Election Study, and has a particular focus on social and political values.

Jeremy Gilbert, is the author of *Twenty-First Century Socialism*, and with Alex Williams co-wrote *Hegemony Now: How Big Tech and Wall Street Won the World (and How We Win It Back)*. His many and varied writings can be found at www.jeremygilbert.org. Follow Jeremy on X: @jemgilbert

Gargi Bhattacharyya is a writer and teacher, author of *The Futures of Racial Capitalism* and co-author with Adam Elliott-Cooper, Sita Balani, Kerem Nişancıoğlu, Kojo Koram, Dalia Gebrial, Nadine El-Enany and Luke de Noronha of *Empire's Endgame: Racism*

and the British State, among other books. Follow Gargi on X: @ Gargi_at_home

Joe Kennedy is the author of *Authentocrats: Culture, Politics and the New Seriousness*. He teaches English and Cultural Studies on the University of Gothenburg's programme at the University of Sussex in Brighton, in between writing on literature, critical theory, politics, music and football.

Neal Lawson is the Director of Compass, which describes itself as 'The political home for everyone who wants to be part of a much more equal, democratic and sustainable future'. Despite being a Labour member for more than four decades Neal was suspended by the Party 2023–24 and threatened with expulsion after advocating cross-party co-operation before being cleared of all charges. Follow Neal on X: @Neal_Compass

Phil Burton-Cartledge is a prolific commentator with daily blog posts at www.averypublicsociologist.blogspot.com. Senior lecturer in sociology at the University of Derby, Phil is the author of *The Party's Over: The Rise and Fall of the Conservatives from Thatcher to Sunak*. Follow Phil on X: @philbc3

Joe Mulhall is Director of Research at the anti-fascism organisation Hope not Hate and an expert on far-right extremism. His books include *Drums in the Distance: Journeys in the Global Far Right* and most recently *Rebel Sounds: Music as Resistance*. Follow Joe on X: @ JoeMulhall_

Hilary Wainwright, with Lynne Segal and Sheila Rowbotham, was co-author of *Beyond the Fragments: Feminism and the Making of Socialism*. Hilary is founding editor of *Red Pepper* magazine and Fellow of the Transnational Institute.

Danny Dorling is a social geographer researching the many forms inequality takes in Britain. His 2024 book *Seven Children: Inequality and Britain's Next Generation* is an account of the varied experiences of growing up framed by social and economic disadvantage.

Danny's website www.dannydorling.org carries all his most recent and previous work. Follow Danny on X: @dannydorling

James Meadway was formerly Economic Adviser to John McDonnell when McDonnell was Shadow Chancellor of the Exchequer. His experience also includes serving as Chief Economist at the New Economics Foundation. James's podcast *Macrodose* is described as 'your weekly fix of everything economics'. Follow James on X: @meadwaj

Jess Garland is Director of Research and Policy at the Electoral Reform Society. Jess has published widely on political participation and political party organisation, and is a regular media commentator on issues ranging from House of Lords reform to the rising influence of large-scale donors on political parties.

Andrew Simms is an author, political economist and campaigner. Andrew is Co-director of the New Weather Institute and Co-ordinator of the Rapid Transition Alliance. His most recent book, co-authored with Leo Murray, is *Badvertising: Polluting Our Minds and Fuelling Climate Chaos*. Follow Andrew on X: @AndrewSimms_uk

Emma Burnell is Director of Political Human, a political communications consultancy. She has worked for the Fabian Society, Trades Union Congress and Institute for Public Policy Research amongst others in a variety of communications roles, as well as being a former columnist and contributing editor for *Labour List*. Follow Emma on X: @EmmaBurnell

Gregor Gall has published biographies of National Union of Rail, Maritime and Transport Workers leaders Bob Crow and Mick Lynch. He is a visiting Professor of Industrial Relations at the University of Leeds, and is a regular contributor to the Scottish newspaper *The National*. Follow Gregor on X: @leftacademic

Yasmin Alibhai-Brown writes a weekly column for the *i Paper*. A widely published author, her books include *Exotic England: The Making of a Curious Nation*, the autobiographical *The Settler's*

Cookbook: A Memoir of Love, Migration and Food and *In Defence of Political Correcteness*. Follow Yasmin on X: @y_alibhai

Eunice Goes is the author of *Social Democracy: A Short History* and previously *Ed Miliband: Trying but Failing to Renew Social Democracy.* Professor of Politics at Richmond American University in London, Eunice has published articles on the Labour Party in journals including *The Political Quarterly*, *Parliamentary Affairs* and *Journal of Political Ideologies.*

Acknowledgements

Without the enthusiastic responses of the 16 chapter authors and one foreword author, to my request to write, and their ready willingness to meet deadlines, respond to any editing, and finally, deliver, this book would have been impossible except as a figment of my political imagination. A huge thank you.

My keynote essay, 'Testing the Limits of Labourism', benefited greatly from the many and varied responses of readers: Adam Gearey, Alan Finlayson, Apala Chowdhury, Beatrix Campbell, Bryn Griffiths, Duncan Thompson, Jane Foot, Joanna Orsatelli, Ian Crompton with his reading group of Jennifer Walker and Mike Gaunt, Jon Bloomfield, Ken Jackson, Martin Pople, Mike Phipps, Pat Stack, Peter Brawne, Tony Dowmunt, Sally Davison and Sue Davies. None of them should be held responsible for my ideological inconsistencies.

The anonymous Pluto Press developmental editors and their incisive picking up on points in my and all the contributors' chapters that I'd missed. Huw Jones for his meticulous copy-editing of the book that was so crucial in producing the corrected and finished version. Dave Stanford for his patient typesetting following one-too-many additions from me.

David Castle, Emily Orford, Melanie Patrick, Robert Webb and Jonila Krasniqi of Pluto Press for their collective faith in *The Starmer Symptom*, putting up with my fusspottery and turning the idea and the manuscript into a book.

Mike Phipps at the Labour Hub website has been generous to afford me occasional space to test out many of the ideas in *The Starmer Symptom*. Most of those ideas I first tested out on my Facebook page. Huge thanks to the many and varied respondents who enabled me to develop my thinking further. If, having read the book, readers want to do the same, adding your responses to my varied political (and other musings), find me at www.facebook.com/mark.perryman.581

For fuelling the inspiration that an organic intellectual culture in and beyond the Labour Party is possible, the Lewes Labour events and Keir Hardie Café crews, including: Amy Turner, Cameron Cove, Charlotte Williams, Dan Turner, David Hendy, Denzil Jones, Eddie Haydn-Smith, Esmé Hilliard, Geraldine Pass, Gill Short, Harriet Lyons, Henrietta Gill, Jane Thomas, Joy Mercer, Judy Wallis, Julie Sleightholme, Kevin Moore, Leslie Doyle, Maggie Symons, Miranda Kemp, Naomi Salman, Paul Grivell, Penny Lower, Pete Knight, Peter Bradford, Peter Brawne, Pho Kypri, Ros Brewer, Sean Tunney, Sophie Gibson, Steve Watts Stuart Cartland and Teresa O'Brien.

Lewes Arms for providing the space for convivial 'afters'.

For enduring my wilder excesses of testing the limits of labourism, Lewes Constituency Labour Party officers Ann Biddle, Frances Hasler and Lindsay Thomas.

For the inspirational experience of taking part in the successful 2024 general election campaigns of Beccy Cooper (Worthing West) and Peter Lamb (Crawley), without whom this book wouldn't have been a feasible proposition. To avoid Beccy and Peter losing the Labour whip, neither are responsible for this book's contents!

For the 2024 general election efforts of Paul Wafer and Tony Dowmunt in helping to ensure voters in Lewes voted for the candidate best placed to defeat the Tory, only to be 'rewarded' by Labour with their expulsion. *La lutta continua.*

For putting up with me shut away in my room working on this book while shouting, loudly, at inanimate objects, my laptop and phone, Anne, Edgar and Daisy the cat.

And for keeping the morbid at bay with the joyful, the combined effects of watching Lewes FC, early-morning runs to Mount Caburn, swimming in Pells Pool and summers spent on the Isles of Scilly.

Mark Perryman, Lewes, June 2025

Index

The Pluto Press Newsletter

Hello friend of Pluto!

Want to stay on top of the best radical books
we publish?

Then sign up to be the first to hear about our
new books, as well as special events,
podcasts and videos.

You'll also get 50% off your first order with us
when you sign up.

Come and join us!

Go to bit.ly/PlutoNewsletter